Nitty Gritty

FEDERAL BUREAU OF INVESTIGATION

FORM NO. 1
THIS CASE ORIGINATED AT   SAN FRANCISCO   CONFIDENTIAL   100-2697

REPORT MADE AT	DATE WHEN MADE	PERIOD FOR WHICH MADE	REPORT MADE BY
SAN FRANCISCO	4/17/41	3/14/41	

TITLE

BEN BURNS
ESTHER BURNS

MRS. BEN BURNS

CHARACTER OF CASE

INTERNAL SECURITY (R)

SYNOPSIS OF FACTS:

BEN BURNS employed by People's World, Communist newspaper, San Francisco, as literary and dramatic editor; residing at 1385 Sacramento Street. Wife, ESTHER BURNS, employed at Housing Authority of City and County of San Francisco and is member of CIO Office Workers Union. Subjects leaving San Francisco for Chicago to be gone several years; future activities and intentions there unknown.

-P-

100-CIA
100 Legat Field
1pc - " Paris
1pc - " Rome
1pc - " Rome

ALL INFORMATION CONTAINED
HEREIN IS UNCLASSIFIED
EXCEPT WHERE SHOWN
OTHERWISE

DETAILS:

_____ advised that _____ residence, 1385 Sacramento Street, San Francisco, is a prospective meeting place for Communists.

_____ advised that the Subject, BEN BURNS, is employed at the People's World, 583 Market Street, San Francisco as a literary and dramatic editor of the paper. He is a former student of the University of Oregon. He desired to dispose of his automobile before license time.

His wife is ESTHER, of the Housing Administration of the City and County of San Francisco, 525 Market Street, Yukon 1661.

He is not on good terms with HARRY KRAMMER, editor of the People's World and frequently uses profane language in referring to him. He is leaving The People's World and is moving to Chicago

APPROVED AND FORWARDED	SPECIAL AGENT IN CHARGE	DO NOT WRITE IN THESE SPACES

APR 22 '41   MAY 1 - 194_

NITTY GRITTY

A White Editor
in Black Journalism

Ben Burns

UNIVERSITY PRESS OF MISSISSIPPI
Jackson

Copyright © 1996 by the University Press of Mississippi
All rights reserved
Manufactured in the United States of America

Print-on-Demand Edition

Library of Congress Cataloging-in-Publication Data

Burns, Ben.
    Nitty gritty : a white editor in black journalism / Ben Burns.
      p. cm.
    Includes index.
    ISBN 1-93411-002-7   ISBN-13: 978-1-93411-002-7
    1. Afro-American periodicals—History. 2. Burns, Ben. 3. Newspaper editors—
United States—Biography. I. Title.
PN4882.5.B87 1996
051'.092—dc20
    [B]   95-32890
                                                     CIP

British Library Cataloging-in-Publication data available

To
Esther,
whose upbeat encouragement,
persevering racial open-mindedness,
infinite patience,
and staunch loyalty
made possible my hectic years
in black journalism and this book

Not to transmit an experience is to betray it.
Elie Wiesel

Contents

Preface

To read a voluminous forty-year-old FBI report on yourself, while confirming a long-held surmise that you were under government surveillance, still is a distressing revelation, like uncovering a dismal secret in a long-buried time capsule. In reading the FBI's stilted words, the pat phraseology, I could not but recognize someone I had known in the past, but was it really "me"? Or was it an entirely other "me" in another life so long ago? I did not see the FBI dossier on myself until 1980, yet I had to recognize that, unseen, it had had a profound impact on my life, on my always limited perspectives, my unceasing fears, my thwarted ambitions, my marked cynicism. I have traveled so far from the Ben Burns of the 1930s. I have evolved through so many different lives since those tumultuous times that I find it difficult to recall, recognize, and identify with that Ben Burns, an eerie revenant returned to haunt me. Yet when I leaf through the FBI's confidential report, page after page, memory flits into focus. For all its ridiculous errors of fact and arcane lexicon, many of the statements ring true. However, today I can find no affinity whatsoever to that Ben Burns. This is another being they describe, but someone I once knew well.

Those were the days when I obviously was considered and listed as a clear and present danger to the system, considering the many staff hours and tax dollars the FBI devoted to tracking me down and compiling its many pages on my "subversive" activity. But in truth I was minuscule Communist small fry, with about as much political significance as a postal clerk's impact on White House policy—and just as threatening.

But perhaps in the FBI's imagery I really was as "dangerous" as the FBI was inclined to describe me. By sheer coincidence, in the course of less than four years, I had become the first and only journalist in the United States ever to work on the three Communist dailies that existed in this country in the 1930s. So I became fair game for the FBI's naive, laughable gumshoes, whose reports were as off-base as some of the slanted stories I used to read on the copy desk at the Communist newsrooms. "A former student at the University of Oregon," the FBI reported in 1941, for instance. At that time, I had never been in Oregon in my life!

"Plump" and "rather disheveled" was how the FBI described my wife Esther. "Plump" she certainly was in her pregnant state, but "disheveled" was no less than insulting in its estimate of her always meticulous appearance. "Literary and dramatic editor," the FBI rated me. The reality was that I wrote movie and book reviews after hours on the copy desk, just to get free movie passes and books.

As a cub reporter on my first newspaper job after graduating from Northwestern University's journalism school, I was able to work my way up to the copy desk of the *Daily Worker*, the oldest and best-known Communist newspaper, reaching that status primarily because other staff members did not relish desk work. From there I shifted, for a short period before the paper went bust, to the first and only Communist daily in Chicago, the *Midwest Daily Record*. Then after a vain job search, there was another short copy desk chore at the *People's World* in San Francisco to stay off the jobless rolls and enjoy for a brief spell the joys of life in the Bay area—and those complimentary movie passes and review books.

The FBI's first report on me came in 1941 when I was already off the Communist payroll after less than four years, all told, as a hack party journalist. I had succeeded in elevating my weekly paycheck in that time from a munificent ten dollars to all of twenty dollars weekly. About to enter parenthood, I knew I had to start earning a respectable living, and I moved into new vistas, new worlds, yet another life in the succession I have led. But J. Edgar Hoover and his minions stayed on my trail for some twenty years and almost three hundred pages of reports (plus contributions by the CIA and the State Department) with an ineptitude that was in the best tradition of an Inspector Clouseau.

Perhaps Hoover's agents had good grounds, for throughout all my varied "lives" I have remained a cynical nonconformist, perhaps best tabbed as a born-again rebel, unwilling to bend to the turgid pedantry and rigid discipline of Marxist theology and Communist orthodoxy or to the accepted business practices and inequities of the supposed free enterprise system.

I have gone through a multitude of "careers," none distinguished but almost all contrarious, perhaps the most unusual being my years as the first (and only white) editor of the foremost black magazines in the nation, *Ebony* and *Jet*, as well as the only white editor-in-chief of a leading black daily newspaper, the *Chicago Daily Defender*. The FBI bloodhounds did not relent in those years, and for all I know their "dirty tricks" techniques may well have influenced my eventual ouster from the *Ebony* editor's post. I turned conventional in later years to earn my keep. As a public relations executive, partner and vice president in the Chicago firm that first brought the McDonald's fast food chain into the public eye, I hoped I was able to close the FBI's books on myself. The world that shaped me, the disparate roads I took—these are what follow. In the words of Rousseau's exemplar *Confessions*, "This is what I have done, what I have thought, what I was": the nitty gritty of my working years as a white editor in black journalism.

I

1941–1945

1

Introduction to the Black Press

My Years with the *Chicago Defender*

With drops of ink
We make millions think.
        Robert S. Abbott, publisher, *Chicago Defender*

I returned to my hometown of Chicago in 1941, jobless, homeless, and about to become a father. For the previous four years I had worked on three Communist daily newspapers across the country—my initiation as a professional journalist. A realistic assessment of my job prospects seemed to warrant the bleakest, most pessimistic outlook on my return to the Nineteenth Street apartment of my parents. How do you begin life anew at age twenty-eight? I asked myself. What hope was there of my finding any newswriting job with a resume that had "Communist" emblazoned all over it? How could I support a family of three when the baby arrived? How could I possibly escape endless tomorrows of working for my father painting houses, the only other craft I knew and where I was assured of a regular paycheck? I had not the shred of an answer to these inescapable questions.

The propitious answers came one summer day in 1942, after months of working as a house painter, when I walked through the front door of a former synagogue at 3435 South Indiana Avenue. It was then the office of the *Chicago Defender*, one of the country's leading Negro newspapers. Hired as temporary fill-in editor, I was soon inducted into another world and in effect began a new existence. I became a *Defender* editor, a "black newspaperman," black in my orientation and thinking, in my concerns and outlook, in my friends and associations, black in everything but my skin color. (My self-designation as a "black newspaperman" would no doubt be justifiably challenged by most blacks, and I use the term cautiously and advisedly—not in any hubristic, feckless pretense of a black poseur, but rather to encapsulate my basic orientation and perception, my beliefs and perspective for more than three

decades.) What begins as temporary often turns out to be permanent, and
before long I became the *Defender*'s full-time national editor, directing the
staff, shaping format, setting much of its policy.

For all my previous editorial experience on left-wing dailies, I fidgeted
nervously, as if applying for my first job, when on a hot July day I first stepped
into the patchwork lobby of the onetime Indiana Avenue synagogue (with
Hebrew letters still carved high on its sandstone facade) that housed the
Defender's offices and composing and press rooms. How strange that I, a
nonreligious Jew, was entering the Negro world by walking into a onetime
Jewish temple. To become a Negro editor, I, a Jew who had never attended
shul, would now spend most of my waking hours in a former synagogue.

A storefront with plate-glass windows was the entry to the *Defender*,
which proclaimed itself "The World's Greatest Weekly"—a slogan purloined
from the magniloquent downtown *Chicago Tribune*, which termed itself "The
World's Greatest Newspaper." Certainly the Indiana Avenue squalor was not
the likely setting for anything "great": a rundown row of limestone-front
hovels lined the street where trolleys still rumbled by every few minutes (in
some buildings lights were kept burning all night to prevent rats from biting
sleeping infants, a legislative inquiry was told). My doubts about whether I
could fit in at the black weekly were not allayed by the tightly watched front
entrance door with its buzzer system like a safe-deposit vault and a uniformed
guard eyeing me like a being from outer space as I waited skittishly to keep
my appointment with the editor-in-chief, Dr. Metz T.P. Lochard. Finally I was
admitted and ushered into a plush, carpeted ground-level office in a blind
corner, its walls covered almost to the ceiling with photos and memorabilia of
the phenomenal career of the *Defender*'s founder and first publisher, Robert S.
Abbott (the office was maintained just as Abbott had left it the day he died
two years before). Behind the only desk in the room sat Lochard, who rose
and greeted me with a beaming smile as if I were royalty.

Communist leader William L. Patterson, for whom I had worked when he
was coeditor of the Communist Party–sponsored *Midwest Daily Record* in
Chicago, had set up my appointment for the job. (If I retain any fondness and
gratitude to any Communist, it would be mostly to Patterson, to whom I owe a
substantial debt for his solicitude and initiative in opening for me the door to
the Negro world, even though I sensed that his motive probably was placement
of a party member in a position of influence in the black community.) Lochard
knew full well of my leftist connections but never queried me about being a
"Red." Rather, he was concerned solely about how I could help him shape a
better newspaper.

His immediate concern was a major project he had conceived: a special "Victory Through Unity" edition of the *Defender*, projected to inspire Negro support for the war effort. Lochard asked me to work on the project part time, and I enthusiastically agreed to join in at a minimal salary. For me it was the beginning of the discovery of a new culture, the once distant black world, about which I knew so little, for all my previous Communist schooling. It also marked the happy initiation of the closest, longest relationship I have ever had with a Negro friend. "Doc" (Lochard had earned his doctorate at the Sorbonne in 1914, and everyone in the office addressed him as "Doc") was the epitome of the polymath intellectual, well read, inquisitive about the universe at large, as truly nonbiased a man as I have ever met, unfettered by racial confines in his thinking, a man in the tradition of the finest black minds of his generation, such as W.E.B. Du Bois and Alain Locke. The Haitian-born Lochard embraced people with his scintillating charm, his pervasive zest, and a warm infectious smile, revealing a mouthful of tobacco-stained teeth. For more than forty years I luxuriated in his friendship, whether under the stress of news deadlines or in moments of leisure in his or my living room probing mankind's inanities.

We spent our first several months working together in compiling a two-part, sixty-eight-page supplement that was to become a notable achievement in black journalism, featuring original contributions from the top names in black and white America. With photos of late publisher Abbott (who had established the *Defender* in 1905 with a capital of twenty-five cents, the legend goes) staring down on us from all sides, I worked on the technical aspects of the supplement, routine chores of writing letters and sending cables soliciting articles, drafting headlines and layouts, doing the copy reading to enliven the often prosaic manuscripts submitted by pundits and politicians ranging from Justice Hugo L. Black and Herbert Hoover to H. G. Wells and Lady Astor. My own written contribution to the supplement (I received no credit in its pages for its editing, a decision designed to softpedal and cover up any white—let alone Communist—connection with it) was an article on job prejudice titled "Let My People Work," written as if I, as its author, were black. By intense reading and research to supplement my still meager knowledge about black life, I was able to assemble the supplement without making too many boners. For what I did not know, I could always count for help on the quick mind of "Doc" Lochard, who was my trusty guide and sponsor in those teetery, early *Defender* days, like some avuncular presence at my side, quick to cover my missteps and to defend me from some of the open hostility from *Defender* oldtimers who openly resented my presence. I was the new kid on the block, subject to all the usual antipathy against a newcomer, an interloper—and a white to boot.

Every day I would stealthily ease my way past the front lobby guard, seeking to be noticed as little as possible by *Defender* editors who were buzzing with the word of a white editor's meddling in their domain. After my first weeks cooped up in Abbott's old office, I would timidly nose my way into the second-floor editorial offices chaperoned by Doc to ask some question about typesetting or other mechanical detail and could sense the antagonism at my appearance. Most open and prickly in his rancor was gaunt oldtimer A. C. MacNeal, a man with an elongated Modigliani neck and tan skin no darker than mine. How was I to know that his venom was not as much racial as simply that I represented a threat to his job? Another whose resentment if not open hostility I sensed was another *Defender* veteran of some years, fast-talking Enoch Waters, whose editorial functions I eventually assumed. I made the mistake of believing I had passed muster with him, when he asked me to join him for lunch one day at a nearby Indiana Avenue basement eatery which rarely had a white patron at its tables. Our lunch was cordial, but yet somehow he remained quite guarded and aloof even after a few beers. Never in all my years at the *Defender*, and even after I left the paper, did I feel comfortable in his bristling presence.

Like some newly arrived immigrant in a strange country, I had to absorb the differing standards and values, the rich culture, traditions, and history of what to me was an alien world despite my previous contacts with Negroes in the Communist Party. I made new friends, adopted many of the mores of the black community, and was soon accepted socially, the only white face at many a black gathering. I became street smart, discovering a new and distinct language—including the offbeat vocabulary of "jive" as well as the banalities and obscenities of South Side street talk. I began to think and feel as a Negro, becoming as angry and bitter at moments as a racial zealot and also having to play the contrite Uncle Tom at times. I became all too familiar with the day-to-day frustrations and humiliations Negroes endured, their indignities and hazards, even if I did not personally experience their abasement. Although I did have to face some initial ill will, when I finally merited as full acceptance as possible, and even a sort of kinship despite my color and background, I rejoiced in one of the most stimulating, gratifying chapters in my life. Just as the back door was for several centuries the customary entryway for Negroes into white America, ironically for me it was also the entryway into black journalism. My initial timorous, tenuous step of part-time editing for the

Chicago Defender's Victory Edition—not only an apprenticeship of sorts to test my editorial competence but also a probationary period in working easily with Negro staffers—led in time to the editorship of more than a half-dozen Negro publications over a period of thirty-five years and to my immersion in the black world.

The Victory Edition was a success, both editorially and financially, as the *Defender* lined up much advertising lineage from blue-chip accounts. It proved the transitional medium to install me as national editor in charge of the influential *Defender* edition sold across the country and particularly in the South, where it had more than twice the circulation of the city edition. I emerged from my initial assignment with compliments even from office antagonists.

My early contacts with publisher John H. Sengstacke were few because he rarely intruded into editorial matters, recognizing his limitations as a relative novice in publishing. Looking like a youngish, clean-cut college student, soft-spoken and easygoing, in the *Defender* offices with its many veteran editors, Sengstacke, the nephew and heir of founder Robert Abbott, appeared like anything but the paper's publisher. Cautious in decision making, Sengstacke obviously was relieved to yield editorial direction for the Victory Edition completely to Lochard and indirectly to me. The wartime atmosphere and the growing recognition that black muscle and brains were essential for the United States in the world conflict gained the *Defender* remarkable responses from the famous people we contacted for articles or goodwill messages. The opening pages of the Victory Edition carried special cables from Generals Douglas MacArthur and Dwight Eisenhower. The Pacific commander-in-chief in ringing words from his headquarters in Australia grabbed the play away from other contributors, such as Wendell Willkie, Eleanor Roosevelt, Pearl Buck, Upton Sinclair, and Nelson Rockefeller. Even though Negro recruits were still placed in segregated army units, MacArthur's moving prose erased temporarily the prevailing stain of Jim Crow in the military. His cable read in part:

> Only those like you who at one time were denied personal liberty can fully appreciate its value. Your heroic struggle up to freedom has given you a sense of patriotism, which is one of your finest characteristics. Your devotion to the democratic cause of freedom has made you a bulwark in every great emergency in our history. I know you will not fail now in this hour of our peril.

If General MacArthur set a high standard in the Victory Edition, caustic, mossback columnist Westbrook Pegler provided the low point in his letter, which we printed in its entirety. "I think your paper is low grade and utterly unscrupulous and is perpetrating a grievous disservice to the Negro people in particular and the United States in general," Pegler wrote. "You have a great opportunity and great responsibility and you are abusing both." Pegler embodied lucid evidence that for all the wartime patriotism and the plethora of appeals for racial unity, anti-Negro bigotry was yet prevalent in an America battling Nazi racism abroad. Too many Americans could and would still echo the words of Adolf Hitler, published in our special edition:

> As for the Negro, it does not dawn upon the depraved bourgeois world of America that it is an absurdity to train a half-born ape until it is supposed to be that a lawyer or doctor has been made of him; that it is a sin to let talented men degenerate while Hottentots and Zulus are trained for intellectual vocations.

If I needed further confirmation of the appalling incomprehension of average white Americans on racial matters, it came in my chance session with an advertising executive assigned by the Advertising Council to pro-bono work helping the *Defender* promote the sale of advertising lineage in the Victory Edition. Lochard requested that I go downtown (something he rarely did) to meet with this executive and enlist his promotional talents on our behalf. For perhaps an hour I sat in the presence of one of the great creative minds in the world of advertising, Leo Burnett. I was astounded by his ignorance about Negroes and their world. I might as well have been talking about some remote Afghan village for all the interest and attention he showed. Obviously, he saw this as an unsavory chore he had been handed, and he approached it with evident indifference and disdain. If I had any illusions about a new public awareness and concern about Negroes because of the war, Burnett dispelled these notions. More than a century after Alexis de Tocqueville had written his somber assessment of racial relations in *Democracy in America*, I found that his words on the vast gulf between the races still rang true:

> I do not think that the white and black races will ever be brought anywhere to live on a footing of equality, but I think that the matter will be harder in the United States than anywhere else. It can happen that a man will rise above prejudice . . . but it is not possible for a whole people to rise, as it were, above itself.

For more than twenty years Madison Avenue, like Leo Burnett, remained reluctant to acknowledge that Negroes were an integral presence in the American scene. It was not until the 1960s that black faces began to appear regularly in television and print advertising. In the 1940s, however, there was a long uphill road to be traveled, one that I proposed to traverse in a very small way in my profession. In time I felt that I had become racially transformed; as the white South African Alan Paton related in his autobiography, *Journey Continued*, "I was no longer a white person but a member of the human race."

The fledgling journalists of my youth all dreamed, passionately but unrealistically, of running their own newspaper. I can recall giddy, speculative discussions in journalism school that projected the ideal career as personal control of your own publication, even if it was a small-town paper. With my doctrinal views of the "capitalist economy," I had scoffed at that vision because I was convinced that advertisers and banks would always have a pernicious influence on editorial policy. But less than a decade after my graduation I found myself quite close to achieving that dream of editorial control. In my post as national editor of the *Chicago Defender*, I achieved almost full direction of its national news and editorial pages with a bare minimum of intrusion or even suggestions from its youthful publisher, John Sengstacke, or my immediate superior, Metz Lochard. From my unobtrusive desk in a faroff second-floor corner where few visitors ever came, I was in day-to-day control of most facets of the twenty-four-page, standard-size national edition. During the war years, the national edition reached a circulation of more than 200,000, its highest figure since the 1920s when it was the key organ of agitation for the black exodus from the South. It was topped only by the established *Pittsburgh Courier*, the first major Negro weekly to switch from traditional Republican loyalty dating from the Reconstruction era to the Democratic camp of Franklin D. Roosevelt in the early 1930s. The *Courier* thereby benefited from the swing of Negro voters to the Democratic Party. During the war years the Negro press generally attained new peaks of circulation and influence; soldiers in combat and in camps zealously read black newspapers for news from home as well as for reports on the mounting clamor for equal treatment of Negro GIs.

In editing the *Defender* I also became a "boss" for the first time, and to my surprise I found that I thoroughly enjoyed my new role—not only because of the exhilarating sense of power to shape staff thinking but also because of the latitude to slant editorial prescripts. I was committed to and exulted in this new life, the most absorbing and stimulating news work I had yet attempted. Despite the initial rebuffs I had encountered, many of my colleagues eventually became my warm and convivial friends. I worked long hours, including Sundays, writing everything from editorials to book reviews to routine rewrites and major features, copy reading, doing layouts and writing headlines for all the national news pages, even devising story lines for the cartoon strips done by freelance cartoonist Jay Jackson.

To take a job at a Negro publication was one thing, but to learn to think and respond as a Negro was another matter, certainly no overnight transition in spite of my political orientation and racial sympathies. I was able initially to identify with Negroes to the point where I began to take heated offense at racial slurs, to feel pride in Negro accomplishments, and also to become guilt-ridden when Negroes got into trouble with the law, whether the crime was rape or political corruption. My reaction to such news was similar to my feeling when Jews were in similar predicaments: "It's bad for the Jews (or the Negroes)."

Even though I had never before held a management post and was well aware of my still limited knowledge of this new world of color I was exploring and enjoying, I assumed my role with confidence in my journalistic skills. More than just a boss, I became a teacher of some of the novices among the underpaid staff, many of whom were newcomers to journalism, eager to learn the craft. But "running the show" with Doc's acquiescence also encompassed hiring and firing staffers—one part of the job that I abhorred. In hiring new employees, I was uncertain in my judgment of people, lacking conviction in my competence to estimate character and talent by a brief conversation and perusal of a scrapbook or resume. When I had to fire anyone, I was dismayed and despondent because of my fallibility in prior assessment of an individual rather than angered by someone's ability to hoodwink me.

There were other inescapable negatives as well. Besides having to make do with an underpaid, insufficient staff, I had problems with long accepted practices in the black press. One such custom was the shortcut editorial technique of covering national news: rewriting the white dailies from a race angle. Although reporters were dispatched out of town on some major stories, these instances were few. The *Defender* retained part-time correspondents in Washington and New York, as well as using stringers in other cities, but most of these space-rate reporters leaned heavily on white newspapers as the basic source of their copy. The *Defender* subscribed to important white dailies, and the staff scrutinized these for stories about Negroes. Editors would "look for the word *Negro*," clip the story, and then rewrite it with a race angle.

In some respects the *Defender*'s national edition was like a traditional community newspaper for blacks in the Deep South states of Mississippi, Alabama, and Louisiana. In a carryover from the 1920s, the paper still boasted more than two thousand agent-correspondents who mailed in typical small-town items about births, weddings, and deaths and then sold the paper to their fellow townspeople. When I arrived, the paper still carried four full pages of such community news each week. A secretary worked full time to decipher scrawled letters from agents who often were barely literate. The agent-correspondents had been the predominant sales force for the *Defender* in the 1920s, when two-thirds of its circulation was outside Chicago. But by the 1940s the Dixie agents had fallen off as new local Negro weeklies started to take away *Defender* circulation. Still, the *Defender* enjoyed substantial readership in the South, continuing its longtime role as the prime mover of the black migration to the North after World War I. In those years Carl Sandburg had reported in the *Chicago Daily News* that "the *Defender* more than any other one agency was the big cause of the 'Northern fever' and the big exodus from the South." In early days one source of news from the South was typical of the penny pinching at the *Defender:* an employee was assigned to go to the railroad yards before the cars coming from southern cities were cleaned and to bring back to the office all periodicals left by passengers, so that the staff could scavenge them for Negro stories.

With the concentrated study of a talmudic scholar, I endeavored in my early *Defender* days to learn as much as I could in the shortest possible time about Negro history and culture. I soon discovered that I was more knowledgeable than many of my colleagues and encouraged the reporters to read more about black history as well as current racial events to broaden their knowledge of subjects that in those days were neglected in school curriculums. But my campaign to induce the staff to read more was not particularly successful. As I grew more confident of the facts, given my own comprehensive reading, I became more ruthless with my copy pencil. My strangest copy-reading experiences occurred with several reporters whom I, the only white on staff, had to importune to make their rewrites from white newspapers much more pro-Negro. These black reporters frequently would perpetuate the pro-white slant of news stories, especially those from the South. "When a white reporter in the South reports a lynching, you can be sure he'll write it from a white point of view," I used to point out. "What we need is a strong Negro angle!" Thus, a "posse" became a "lynch mob" and a "big burly Negro rapist" became a "suspect." Sometimes, however, the race angle could get out of hand. I had occasion to cite a horrendous example in one black weekly after a tornado had hit a big city, resulting in dozens of casualties. In a three-inch "scare" headline, the paper proclaimed: "TORNADO BY-PASSES NEGROES."

Many of the old-timers at the *Defender* had begun their newspaper careers in barbershops, where so much community gossip was exchanged. When Abbott founded the *Defender* in 1905, he turned to the barbershops to fill his news columns. When he spotted a barber or customer who seemed to have a gift for collecting gossip, he promptly took that individual on as a reporter. The *Defender's* executive editor when I arrived on the scene, Lucius Harper, had been a barber and then a bellboy before becoming a journalist.

Of all the staff, aside from Lochard, I received the most help in my early *Defender* days from Harper. He had apparently had his fill of hard work during some thirty years of newspapering, and by the time I arrived he was coasting on past glories: never in his office more than four hours a day, passing the time in writing his front-page commentary, "Dustin' Off the News," and reading his fan mail. A delightful raconteur, the loquacious Harper would keep a circle of editors in stitches with his tales. Mimicking the late publisher's high-pitched voice, he would recount Abbott's imaginative news techniques, such as inventing stories when major headlines were scarce. A racial militant, Harper took much pride in displaying his unusual driver's license. Back in the 1940s the state of Illinois still insisted on designation of "race" on licenses, and Harper had written on his application, "human." The secretary of state never challenged him on that listing.

Along with every other *Defender* editor in a position to determine what went into the paper, Harper had his "musts"—stories he wrote that had to go into the paper no matter what important news might have to be omitted. These "musts" of all top editors were invariably straight paid-for publicity pieces. Once Harper told me, "The day before Christmas I'm always on Forty-seventh Street [in the heart of the 'Black Belt']. It's worth five hundred dollars to me to walk down the street that day." The money came from merchants who wished to remain in Harper's good graces. Sometimes the substantial exactions that editors were able to pocket were the subject of furious contention. Several years after I left the *Defender*, city editor David Kellum quit in a huff when the management insisted he turn over to the publisher a brand-new Packard that had been given to him by South Side merchants.

Kellum was a *Defender* fixture, striding across the city room with a Groucho Marx–like gait. He had started work at the *Defender* clipping items about Negroes out of white dailies, worked as Abbott's chauffeur until he sideswiped another car, and then became editor of the Bud Billiken children's page. ("Bud Billiken" was a fictitious character whose name was suggested by Harper for the children's page.) He retained that post along with the city editor's job (for which he was paid only forty dollars a week). We became friends from the first, with nary a disagreement. I gave full recognition to his role with the city edition, and he acknowledged mine in shaping the national edition.

The usual method of passing along cash to editors was an "open drawer" technique: a news release dropped furtively into an editor's drawer with anything from a five- to a twenty-dollar bill attached. I had first learned of this practice while doing publicity for Alderman Earl Dickerson, when I found that his aide, John Johnson, had much better luck than I did in getting press releases in the *Defender*. Finally he explained to me that he always attached a five-dollar bill to a press release when he handed it to Kellum. Management also had its strategy of collecting "loot"—especially around election time, when the bigger Negro papers could net as much as fifty thousand dollars in advertising and sometimes outright payoffs for political support. My journalism-school training rebelled at the selling of news-column space, whether it was a reporter or editor soliciting payoffs or management offering editorial endorsement to the highest bidder. In my view the open deposit of cash in an editor's drawer along with a press release was an outright scam and flaunted every journalistic principle I had ever learned in college. How could a publication pretend to present a fair, unbiased view of the news when its reports were bought and paid for? Such was the accepted journalistic wisdom. In time I learned that the custom went back many years at the *Defender*, which had begun charging space rates for publishing personal news items before World War I. The practice became established and was accepted by most of the black community. I had no choice but to ignore and pretend I knew little about what I viewed as a kind of bribery. Reasoning that the stratagem was defensible because black journalists were so underpaid, I finally became resigned to editorial payoffs at black newspapers. I viewed the situation as the result of racial restrictions on job opportunities and income potential for black journalists. I learned to recognize stories that had a pricetag on them and wielded my copy pencil cautiously, lest I upset the offending editor or the news source that had paid the asking price for a story.

Like other editors, I, too, had my special "loot." I never accepted a single dollar to place a story in the *Defender*, although the temptation was presented to me on numerous occasions. My "payoff" consisted of books. When I became book reviewer for the *Defender*, I would take home up to a dozen books a week. Most of them were on racial subjects, and I pored over these books incessantly to learn more about the rich history of centuries of ceaseless Negro endeavor to win a measure of equality in America. I welcomed Gunnar Myrdal's *An American Dilemma* when it was first published in 1944, and

I was one of the few people at the *Defender* who read the ponderous tome from cover to cover. My book reviews appeared on the op-ed page along with columns by such luminaries as W.E.B. Du Bois, Langston Hughes, Walter White, secretary of the National Association for the Advancement of Colored People (NAACP), and S. I. Hayakawa, then an English teacher at the Illinois Institute of Technology and later to become a U.S. senator from California. I was in the curious position of reading copy by these well-known writers, keeping after them to observe deadlines, correcting their spelling and the occasional solecism, and watching for factual errors. In my first months on the job I was discreet, but not timid, in revising copy, unimpressed by the fame of the writers I was assigned to edit. "No passion in the world is equal to the passion to alter someone else's draft," wrote H. G. Wells, and I certainly was seized with that passion. Du Bois in particular could be a problem, with his scholarly, intricate sentence structure that benefited from the addition of an occasional comma, semicolon, or paragraph break to make for easier reading. I do not recall any complaints about my revisions. I was sheltered by my geographical distance from the celebrity columnists whose copy I was checking and altering, almost on deadline. There was no time for long-distance discussion or dispute over my changes, mostly minor but sometimes significant, until long after the *Defender* had rolled off the press. In my years of copy reading of Du Bois's weekly columns, cogent but often didactic, I never once personally met or spoke on the telephone to the giant of black scholarship, who at that time lived in Atlanta. His leftist political views were close to mine, and my revisions to his copy were mostly technical, rather than substantive.

Another distant columnist was Walter White in the NAACP offices in Manhattan, whom I did not meet personally until long after I left the *Defender*. We spoke on the phone occasionally, but that was the extent of our contacts. White, who in another time would have made a consummate politician, could call off a dozen U.S. senators whom he knew by their first names. Often he amazed people in high places by this habit. Eleanor Roosevelt related in an article in *Ebony* that she was amazed when on their first meeting, White called her Eleanor. She accepted it with typical grace, later saying: "It was the thing he wanted to do. I accepted it because most people don't dare." In the early 1950s, when I was editor of *Ebony*, White arrived at our building one day with a *Look* magazine editor in tow whom he was trying to impress. He approached my glass-walled office with publisher John Johnson as his guide and asked: "Is that Ben Burns in that office?" When Johnson told him it was, he bounded into my office with a flourish, extending his hand as if I were an old friend, and greeted me effusively, "Hello Ben, how are you? It's been so long since I've seen you." Taken somewhat aback, I hesitated to address him as Walter even after the hearty greeting from the nation's foremost racial leader. I was able to avoid the issue by never once using his name in our meandering discussion of Negro magazines.

In contrast to Du Bois and White, Langston Hughes visited periodically from his Harlem apartment, usually when he was in town on a lecture tour, and we quickly became firm friends. Never did he offer a word of objection to any changes or cuts I inflicted on his clean, sprightly copy. By the early war years Hughes had already begun to drift away from his Communist sympathies of the 1930s and the rigid party line expressed openly in the words of one of his controversial poetic fantasies, such as "Put One More S in the U.S.A. and Make It Soviet," and *Goodbye Christ*. These poems became the particular target of right-wing veterans' and religious groups, which sometimes picketed his appearances. The harrowed, dismayed Hughes, pressured by lecture cancellations, chose in late 1940 to repudiate the lines of his leftist days that had so rattled conservatives.

As one of my last book columns while working at the *People's World*, the Communist daily in San Francisco, I had loyally echoed the party condemnation of Hughes as a "turncoat" for denouncing his own radical poems—ironically, a label I was to merit myself in coming years. Maliciously mocking him in stilted Communist hyperbole, I jibed at Hughes as "bitten by the war bug" and "pimping for ye imperialism" with his apology for *Goodbye Christ* instead of "defending the poem which appropriately said goodbye to Christ because of all the sins against Negroes committed in his name." In my book column I read Hughes out of the "movement." (This story was retold in Arnold Rampersad's biography, *The Life of Langston Hughes*, published in 1986.) "This is where you get off," I bade farewell to Hughes in my regrettable 1941 column. Just four years with party publications had burnished all that is standard in denunciations of deviates from the official party line, and I fully exercised this Communist Party art in my fulmination in the article that was in effect my coda in Communist journalism. I soon came to empathize with Arthur Koestler's lament, "Since my schooldays I have not ceased to marvel each year at the fool I had been the year before. Each year brought its own revelation and each time I could only think with shame and rage of the opinions I had held and vented before my last initiation."

Less than two years after my denunciation of Hughes, when I joined the *Defender* staff, he and I began to develop a close working relationship. He never mentioned a word about my *People's World* diatribe. As my own

Communist allegiance became more and more shaky, we could and did find a measure of political common ground, I an admirer of his humor and prose and he respectful of my role as editor of his columns. My flip-flop on Hughes was just one of many twists and turns in my political views and personal attitudes over the years, which kept me always looking back at what a "fool" I had been.

I edited all of Hughes's early "Simple" columns that later became racial classics in his books. I was always an admirer of Langston's subtle, penetrating humor. I did learn in time to be temperate in editing, particularly of well-known authors more likely than Hughes to explode in bursts of temperament. "Editing is the same as quarreling with writers—same thing exactly," once observed *New Yorker* editor Harold Ross, but I learned that an editor's function is also to imply that no quarrel exists with writers while placing on paper his or her differences with them.

The only local columnist on our op-ed pages was taciturn S. I. Hayakawa, who would quietly ease his way into my office each Friday right on deadline to deliver his neatly typed column into my hands. He turned out such precise, clean copy that any editing was invariably superfluous, and all I had to do was designate typefaces and write subheadings. Hayakawa was in every sense a liberal on racial issues, even though he turned to the right politically in later years. I cannot recall ever differing with his constrained but pointed litanies on the "problem," as we usually described America's racial dilemma.

In the 1940s, twenty years before the black revolution that shook up white America in the mid-1960s, among the nuances of Negro life I had to learn immediately in turning out copy for the black press were lessons in racial terminology. *Black* was rarely used then, and *Negro* was the commonly accepted and preferred racial designation with but few exceptions, the most notable being the *Afro-American*, a regional chain of four weeklies based in Baltimore, which sought to avoid any racial mention at all and would write of "our congressman" or "our alderman." The *Chicago Defender* for years had favored *race*, as in "race politician" and excluded *black, Negro,* or *Afro-American*, allowing only occasional use of *colored*. When I joined the *Defender* staff, *Negro* was the preferred word, and I was schooled so rigorously in its usage that to this day I often wince at the term *black*. This is partly because during my years as an editor, *black* was the pejorative description used for natives by South Africa's racists as well as by colonial powers and also because the term is inaccurate in describing a primarily brown-skinned people. As Du Bois wisely observed, " 'Black' is a relative expression: no human skin is absolutely black." He might well have added that there is no absolutely "white" skin either; the skin of so-called white people ranges in color from pink to tan to gray.

The term *black* was rarely used by race publications until the 1960s. The only popular weekly in the country with *black* in its name in the 1940s was the *Oklahoma Black Dispatch*. In the decades after 1838, when the first race magazine was published, not a single periodical used *black* in its title, while the majority had no racial identification at all in their names. Among those that did indicate race in the nineteenth century, the favored terms were *Negro* and *Afro* or *African*. *Black* in a magazine title was perhaps first used by nationalist Marcus Garvey in his monthly *Black Man*, printed in Jamaica for a short time in 1933. Only after the 1960s and the black revolution did *black* come into common usage by periodicals such as *Black Enterprise* and *Black Sports*.

Black is easier to accept and adopt as a descriptive adjective than as a noun, since as a noun it bears a strong reminder of how white South Africans distinguished sharply among "blacks," "whites," and "coloreds," denying rights to pure-blooded Negroes that were granted to those of mixed blood. For me *blacks* always brings memories of the insulting way *schwarzers* were disparaged in Yiddish, when in my teens I worked at a Harlem seltzer-bottling shop and later at a Chicago watermelon freight yard.

Quite a few Negroes of an older generation agree with my aversion to *black* and recall, like Russell Baker in a *New York Times* column recounting yesterday's now discarded notions, the time when "it was racist to refer to people of African ancestry as 'black.'" When *Ebony* was started in 1945, some people objected to the name, recalled publisher John Johnson. He noted in a *New York Times* interview forty years later: "Quite a few people wrote letters and said: 'Why are you calling us black? We're not black. We're Negro.'" Johnson remembered those days as a time when it was considered disparaging to be called "black" and the name *Ebony* was resented by many as insulting. But today, in what William F. Buckley, Jr., has described as "the anachronization of the word 'Negro,'" the reality is that "nobody uses the word *Negro* anymore, except maybe the United Negro College Fund." The bitter controversy over racial designations has continued unabated for well over a century to today, when *African American* is increasingly used. Back in 1848 abolitionist Henry Highland Garnet sagely observed: "How unprofitable it is for us to spend our golden moments in long and solemn debate upon the questions which we shall be called—'Africans,' 'Colored Americans,' or 'Africa-Americans' or 'Blacks.' The question should be, my friends, shall we arise and act like men, and cast off this terrible yoke?"

The first fifty dollars I was able to save after returning to Chicago went for what had become for me a necessity—a car to criss-cross the spread-out city. I chose a Model A Ford flivver with an outside rumble seat. Wartime rationing of gas made fill-ups increasingly problematic. To bypass rationing restrictions, I resorted to the same subterfuge as other *Defender* employees— listing my address as the Indiana Avenue office of the *Defender*—to get a gas allotment based on "special" standing as a journalist. The chairman of the local ration board was the publisher of the *Defender*, and that was convenient in obtaining extra gas stamps for a "war-related" necessary job. Since cheating on rationing was as common in Chicago as fixing traffic tickets with precinct captains, I had no hesitation in using my extra stamps. The issuance of the ration stamps, however, led to an incident that jolted me into recognizing that I was still ignorant of racial argot. I had routinely gone to the State Street ration board office, where I was shuffled around from one sullen, indifferent clerk to another until I complained to one woman about the delay, telling her my ration stamps were supposedly to be issued at her desk. "Who told you that?" the surly Negro clerk asked.

"That gal over there," I innocently responded, pointing to another black clerk.

"What did you say?"

"That gal over there," I repeated.

Thereupon she launched into a bitter denunciation of me and of my use of the term *gal*, equating it with the insulting use of *boy* in reference to adult black males. Like most white Americans of the time, I was still unaware that some expressions then in common use, such as *gal*, were considered demeaning and offensive by Negroes—and now also, of course, by women. I had to listen, subdued and meek, while taking my lumps. The word *gal* thereafter became taboo in my vocabulary whenever in the presence of black women.

If gas-rationing stamps were one of the fringe benefits of working on the *Defender*, replacing a blown-out tire on my venerable Model A was not included. For that, John Johnson volunteered his connections to what was a black market in more than one sense. He directed me to the owner of a fleet of cabs that operated along South Parkway picking up and dropping off residents of Chicago's "Black Belt." This man provided the right size tire when I mentioned Johnson's name, and he also proffered just about any kind of ration stamp I might want to buy. But I was fearful of buying even the "illegal" tire, let alone any ration stamps. Timidly I drove out of the jitney garage with my brand-new tire as if I were making a furtive getaway after a daring heist. I never did learn just how the black-market stamps and merchandise were obtained.

In later years I came to believe that whenever some seemingly impenetrable barrier faced us at his magazines, Johnson invariably would devise some offbeat tactic or find some shadowy character to enable us to bypass any roadblock. Perhaps it was just the power of the press that gave him his astonishing clout. I could not entirely discount what a press card and a newspaper connection could accomplish after I avoided a speeding ticket one day. Stopped by a plainclothes officer downtown on Randolph Street for driving too fast, I was asked to produce my driver's license. He slowly examined the card and then stared intently at me. "You live at 3435 South Indiana Avenue?" he asked.

"Nope, I just work there."

"You colored?"

"Nope."

"What you doing at that Indiana Avenue address?"

"I work for the *Chicago Defender.*"

"Oh, is that right? Do you know Dave Kellum down there?"

"Of course. We work together."

Thereupon his abrupt attitude changed entirely, as he claimed the much befriended Kellum as a longtime "buddy." He still wondered, however, why a white was working for a Negro newspaper. "Things are tough. It's a job," I told him, not attempting to explain my commitment to racial equality. He returned my license with the smiling admonition to "take it slow" and "give my regards to Dave."

Kellum and I divided day-to-day *Defender* chores, he presiding over the city edition while I edited the national version of the weekly. The ragtag reportorial staff we had, poorly paid with irregular hours, overtime pay unheard of, and expense accounts minimal, was a continuing parade of new faces. Most memorable for me was a small clique of no more than a half-dozen people who worked closely with me and whom I was able to enlist in the Newspaper Guild. Our star investigative reporter and feature writer was former radio scriptwriter Richard Durham, whom I had induced to take a reporter's job even though he had no journalistic background. A fast learner, Durham was slow and sometimes careless in his copy but highly creative in his feature interviews with big names. He was also persistent and penetrating in his exposé stories, such as his scoop on a mayoral candidate who had signed a restrictive covenant, which helped defeat the Democratic primary contender. Left-oriented at the *Defender*, he later shifted to the Black Muslim ranks to edit the newspaper *Mohammad Speaks*, and he then ghosted the autobiography of heavyweight champion Muhammad Ali.

A sterling backstop staff member was bright-eyed gnome Robert Lucas, a slow talker and fast writer who was also a would-be radio scriptwriter. His neat, clean copy was always a pleasure to handle. Jackie Lopez, a tall, attractive woman from Harlem, came to the editorial department as a beginner. I struggled to shape her roughly written news stories, patiently coaching her in reportorial basics, but she could not manage to master the craft before her departure. A transient beat reporter, barely literate but eager to learn, Hilliard McFall turned in scribbled notes on criminal court cases he covered, but often his barely decipherable writing was shaped into the *Defender*'s frequent sensational front-page crime headlines, though these were sometimes inaccurate because of his blunders. His talent was mainly in knowing how to get into places barred to most reporters, and I grew to admire his good-natured response to my occasional withering criticism. Another staff short-timer was pert Jackie Ormes, who was always upbeat but who, for all my attempts to shape her clumsy writing, never could measure up as a competent reporter. She achieved some later prominence as the creator of the first commercial Negro dolls on the market, Patti Jo and Benji.

Benji, a male doll, became the source of a racial mixup in our personal lives when I bought one for our son, Rich, then five. Benji and Rich became fast friends, and when a neighboring child grimaced on seeing Benji and remarked what a "funny" doll he was, Rich quickly came to Benji's defense.

"What do you mean, he's funny? He's just colored."

"Yes, but he's funny."

"Oh, no, he's not. He's colored, just like me. What's wrong with that?"

No one had ever told our youngsters they were colored or white, but with members of both races constantly in and out of our house, they had no racial awareness—we thought—until Rich cleared up our assumption with his claim to be colored.

In the daily war headlines, I increasingly perceived that the maelstrom in Europe and the Pacific was closing in on my refuge on Indiana Avenue at the *Defender*. I knew a day of decision on my future course was approaching in the form of the draft. Like many of my generation, I had to confront a vexing disparity after Pearl Harbor. Confirmed pacifists since the 1920s, raised on antiwar novels and propaganda, we were jolted into military awareness by Hitler's sweep across Europe and the anti-Semitic atrocities of the Nazis. Despite my leftist beliefs, I was not quite ready to follow the prescribed path of Communists, for whom concern for the Soviet "motherland," the heart and soul of world Marxism-Leninism, was the prime consideration. Many enlisted in the military immediately, but some of those who were known to the FBI discovered that instead of fighting on the frontlines, they were relegated to remote army camps where they were kept under close surveillance not unlike suspected Nazis. There, considered almost as enemy aliens, they worked at common labor, although Washington still loudly proclaimed its close alliance with Moscow. An unwritten but hard-and-fast dichotomy was maintained by the government between "disloyal" U.S. Communists and "friendly" Russian Communists. Some party members I knew managed to burrow through the FBI net and get into army uniforms. They were among the first casualties in battle.

My own ambivalent feelings—my long held pacifist convictions pitted against my knowledge that only superior armies could stop Hitlerism—were further complicated by my self-recognized cowardice. What kind of sorry soldier would I make? Could I ever put up with the rigid discipline of army training? Would I chicken out at my first exposure to gunfire? Should I register as a conscientious objector? Would I, as a Communist suspect, wind up in one of the isolated camps where known Communists were being sent?

For months I had no need to face up to these portentous questions since I was exempted first as a father, then as a journalist. But the inescapable reckoning was coming ever nearer. I sought to evade the draft by applying as a *Defender* war correspondent, attempting as much as possible to cover up my Communist Party connections, but even as I completed the War Department application, I sensed that my background would never pass muster in Washington. Although I did not know it then, the FBI file on me was already voluminous.

I clung to a tenuous hope of escaping army service, based on the unaccountable fluke of having slipped through a War Department clearance check in 1943 when I covered war games of the all-Negro 93rd Division in Louisiana. I flew down to Leesville on an air force plane with a score of Negro editors and top army brass, including the highest ranking Negro in the army, General Benjamin O. Davis. Watching army maneuvers in the muck and grime of Fort Polk and observing the GI regimen in barracks and tents confirmed my belief that the army was not for me and reinforced my resolve to stay out of military uniform.

One evening all the editors assembled in an officers' tent for a heated session with General Davis and Truman Gibson, then an assistant to the secretary of war, to question the army's still rigid segregation policy. I listened in amazement as incensed indictments were tossed freely at the two officials, who vainly sought to defend their "gradualist" stand. The editors, who included some of the top names in black journalism, blistered the army as aggressively in person as they regularly did in their editorial columns, and I restrained myself from openly applauding their pugnacious outbursts. For his part the general in his defense seemed to echo the World War I words of former president William Howard Taft: "The editors of the colored press should be reasoned with to cease publishing articles, however true, having inciting effect." In Washington, there had been talk of indicting the more vociferous black editors for sedition because of their harsh criticism of the War Department and its racist policies. President Roosevelt had delegated J. Edgar Hoover to oversee censorship, and some black editors could recall Hoover's recommendation after World War I to ban at least the most militant publications. He had urged that "something should be done to the editors of these publications as they are exciting the negro [sic] elements of the country to riot and to the committing of outrages." Attorney General Francis Biddle had warned Sengstacke in a Justice Department meeting that if papers like the *Defender* did not temper their blasts (many written by me) against army and navy discrimination, he would "shut them all up." Sengstacke had stood his ground, however, defying Biddle to "attempt it." To his credit, on his return to Chicago he never in any way sought to curb or tone down either our news reports about racial clashes in the military or our editorial attacks on discrimination in the armed services.

In contrast to some of the antipathy I faced at the *Defender*, the black editors on the press junket were all affable and considerate. On this, my first trip to the South as a "white Negro," I was the only non-Negro in the journalistic contingent. But because I was a *Chicago Defender* editor, many of the others assumed that I was black, even if light-skinned. Such was also the presumption of local police when one night a group of us went into town to the for-Negroes-only tavern and poolroom. I could have been legally prosecuted for eating and playing pool there, because racial segregation was a matter of state law, and a white no less than a black could be jailed for racial mixing. No one ever questioned my race, however, and I was never perceived as different from any other journalist on the junket. I learned a primary lesson in race relations of the times: if you associate with Negroes freely, people will assume you are a Negro. This was true not only in the South but with whites generally, and sometimes with Negroes too.

My status as national editor at the *Defender* sometimes caused embarrassment and discomfort among some staff members, when they had to introduce black visitors to their white editor. At the *Defender* and later at *Ebony* magazine, I wound up in the most remote office from the building entrance, relegated to the shadows like an outcast to avoid the quandary of being spotted as the "white boss" of a Negro publication. I could well understand the reasons why and readily accepted my sequestered role.

In the three years I worked for the *Defender* in the 1940s, few readers ever suspected that I was white. My byline appeared regularly on weekly book reviews and an occasional news story or feature, but the issue of my race was never raised. I scrupulously avoided publicity, striving to be accepted as just another editor.

I realized that my days at my *Defender* desk were numbered as news reports on the draft indicated that the military was enlisting any man it could. My inquiries to Washington about the status of my application as a war correspondent went unanswered, and I lost faith in my chances when several staff members with far less qualification than myself received approval for correspondent status. I began marking time until the fateful 1A classification would arrive.

Among the friendships of a lifetime that I treasure most was my rapport with Dan Burley, an irrepressible, dynamic scrivener for whom I immediately developed the warmest affection when we met for the first time during my Fort Polk stay. I was quartered in a two-person tent with Burley, who was covering the 93rd's maneuvers for the *New York Amsterdam News* of which he was then managing editor. Over the years he won my fullest admiration and respect for his mastery of the writing trade, his shrewdness, his wry sense of humor, his keen understanding of whites as well as of his fellow blacks, and on our introduction at Fort Polk, his prodigious ability on his portable typewriter. On that trip he filled endless footage at machine-gun speed on the roll of wire-service teletype paper he had brought with him, his copy billowing out of the typewriter. Burley was a walking encyclopedia on Negro life from jazz to politics, from sports to black history. Our couple of nights sharing an army tent marked the beginning of a staunch friendship that lasted until his death in 1963. Somehow our working paths seemed to coincide time and again, and I was to find myself on and off working in the same office with him for many years.

An accomplished self-taught boogie-woogie pianist and composer, Burley could easily have been a professional nightclub entertainer, but his love for words kept him at his typewriter despite many frustrations in a succession of underpaid jobs with Negro weeklies. In another time he would have been a star journalist on a metropolitan daily, but coming out of Chicago's gutter, uneducated and unpolished, resigned to the racism of white journalism in the 1930s, he remained trapped making the rounds of black publications. A self-described hustler in the tradition of the craft, he knew just how and where to palm a fiver for a news story, to partake of favors and handouts. But for all his slick ways he was always broke, incessantly cadging money that he rarely paid back, yet so ingenuous he could easily be forgiven and always come back for still another "touch." Always great company, he was buoyant with others no matter how he might feel inwardly. He was as generous and endearing with friends as he was waspish, gruff, and openly fractious with those he disliked.

In contrast to my close friendship with Burley, my relationship with most of the myriad contacts I cultivated in the black community for some thirty-five years rarely went beyond passing acquaintance, sometimes lasting a couple of years and rarely extending beyond our job association. Although I sought out blacks with whom I could find common interests beyond racial concerns—in intellectual or cultural matters or in hobbies or travel—I was only able to cultivate a handful of intimate black friends. I hopefully invited a stream of black visitors to our home for dinners, usually people whom I had met in the course of my editorial work, but when the conversation gravitated away from racial themes—perhaps to classical music or art, the theater or literature—somehow we would lose our black guests. This was not necessarily because they were unfamiliar with these subjects but rather because when they were with us, their interests lay more in what was, after all, the basis of our relationship—"the race thing."

Rarely was there a reciprocal invitation; we were seldom asked to parties on the South Side. Were my wife Esther and I pretentious snobs, too distant and remote from black life? Where had we failed in our attempts to welcome black visitors to our home? Somewhat bewildered, we probed deeply into our behavior and attitudes, stewing over whether we had displayed some kind of prejudice or committed some faux pas. But neither of us could think of any possible reason for the slights. We discovered that we were not alone among whites who vainly sought to cultivate more than just casual Negro friends. I was intrigued to read the comment by Eleanor Roosevelt in an *Ebony* article in the 1950s: "One of the odd things about my Negro friends is their consistent failure to invite me to their social gatherings. I am rarely invited to their weddings, musicals or teas. I invariably invite them to my house, but the invitation is not returned." With her typical graciousness, she speculated that the reason was perhaps that Negroes were "a little shy" or else thought she was too busy.

My own sense after many years working with blacks is that too many still find it difficult to relax and unbend socially with whites, always thinking they have to be on their best behavior. "No matter how I try I just can't seem to relax with white people," John Johnson once confessed to me. "Maybe it's Arkansas in my background but I guess I always have my guard up."

My first experience at the *Defender* in being taken for a Negro admittedly flustered me momentarily. Later I became more apt to smile at these incidents, which occurred with increasing frequency. In my introductory months at work, Lochard often found it convenient to assign me to some of the less agreeable chores around the office, among which was that of lecturing to visiting journalism students. When a class from Northwestern University along with their instructor, Curtis MacDougall, was due to arrive one particular Wednesday, Lochard passed to me the assignment of speaking to them about the Negro press. I managed to make the grade, at least until one woman demurely asked, "Do any white people work on the *Defender?*"

I must have squirmed subconsciously and then replied instinctively, since I did not have time to think about my answer. "But I'm white," I responded. I have never forgiven myself for the "but," which seemed almost defensive of my racial status as a white working for a Negro newspaper. I thought later that it amounted to an acknowledgment that there was something unworthy in being a Negro. The other students tittered when the questioner added to my discomfort by purring, "Oh, I'm so sorry." In calling me a Negro, obviously she thought she had insulted me and was quick to make her apologies. For both of us, the exchange was a sorry bit of politesse illustrative of societal prejudices of the day, and I in my denial was as guilty as she was.

In later years I often found curious reactions from people who learned that I worked for a Negro publication. Even when they knew I was not black, they were aware of my testiness on the matter of race and would be on their best behavior when talking to me about Negroes. Once a neighbor, who knew where I worked, casually mentioned while talking about cooking: "Only jigs know how to make barbecue." Then she flinched and added, "Oh, I'm sorry I said that." There were many acquaintances whom I recognized as confirmed racists and whom I realized were free and easy with such epithets as "nigger" and "coon," but they rarely used these words in my presence. When they did, I sensed that they were striving to sound me out, to see how far they could go in speaking their minds in their usual insulting prattle about Negroes. Sometimes I became unduly sanctimonious, putting them in their place for using frowned-upon words like *Negress*. I often regretted this assumption of righteousness.

No pangs of conscience upset me in one racial tangle, which made me aware of how little I knew about leftist friends who were supposedly sympathetic to the black cause. Several weeks after I had begun working at the *Defender*, one close friend phoned me at the office with her congratulations. Then she guardedly inquired: "Say, I've got a problem. Maybe you can help me. I've been looking high and low for a maid and just can't find one. Now that you're working at the *Defender*, maybe you can get me one down at your office." With much bitterness and restraint I informed her that "reporters, not maids" wrote for the *Defender*.

I heard similar stories from black professionals and businessmen. When one South Side minister was asked about a maid by an inquiring white friend, his pointed riposte was: "No, I'm afraid I can't help you. I too seem to be having trouble locating a maid. Do you know where I can find a white maid?"

2

The First Commercially
Successful Negro Magazine

The only truth is race; there is no other.
Benjamin Disraeli

T he idea of starting a new Negro magazine was first broached to me in the summer of 1942 by John H. Johnson during our political campaigning for congressional candidates Earl Dickerson and William L. Dawson. I first met Johnson in Dickerson's lawbook-lined second-floor offices at South Parkway and Thirty-fifth Street above the headquarters of the Supreme Liberty Life Insurance Company (of which Dickerson was legal counsel), and we soon became close friends.

An aspiring, well-groomed, resolute youth four years younger than I, Johnson was still hopeful of one day graduating from the University of Chicago (which he never did), while working as an underpaid, fifteen-dollar-a-week factotum on insurance company publicity. He had observed my versatility and celerity in both writing and editing while working on the Dickerson and Dawson campaigns; watching me, he became persuaded that I was the editor he needed—or at least the best available to him—in his dream of becoming a magazine publisher. Our working relationship had been smooth, supportive, and collegial in our months of politicking, and our friendship had become closer than just routine political contacts. If opposites attract, we were well matched: he the ambitious pragmatist with the goal of making money and I the radical, self-effacing workaholic. If not a marriage of minds and aspirations, ours was nevertheless a joining of professed journalistic pursuits. When he broached his magazine concept, I readily accepted his proposal.

His idea was simplicity itself: a compendium of the best and most significant articles on the Negro appearing in white as well as black publications. The obvious title: *Negro Digest*. The model: *Reader's Digest*. Yet what appeared a promising publishing venture had many negatives to raise doubts about its viability. The history of black publishing was strewn with repeated magazine failures. The only survivors in the early 1940s were *Crisis* and *Opportunity*, the organization-supported journals of the NAACP and Urban League, respectively, both of which stayed afloat only through membership dues. The last attempt at a popular mass-circulation magazine had been *Abbott's Monthly*, several issues of which were published by the *Chicago Defender* in October 1929 before the venture succumbed to the effects of the stock market crash and Great Depression.

While many black newspapers began to thrive after the turn of the century, black magazines were consistent, short-lived flops. The first Negro publication, *Freedom's Journal*, issued by John B. Russworm, America's first Negro college graduate, and Samuel E. Cornish in New York City in 1827, had the format of a magazine but is generally classified as a newspaper. It earned its place in journalistic history by printing what white publications of the day would not: the militant abolitionist protests aimed at organizing Negro support for freedom of all slaves. As an out-and-out protest organ, it was highly effective in accomplishing what nobody else was doing, not even white abolitionists. It survived just two years and was followed by a succession of transitory Negro newspapers and magazines, all basically protest organs until the late nineteenth century, when the budding Negro press began to turn its attention to the new black society created by emancipation. For the first time columns were devoted to social doings in papers like the *Philadelphia Tribune*, which commenced publishing in 1884 and has managed to survive to today.

Militant black journalism began in the early twentieth century, when a new racial awareness was aroused by the birth of such crusading groups as the NAACP, formed in 1909. In the following years, when lynching and the Ku Klux Klan were at their peak and Negro morale at its lowest, Negro newspapers rose to their highest circulation figures as they became the most bellicose voice of the race and flourished as negative protest journalism.

Black magazines, however, never could succeed in the decades when Negro newspapers blossomed. Between 1838, when the first Negro magazine, *Mirror of Liberty*, was initiated by David Ruggles, and 1909, no fewer than eighty-four magazines were founded, according to a survey by University of Michigan researcher Penelope Bullock. All of them quickly expired. (Oddly, one of the failures, published in Philadelphia in April 1906 by Thomas Swann, was titled *Ebony*, a name that was used again in 1945 by Johnson to launch the most successful Negro magazine ever published.) All the race magazines confronted the same problem Ruggles had faced with his *Mirror of Liberty*. Six months after his first issue, Ruggles wrote of "the rough and inclement season of adversity which we have been called upon to endure since the appearance of the first number of this periodical." He was unable to make ends meet because of inability to collect sufficient subscription monies, the main source of income when advertising revenue was minimal.

Many of the black magazines of the nineteenth century were religious organs, and all of these quickly became defunct despite church collections for their support. Among those who failed as publishers was Frederick Douglass, whose magazine *Douglass' Monthly* (successor to his weekly newspaper, *North Star*) survived for five years. The great antislavery leader ceased publication of the monthly in 1863 "for want of what is justly due us," his way of describing the problem of collecting from delinquent subscribers.

To me the prospects in 1942 for *Negro Digest* or any racial magazine finding a broad readership and prospering when so many periodicals had perished in the past seemed dim indeed. When I learned that another *Negro Digest*, with exactly the same title as the sanguine Johnson's, had died after several issues, I began to believe that Johnson was pursuing an idle dream, and I conveyed my pessimism to him. But he remained confident of his scheme and even asked me to invest in it: five hundred dollars would buy a partnership. I refused, however, in the belief that *Negro Digest* would not succeed with a couple of novices at its helm and for lack of five hundred dollars in my threadbare bank account.

Moreover, Johnson's resume at that time did not inspire much confidence or sketch the picture of an imaginative, bigtime "Henry Luce in sepia," as he was called in a *Vanity Fair* panegyric some forty years later. At that time Johnson better fit the description of him in an *Advertising Age* piece in 1965, as looking like a "reticent bookkeeper." If his business experience was zero back in 1942, still my months of working with him in politics had convinced me of his doggedness, ambition, and readiness for hard work even if he sometimes lapsed into lassitude. Though he had edited his high school newspaper, he was self-critical and apprehensive enough about his own skills as a writer and editor to impel him to turn to me to edit his projected magazine, even if *Negro Digest* was to consist mainly of reprinted articles. For my part, I was not about to allow this opportunity to edit a magazine to slip by, even though the proposed salary seemed to amount to a mendicant offering a pauper a piece of a possible handout. Even though our first venture—Dickerson's ill-fated congressional campaign (he was defeated by Dawson)—had been a failure, I was willing to gamble a second time on a possible success with Johnson.

Indefatigable and not easily dissuaded, Johnson had been looking for financial angels everywhere. The Negro businessmen he had approached had turned him down, including his initial benefactor, Harry H. Pace, president of Supreme Liberty Life Insurance, who had taken Johnson under his wing upon his high school graduation. Pace had originally given Johnson the incentive and idea for *Negro Digest*. Pace himself had faced a touchy predicament as a busy insurance executive: Too busy with mortality charts and risk rates to keep up with racial events, yet feeling he had to know what was going on in the world of color, he turned to Johnson for a prudent solution to his problem. In Johnson—a promising entry-level employee hired at fifteen dollars a week—Pace found a ready answer to his need to know everything of significance in print in the white press. Johnson's assignment was to riffle through dozens of papers and magazines and "look for the word 'Negro,'" as he recalled some years later. If his boss wanted a "digest" of this sort, Johnson concluded, there must be a market in the black community for such a product.

Scoffing at this idea, I asked Johnson, "How are you going to sell a quarter magazine when the Negro papers are just getting through by the skin of their teeth on a dime?"

"You know there's a war on," countered Johnson. "Big things are in the air and we can get in on them if we make the right moves. The magazine can't miss."

He was right, and I was wrong. In spite of the lack of investors, the irrepressible, headstrong Johnson decided he would go ahead on his own if I would agree to handle the editorial end of the magazine. Dubious as I was about its possible success and even doubting my own ability to piece together a magazine, since I had no experience in magazine publishing, I still reluctantly agreed to Johnson's proposal. I did all the editorial work and makeup on the first issue at home on my kitchen table, much of it after a long day of house painting in the morning and followed by hours of work at either the *Defender* or the Dickerson or Dawson campaign offices.

My desire to get back into journalism plus my gullibility in embracing a worthy cause made me an easy mark for Johnson's proposal that he pay me all of twenty-five dollars to put together the first issue of *Negro Digest*. But after agreeing to accept twenty-five dollars per month, my liberality did not extend past the first three issues; just in case, by some miracle, *Negro Digest* was a success, I wanted my gamble to pay off. I proposed that after the first three months my monthly stipend be doubled to fifty dollars, and Johnson readily agreed. I became more confident about being able to produce a saleable professional product after carefully perusing back issues of *Reader's Digest*. Clearly, its format would be easy to replicate. Even though I lacked magazine experience, I did understand the practice of journalistic mimicry, not uncommon among media practitioners, and I could easily imitate the typefaces, layout, and style of the nation's most successful magazine.

With his editor lined up, Johnson set out to find a printer with adequate equipment and inadequate business sense willing to speculate and take the *Negro Digest* job on credit. In view of his limited capital assets, however, he found no takers. Nonetheless, by what began as a ruse, the fledgling publisher managed to get five thousand copies of his first edition off the press. As part of his insurance company job, Johnson handled a monthly house organ produced at Progress Printing Company on Halsted Street near Thirty-third. The not-too-alert composing room supervisor who processed the insurance company copy did not suspect that the copy Johnson gave him one day was for his projected *Negro Digest* instead. The cagey Johnson kept telling the printer what "they" wanted, and the gullible supervisor assumed that "they" was the insurance company. He accepted the copy as regular insurance company material and processed it accordingly. In fact, the copy was manuscripts—actually pages torn out of white magazines and newspaper columns—that I had condensed, edited, and prepared for typesetting in spite of serious doubts whether it would ever see the light of a Linotype machine. I was very surprised to get it back in neat galley proofs, ready for pasting up on dummy pages. While *Negro Digest* was being handled as regular insurance company billing, the printer, whose nickname I recall as Gabby, finally became aware that something was amiss. Johnson confessed his trickery and then, by guile and persuasion, convinced Gabby that since he had already set most of the *Negro Digest* copy, he might as well finish the job. He swore that he would somehow manage to pay the printing costs. Gabby grudgingly agreed to gamble on Johnson's promises and projections of a major magazine job in his small shop in months to come, although probably believing that the proposition was as risky as a Las Vegas roulette spin.

In the disorderly storefront print shop, I was called upon to struggle to make up magazine pages with compositors whose previous experience seemed to be limited to business cards and sales throwaways. The two painfully slow Linotype operators in the shop were a Pole and a Lithuanian, whose knowledge of English was shaky at best, and the stonemen pied (jumbled) two pages of type out of the sixty-eight pages before we were able to start running on the press. For all my hours of proofreading, half the line breaks in the magazine split words in the wrong place. The most grievous flaws were the occasional "blackheads"—printer's lingo for space slugs that worked their way up to blemish pages with black blobs when printing from original type, as we did with our short press run of only five thousand copies.

Johnson raised some cash by borrowing policyholder lists from the insurance company, where he still worked, and soliciting charter subscriptions at two dollars a year, even while *Negro Digest* was as yet a figment of his imagination. He later said that he paid for that mailing with five hundred dollars borrowed on his mother's furniture. Since he confessed that writing was not his strong suit, I was called upon to help draft solicitation letters, the first of many subscription promotion pieces I created in the early years of *Negro Digest*. Patriotism mixed with commercialism in the appeal I wrote for subscriptions to be sent to black GIs by relatives back home. For servicemen the low rate was only two dollars a year, and before long the military addresses were plentiful in sacks of *Negro Digest* mail. In Dickerson's private offices, Johnson and his wife Eunice mimeographed the initial mailing of some twenty thousand letters to potential subscribers and prayerfully dispatched the sacks of mail. The response from some three thousand subscribers was enough to keep *Negro Digest* afloat until payment for newsstand sales began trickling in.

In spite of its shoestring debut, *Negro Digest* filled an immense gap on newsstands in black communities; in November of 1942, when it made its appearance, there were no generally circulated Negro magazines. The lineup of writers—including Carl Sandburg, Langston Hughes, Roland Hayes, Quentin Reynolds, Marquis Childs, Walter White, Bishop Bernard J. Sheil, and Roi Ottley—would have done any white magazine proud and would surely attract black readers who had never before had a publication of this caliber.

Although short on bulk and long on typographical errors, the package with its two-color cover was still quite professional in makeup, printing, and paper quality. Comprehensive as well as entertaining, it included initially a book digest by popular newsletter editor W. M. Kiplinger from his *Washington Is Like That*; humor, which was rare in black weeklies; and controversy in a debate, "Should Negroes Demand Equality Now?" with southern editor John Temple Graves staunchly upholding the traditional Dixie negative and a *Negro Digest* poll by "Wallace Lee" on the same subject. ("Wallace Lee," the poll director, was the first of many assumed names I adopted in my years of working for the Negro press. My sample polling to reflect national opinion was usually no more than a dozen acquaintances, but my margin of error was probably no greater than those of so-called scientific polls.) As a paste-pot product pieced together on my kitchen table, *Negro Digest* was a creditable pastiche of what the white press as well as the black weeklies were publishing about Negroes.

Much of that first issue still seems timely and valid today, a half-century later. Certainly Sandburg's prophetic words are still meaningful as ghetto life gnaws at the vitals of America's cities:

> The slums get their revenge, always somehow or other their retribution can be figured in any community. No slum is separated from its community. Thousands of mean and sinister streets stretch out indefinite bonds from the slum to the outer world.

In my race-angled duplication of the *Reader's Digest* format, mimicry was not restricted to its type styles and page arrangements. We also imitated such familiar features as "Quotable Quotes," which became "Potent Prose" in our pages, and "Most Embarrassing Moments," which became "My Most Humiliating Jim Crow Experience" in *Negro Digest*. Our front cover was an exact look-alike of the *Reader's Digest*, listing titles and authors in similar typefaces. If Johnson had any trepidation that he might be subject to legal restraints in this outright reproduction of *Reader's Digest* in a Negro version, he showed no fear and seemed confident that there would be no outright complaint. This was partly because we were such minor-league players but also because he sensed that *Reader's Digest* would either be flattered that Negroes would poach its image or be hesitant to seek legal redress lest it be accused of racial bias.

One *Reader's Digest* feature, however, we did not copy: its payment to authors of perhaps the highest word rate of any magazine. Our total editorial outlay averaged no more than two hundred fifty dollars an issue, no doubt the lowest of any periodical of the day. For the first issue the editorial costs added up to less than two hundred dollars, including the twenty-five paid me to edit the package. Our rates for reprints ranged from a low of ten dollars per article to a high of twenty-five. In requesting permission for reprints, Johnson's letters offering a meager "token fee" were in the Yiddish tradition of *schnorren*. He played the part of the impoverished, struggling publisher of a praiseworthy but destitute racial-cause magazine, and almost invariably the tin-cup stratagem worked in the early years of *Negro Digest*.

In a sense *Negro Digest* was an entirely new publishing concept for the black press: the first time a black publication did not polemicize, was not agitational, did not protest, did not editorialize in any way, did not plead the Negro's cause. Its sole aim was to reprint what was most significant in the white and black media about Negroes, even if the material was unfavorable to the race. As such, it was acceptable even to white southerners, though few had enough interest in race relations to read *Negro Digest*.

Johnson's stated editorial aim was to escape the "radical" label that had been stamped on the Negro press because of its truculence in seeking immediate racial equality as the price of Negro support for the war effort. The *Pittsburgh Courier*'s "Double V—Victory at Home and Abroad" jeremiad set a clamorous, disputatious tone that was followed by most other black weeklies, which balked at conforming to wartime pressures to curtail if not eliminate their protests against racial discrimination. In the South, white editors and politicians returned Negro press invective in kind. This was true even of southern liberals, such as Virginius Dabney, who complained in the prestigious *Atlantic Monthly* about the "astounding and alarming" way in which "incendiary" Negro newspapers "harp constantly in racial grievances." Dabney warned that "riots would probably break out if they were widely read by whites."

Johnson wanted *Negro Digest* to set a moderate tone, which remained the mark of his publishing ventures for years to come, and it was my finicky, discretionary assignment to set a middle course in assembling *Negro Digest*'s contents. If I had any compunctions about this "neutral" policy, I remained ultra-defensive, fearful of being smeared with a "Red" label, unwilling to battle strenuously for my views and retreating hurriedly when I sensed danger. Thus, some strange pieces appeared in the magazine. For example, as if there were possibly some merit to the opposite side, in our second issue we ran "both sides of the question" on the topic, "Is Lynching Justified?" We made use of a hysterical letter to the editor defending lynching as "necessary in a state where more people are colored than white," which was published in the New York daily *PM* as a reply to its antilynching stand.

I was able to contrive at least one *Digest* feature that targeted some of the worst expressions of southern racism, which was at its peak in response to steps taken by President Roosevelt to ease racial restrictions. Called "Dixie Drivel," the page ferreted out statements from top state officials and atavistic Klansmen. The page included quotations such as these:

> I firmly believe that racial discrimination is a divine thing. The South loves the Negro in his place, but his place is at the back door. (Eugene Talmadge, governor of Georgia)

If a nigger ever tried to get into a white school in my part of the state, the sun would never set on his head. (Ellis Arnall, governor of Georgia)

No white man should be forced to sit next to a fellow American who is dark; that is one of the four freedoms. (Millard Tydings, governor of Maryland)

White people have had generations and generations of experience in the taking of fares from the public. Negroes do not have the years of cultural experience behind them. (E. D. Merrill, president of Capitol Transit Company, Washington, D.C.)

After some months, however, Johnson found that the "Dixie Drivel" headline "offended" some southerners and in May 1943 it was changed to "Chatter Box" over my feeble objections.

As if I were not doing enough editorially, I also was called upon to write press releases on the highlights of each month's issue. These were used regularly in the Negro weeklies and also were picked up by the wire services and white dailies around the country. I also took over from Johnson the careful foraging through dozens of magazines and newspapers for any mention of Negroes: it was a fatiguing job, but it fit in conveniently with my work as national editor of the *Defender:* I could reprint the clippings in the *Digest* and rewrite them for the *Defender.* To expand *Negro Digest* beyond mere reprints, after several issues I devised the first of our original features: quizzes and puzzles for readers on subjects from black history, literature, and current events, a kind of racial Trivial Pursuit. Heartened by prominent white writers' encouraging contributions to our "If I Were a Negro" series, which began in our second issue, I began soliciting original articles for the *Digest,* in spite of our low rate of pay for authors. Both Marshall Field and Orson Welles were among the early contributors of "If I Were a Negro" commentaries; they were paid only fifteen dollars for their pieces. *Time* magazine gibed that they were more "hot and bothered about the race question" than Johnson himself. Book publishers welcomed our use of excerpts from racial works and began sending advance galleys for our perusal and possible use. A notable coup was publication of a chapter from Lillian Smith's controversial novel *Strange Fruit,* before its publication date. Part of Richard Wright's *Black Boy* ran in *Negro Digest* before the book was published.

By July 1943, less than a year after its start, we could proudly proclaim that *Negro Digest* was "the biggest Negro magazine in the world, barring none"— a hollow claim of sorts because there were so few other Negro magazines in existence, yet meaningful in our pioneering of a successful popular Negro periodical when all previous attempts had failed.

My name was not on the first issue of *Negro Digest*, although I had single-handedly put the magazine together. Not until August 1944 was I finally listed as associate editor. Until then Johnson's was the only name on the masthead, as managing editor (he added the title of publisher only after a full year of publication). His identity as a Negro and as the sole personality behind *Negro Digest* was critical to the magazine's acceptance, he insisted. He was fearful that self-demeaning Negroes, seeing a well-crafted product and lacking faith in their own talents, would be apt to mutter disparagingly, "Must be some ofay behind it," and I believed his contention. Recognizing the risks involved in disclosing my color, I readily accepted my anonymous role—not only because I was an "alien" white but also because it could prove an embarrassment if my Communist Party ties were uncovered. I did, however, manage to get the name of "Burns" into the table of contents by a ploy: we began a new feature, "Color Craze," in August 1943, shortly after my son Richard was born, and I used his name as a byline.

Although Johnson had no role in editing *Negro Digest*, in spite of his title of managing editor, in later years he embellished his personal success story by claiming to have edited the *Digest*. For example, an article by Richard Dunlap, published in 1986 in the American Airlines publication *American Way*, stated—no doubt based on Johnson's own words—that "Johnson and his wife prepared the copy for the first issue." The only "preparation" Johnson did was to pick up copy from my home and deliver it to the printer.

From the first day we met in Dickerson's office, Johnson had known full well of my Communist background, having been privy to Dickerson's frequent strategy sessions with William L. Patterson, my party sponsor. But he never questioned my leftist politics when we commenced working together on *Negro Digest*. Despite my Communist affiliation, he needed me at that particular time for what I could bring to his young venture as well as for my willingness to listen to, even if not to accept, his sometimes waffling racial views. For my part, being unsure and unversed in black journalism, I believed that as a Negro Johnson knew best about racial matters and that I should heed his guidance. I also recognized that Johnson would provide entry for me into the then untested field of Negro magazines. In our symbiotic relationship over more than a dozen years, my leftist inclinations were never discussed or mentioned by Johnson, although we frequently disagreed, sometimes loudly, about his now conservative, now militant opinions and particularly about his irksome penchant for truckling to financial considerations in his editorial thinking.

Johnson's juggling of debits and credits at the inception of *Negro Digest* lay outside my restricted area of interest, especially because I had by that time become a full-time editor of the *Chicago Defender*. The *Defender* occupied most of my time, and for me it was the greatest challenge, the concern that was uppermost in my thoughts, the most stimulating job I had ever had, and the one that offered the greatest potential. *Negro Digest* for me was supplementary to my *Defender* job, a moonlighting project for extra income, one that fit conveniently into my *Defender* schedule as well as my racial interests. Yet in editing the magazine, I inevitably became concerned in its financial welfare, which depended on its circulation. This primed my editorial orientation to invest the magazine with freshness aside from routine reprints, to make its pages alive and not just a rehash, to find provocative articles that would prompt browsers at magazine racks to buy *Negro Digest*. The search for sales-stimulating articles in time brought about the partial abandonment of our reprint-only policy, and as was the case with *Reader's Digest*, our articles soon came from a growing stable of freelancers as well as from well-known writers.

Among Johnson's talents was his ability to wheedle articles out of prominent writers for ridiculously low, "token" payments. I initiated story ideas with circulation appeal, and Johnson would draft a letter soliciting a designated writer for a contribution. Our payments were never higher than twenty-five dollars. The fee was certainly no lure, but I hoped that the subject would be challenging enough to provoke a response to Johnson's solicitation letter, which always appealed for a writer's "help for a new worthy publishing venture" that lacked the necessary income to compensate writers at their "true worth." That our publication was Negro was also, of course, an influential factor. In most cases the strategy worked. Our list of writers of "begged" originals for several years included the outstanding names in the craft.

Over the years Johnson came genuinely to believe that he personally had originated many of the new features in *Negro Digest*. A typical instance was the idea for the much publicized "If I Were a Negro" series, which originated under that title as an article in the *Chicago Daily News*, written by its financial editor, Royal F. Munger, and reprinted in the second issue of *Negro Digest*. Thereupon, I drafted a form letter to nationally known individuals requesting similar articles and offering them a token payment. Eventually we were surprised to receive a contribution from Eleanor Roosevelt, which impressively boosted the circulation of our October 1943 issue and proved a turning point in the magazine's profitability. When Johnson later retold the story, however, as he did in a *New York Post* article by Helen Duder in 1962, he claimed, "I got the idea of running a series of articles by prominent white people on 'If I Were A Negro.'"

The distribution aspect of the magazine business was entirely new to Johnson, and he soon learned to his dismay, after the heartening initial subscription response, that it was not as simple as it seemed. The biggest Chicago wholesaler balked at handling something entirely new, a Negro magazine. To prove there was a market for *Negro Digest*, Johnson turned to something like an old theatrical gambit—papering the house with free passes to make a play look like a hit. He induced friends to make the rounds of the South Side as well as downtown Loop newsstands seeking to buy *Negro Digest*. When they were told that a newsstand did not carry the magazine, they would request that the dealer obtain copies. The tactic worked, and the wholesaler agreed to distribute this Negro magazine on a regular basis. To make certain the distributor would keep the title in stock at outlets, Johnson used whatever spare cash he had to go around buying up copies of his own magazine to prime the market. Audacious and determined, Johnson spared no detail to succeed in his venture. He remained undaunted by discouraging predictions of his downfall, including a warning from NAACP executive and *Crisis* editor Roy Wilkins that "you'll never make it." In his ambition to make *Negro Digest* a viable business, he was driven by his youthful indigence and privation as I was by my striving to find a better life. He never slowed in his pursuit of wealth even when, after twenty years in business, he finally attained it.

I had grown up in the Chicago slums, but Johnson had had to climb up to them from his early years in the river town of Arkansas City, Arkansas, across from Mississippi. In those cotton-growing bottomlands the worst of southern Jim Crow was part of day-to-day existence. For him, like myself an only child, early boyhood was spent without a father. Mine had abandoned me when I was a baby, and I never knew him until I was ten years old; his had been killed in a sawmill accident when Johnson was only six years old. In the early days of our relationship, he never mentioned his background of poverty, nor I mine. We never talked about the past, but always about the future, striving to erase yesterday's penury from our minds and hoping for a better tomorrow. Much of his by now legendary rise I learned for the first time in news clippings rather than from Johnson himself, despite our long years of association: how he went through the eighth grade twice because his Arkansas hometown had no high school for Negroes; how he spent days in a Red Cross tent colony one spring during a Mississippi River flood; how he first came to Chicago with his remarried mother at the age of fifteen to attend high school while his mother worked as a housemaid for four dollars a day; how he lived on relief for eighteen months after his mother lost her job; how he was elected class president at DuSable High School; how he obtained a part-time job through the National Youth Administration while his stepfather worked on a Works Projects Administration project to support the small family; and how during an Urban League honors convocation, the young man caught the eye of insurance company executive Harry Pace, who offered him a part-time job while he attended the University of Chicago, which he left to work full time at Supreme Insurance. And then came the gestation and birth of *Negro Digest*.

Within a year the magazine was selling more than 150,000 copies each month, its circulation stimulated by Negroes' increased income from jobs in World War II defense industries. This was the time when many rural black migrants to big cities began to enjoy their first big paychecks and a higher standard of living. In those days the United States was suddenly discovering the Negro in its midst. Washington dispatched to bigoted bureaucrats across the nation the admonition that black hands could be as vital as those of whites with lathes and mortars. The federal government began to advocate racial mixture at home and at the front. The print media, as if by prearranged signal, published a deluge of lachrymose pieces about the plight of the "darker brother." The sudden attention caused the Negro press to issue jarring reminders about past racial transgressions and to make uninhibited, strident demands for full equality for the tenth of the nation that was black. The Negro public savored their new economic status and aspired to a better life, and they found joy in reading about the surging momentum for equality, sparked by eloquent claims about the brotherhood of man and by the antiracist propaganda crusade against Hitlerism. It was a period when all race publications attained new circulation highs, and *Negro Digest* grew apace. With more readers buying the magazine, we were able to increase its size, which reached 102 pages by August 1943. Even so, in the early war years so much was written about the Negro that we had to discard for lack of space much that was percipient and approbatory in white journals.

By late fall 1943, Johnson felt assured enough of his future as a publisher that he vacated the office space he shared with Dickerson and rented a storefront for his circulation operations at 5619 South State Street, close to the Club Delisa nightspot. For all practical purposes, the editorial offices still remained my kitchen table, but the table had been shifted to a new address.

My family now resided in what for us was a sumptuous, six-room apartment at 3725 South Lake Park Avenue, square against the Illinois Central rail tracks. Esther and I had decided to move closer to the black community, even though Lake Park Avenue then was lily-white, blanketed by a restrictive covenant that mandated Cottage Grove Avenue, just two blocks away, as the arbitrary frontier between black and white neighborhoods.

Up to the time of our move, I had only been writing about racial problems, denouncing housing discrimination in editorials for the *Defender*. In our new location we found ourselves squarely in the midst of the racial problem of the times, living in a racially contested pustule of realty where Negroes legally could not rent or buy homes. In this tense area, racial lines were beginning to break down as Negro families periodically filtered across the Cottage Grove Avenue boundary despite stubborn legal attempts by white real estate agents to keep them out. This was before the U.S. Supreme Court ruled that restrictive covenants were unenforceable by law. Like some of my leftist associates in the Lake Park Avenue enclave, we were disquieted and conscience-stricken to find ourselves residing in what amounted to a Jim Crow enclave in the midst of the South Side. In our close neighborhood social circle, we stayed quite chummy with Negro friends from "across the line," all of us quick to bemoan and berate the covenants and the realty racists who sought to uphold them.

The two-flat building where we lived belonged to the Home Owners Loan Corporation (HOLC), a government agency that had taken it over after foreclosing the mortgage. The HOLC agent to whom I paid fifty dollars in monthly rent informed me one day that I could get a good buy on the building and make myself some "easy money." The asking price for the two six-room apartments, both of which were in good shape, was only six thousand dollars, of which I need only deposit a six-hundred-dollar down payment. Paying off the rest would be not much more difficult than paying monthly rent. With a mischievous smile he observed that I could make a big profit when I resold, assuring me that Negroes were bound to start moving into Lake Park Avenue before long and that I would have to get out. Incensed at his gratuitous presumption and slightly pompous in my response, I assured the HOLC agent that I was not the kind of white who "ran" when Negroes moved into the neighborhood. I summarily rejected his tempting offer. The notion that I could profiteer on racial discrimination—an idea the HOLC agent took no pains to disguise—was reprehensible according to all my interracial inclinations, zealous and magnanimous as I was in my dedication to the Negro cause.

Several years later, however, I had to question whether my self-righteousness had not been fuzzy thinking and bad business sense. When James

Baldwin reproved the ultra-virtuous, "No one is more dangerous than he who imagines himself pure in heart," he might also have added how masochistic they can be. As the agent had predicted, we did move out of the apartment— not because of a black invasion of the neighborhood but rather because I went off to become a sailor in the merchant marine. The building was sold to a white real estate agent, who resold to a Negro family at a three-thousand-dollar profit in less than a year. I was surprised to learn, upon my return from a couple of months at sea in the late spring of 1943, that the apartment we had occupied had become the home of Rep. William L. Dawson, for whom I had campaigned just a couple of years previously. Why the well-to-do Dawson had moved into the modest Lake Park Avenue house I could not fathom. I knew he could afford much better. But was there much better available in the district he represented? With the knee-jerk reactions of my radical years, I found myself contemplating the irony in racism that would oblige a well-heeled black member of Congress to make his home the onetime low-rent flat of his former meagerly paid white employee. Years later I learned the hard fact that Dawson had bought the house simply as a "good investment."

Day-to-day living on Lake Park Avenue adjacent to the heart of what in the 1940s was called Chicago's "Black Belt" could sometimes be tense and hazardous. Often when our Negro friends were not within hearing, our left-wing crowd would candidly face up to our personal concern about crime in our immediate neighborhood. For our tightly knit group of radicals, the embarrassing discrepancy between our expressed belief in the right of Negroes to live where they wished and the acknowledged facts of black crime was troubling. Working for two Negro publications and writing editorials in the *Defender* impugning whites who insisted that Negroes had criminal tendencies, I found it particularly disconcerting to face the Lake Park Avenue dilemma. I did not dare speak to my Negro friends about my bewilderment and chagrin for fear they would brand me as prejudiced. We could not escape the dilemma by moving out of the Lake Park Avenue apartment, not only because it might appear that we were fleeing an adjacent Negro neighborhood but also because by then the flow of wartime workers into Chicago had already filled the available supply of housing. The only practical solution seemed to be to install more locks on our doors and windows and to behave cautiously, always on the lookout for possible intruders or muggers.

Not too many years later, when I became closer to my Negro friends and was able to speak more freely about race and crime, I found that we were only doing what many Negroes had to do. They did not attempt to deny that crime flourished in black neighborhoods and their outskirts, and they even hesitated to take obvious refuge in ghetto poverty as the cause of black crime. Rather, to them black crime became an immutable fact of black life in America, another facet in the nefarious web of racism that entrapped Negroes from the day they were born.

"There exists among the intolerably degraded the perverse and powerful desire to force into the arena of the actual those fantastic crimes of which they have been accused, achieving their vengeance and their own destruction through making the nightmare real," wrote James Baldwin. Thus, the Wabash Avenue police station on Chicago's South Side was one of the world's busiest— a logical consequence of forcing many Negroes to labor at the nastiest, lowest paying jobs in Chicago, if indeed they had jobs at all. Contemptuous of white man's laws designed to keep them harried, harassed, and hemmed in the ghetto, blacks could find reason enough to make the white "nightmare real," as Baldwin wrote.

The net of the bedeviled South Side trapped not only the underclass (a sociological term not yet coined in the 1940s) but also the emerging black middle class, as well as thousands of law-abiding black workers condemned to live in restricted, crime-plagued black neighborhoods. In sheer self-interest, better educated Negroes with higher incomes were more concerned with black-on-black crime than with black-on-white crime. To them, blacks murdering blacks—a far more prevalent type of crime than blacks killing whites—was just another aspect of life in racist America. They had to stay put, install more locks on their doors, and keep a wary lookout for muggers when out after dark, if they dared venture forth at all. That is what we, too, did on Lake Park Avenue, and never once were we robbed or disturbed during those years, although we often came home at all hours of the night. In fact, the only time our home was broken into and robbed was when we moved to a white suburb years later.

At the *Defender* office I heard stories of single Negro women who never dared go out alone after dark. Curiously, this provided solace for my disturbed conscience, easing my apprehension that I might be guilty of casuistry concerning the facts of Negro crime. Yet I wondered: was I being entirely honest with myself concerning my full acceptance of the simple postulate that poverty makes crime? Was there more than just slum misery behind the high black crime rate? Why did so many black gangs thrive while committing mayhem against their own people? What could account for the many domestic murders of blacks by blacks, described by a black police commissioner in New York, Benjamin Ward, as "our little secret"?

Many years later Jesse Jackson, in a frustrated outburst at a Chicago meeting, decried "black on black murder . . . the leading cause of death in black males ages fifteen to forty-four." Jackson voiced the personal fears of many black urban residents: "There is nothing more painful for me than to walk down the street and hear footsteps and start thinking about robbery—then look around and see somebody white and feel relieved."

Adding a further, regressive twist to my disturbing apprehensions about black crime was the advice from my *Defender* cronies that front-page headlines on crime sold more papers than any other news category. For me at that time, just to ponder the subject of black crime was enough to evoke qualms about my commitment to racial equality and self-questioning about my freedom from all traces of prejudice. Still a raw recruit into the Negro world and black journalism, I mentally castigated myself for even the flickering thought that black crime might have causes beyond environment and racism. "Violence can be a potent drug for the oppressed person," black psychiatrist Alvin Poussaint has written. "Reacting to the futility of his life, the individual derives an ultimate sense of power when he holds the fate of another human being in his hands." In simpler terms, a community leader in Liberty City, Florida, named Otis Pitts, summed up black crime as the Negro response to racism in a 1989 *Time* magazine article: "Crime is a subtle form of revolution. Every robbery is somebody's personal riot." For me that statement, neatly tailored to all my assumptions in those early *Defender* days, helped placate my troubled conscience and explain even the most heinous of black crimes.

3

A Premature Anti-Racist

The trouble with colored people is that they never ask for enough: they should ask for everything—then they might get something.
Lincoln Steffens

Accustomed for most of my young life to "the worst of times," having become a confirmed pessimist after continued jolts of adversity, I could only anticipate some new calamity to end my idyll in editing both a weekly newspaper and a monthly magazine. Realistically, I recognized that my days as a civilian were numbered. My application to obtain war correspondent status went unanswered, and as I watched other *Defender* staffers (including an unqualified legal hanger-on with no journalistic experience whatsoever) dodge the draft by receiving accreditation as a correspondent, I finally turned to a last resort to stay out of the army: I opted to enlist in the merchant marine in spring of 1944, after a year and a half of working for the *Defender* and *Negro Digest*. Although I had no sea-going experience, I was able to sign on as an ordinary seaman through the CIO National Maritime Union (NMU).

I knew my departure from the *Defender* would present no logistical difficulty, given its adequate staffing, but leaving Johnson alone to handle the editorial end of *Negro Digest* was more problematic. Johnson himself had succeeded in winning draft exemption through his status as publisher, giving him a classification as vital to the war effort. At his behest, in the weeks before I departed I labored at a breakneck, slapdash pace to assemble in advance as many issues as possible.

At home, too, my leavetaking, like all wartime family disruptions, represented a major upheaval. It was hard to face a lengthy separation from Esther and our two babies. But I did have at least one gratification: a farewell telegram from publisher John Sengstacke reading, "Your loss to the *Defender* will be felt tremendously by all of us and me personally." I had an eerie sensation of reading a condolence message to mark my passing. In a few short days I was one of the sweaty, roughneck crowd of seamen at the NMU hiring hall in Manhattan waiting to sign up as Liberty ship crews. With my union card and Coast Guard pass in hand, I truly was an "ordinary" seaman, never having been to sea before and being ignorant of maritime knowledge. My ship assignment came swiftly, to a ship named in honor of the late mayor of my Chicago birthplace, the *S.S. Anton J. Cermak* (Mayor Cermak had been slain in the assassination attempt on President Roosevelt in the early 1930s).

My transformation back to "proletarian" was abrupt, but even more startling and chastening was my overnight change from a thriving family life in a comfortable home to life as a bedraggled sailor sleeping in a narrow upper bunk in a small cabin on a rocking Liberty ship on the high seas, earning all of eighty-seven dollars a month. War had finally hit home for me personally, as it had for millions of others the world over. War strips the human animal down to bare emotions and raw behavior, and in my couple of months in the floating zoo on the *Cermak* I witnessed the worst and very little of the best of the species.

If I had had any misanthropic inclinations before going to sea, they had been reinforced by the time of my return home, so that I could empathize with the character in Dostoyevsky's *Brothers Karamazov* who observes, "The more I love humanity in general, the less I love man in particular." It was with that disposition that I headed back home from a Mediterranean voyage to Algeria and Sardinia. When we finally landed at Newport News, Virginia, after some sixty seasick days, I walked ashore limp and lethargic, some fifteen pounds lighter than when I had left the States. I vowed that I would never again set foot on any kind of seagoing vessel, even a rowboat. I was now resigned to being drafted into the army. But to my surprise, I failed to pass an army physical, and I went back to work at the *Defender* and *Negro Digest* with renewed zest.

An article I had written at sea for the *Defender* on race relations in the merchant marine had not been used, and I was able instead to sell it to *Crisis* magazine; it was then reprinted by *Catholic Digest*. Another article I wrote for the *Defender* on my ship experiences I picked up for reprint in *Negro Digest* in the June 1944 issue. This was the first time the name of Ben Burns had appeared in the magazine, although I had been its sole editor for more than a year and a half. I even found time to assemble a long projected book, *The Best of Negro Humor*, which Johnson planned to use as a circulation promotion for *Negro Digest*, a copy to be given away free with each subscription. Although I edited the 112-page book, published in 1945 with an introduction by Langston

Hughes, the title page read "edited by John H. Johnson and Ben Burns." At least my name had not been omitted entirely, as it had in the early issues of *Negro Digest*. A collection by category—politics, church, military, sports, African—of jokes published in the first years of *Negro Digest*, the book also included some of Hughes's "Simple" stories, later published separately. More than a decade later, Hughes himself compiled a volume of Negro humor, which was published in 1966.

Coming home from the high seas was almost as traumatic as my hurried departure for the merchant marine, given the housing shortage in Chicago. Esther had heard from a close friend that she was about to leave her West Side flat since her husband was going into the army. Knowing that it would be impossible, except with a substantial under-the-table payment to the landlord, to take over the flat, Esther simply moved in while her friend was still there and remained when she departed, presenting the landlord with a fait accompli. Our boxed-up belongings were moved in after dark and piled high in the living room and kitchen. When I arrived home, the landlord was outraged to learn that we were camped in his apartment. But I was in no mood for confrontation. Rather, using my old housepainting skills, I speedily redecorated the apartment. When the landlord arrived to issue legal warnings, he was so impressed that he resigned himself to our remaining as tenants.

Some months later, however, the landlord voiced a preposterous complaint about us to another building tenant. My editorial work on *Negro Digest* was done at home, and a regular caller to our apartment was John Johnson to deliver a stack of type proofs. Usually impeccably dressed, he would drive up to the front of the house in his big black Cadillac. It was this spectacle that alarmed our landlord. Who could this hulking black man in a big black Cadillac be, perhaps a gangster? And what was my connection with him? "When a maid comes, that's okay," the landlord whispered to our neighbor. "But this Burns, he has niggers in fancy Cadillacs. What kind of business is he in? I don't like it at all."

Not only was our landlord discomforted by our presence, we also found reason to be perturbed by our address at 4438 West Jackson Boulevard. Residing in a white neighborhood distant from my two jobs and from the Negro community was an inconvenience and also increasingly a cause for personal misgiving. Had I abandoned the principles I was espousing in editorials in the *Defender*? Was I hypocritical in living "white" while championing the Negro cause?

An opportunity to test my racial beliefs came unexpectedly when I heard that a wealthy Negro attorney I knew had purchased a big building on Drexel Boulevard in the heart of one of the better black neighborhoods. He had three ten-room apartments at the affordable rent of $175 a month. I quickly phoned him to inquire if I might be able to lease one of his apartments. "Well, Ben, I'd like to help you but I'm afraid I can't. You see we're subdividing," he told me. "Subdividing" was a euphemism for creating what were called kitchenettes in the ghetto, a way of getting around rent controls.

"But I'm willing to pay more than the ceiling rent," I offered. "I'm really in a jam and need the place badly."

My appeal was in vain, and later I learned that he had kept one of the large apartments for himself and divided the other two into six smaller flats renting for $125 each, thereby netting himself $750 monthly compared with the previous rental of $350. As another instance of disillusionment with professed liberal—if not radical—Negro friends, the incident was particularly exasperating, since that lawyer became one of a legal team that convinced the U.S. Supreme Court that restrictive housing covenants should not be enforced by judicial edict. That wealthy Negroes were as apt as whites to exploit critical housing hardships and to bilk "black brothers" was not a new lesson but still disturbing.

Housing has always been among the most vexing of racial impasses, and it also became a hardship for Esther and me. Finding a suitable apartment and later seeking to buy a house was a continual headache once I began listing a Negro publishing company as my place of employment. I found that I had to "pass" for white to obtain a place to live. I was introduced to this aspect of racism while I was at the *Chicago Defender*. My experience in seeking to rent from the attorney was followed by my pursuit of another large apartment in a white section of the South Side. When I met with the realty agent, everything seemed to be going right until he asked where I worked. I sought to avoid the query by giving the name of the firm that published the *Defender*: "The Robert Abbott Publishing Company."

"Where are they located?"

"Thirty-four thirty-five South Indiana Avenue."

"Isn't that a Negro neighborhood?"

"Yes."

"What do they publish?"

"A newspaper."

"Isn't that the *Chicago Defender*?"

"Yes, it is."

"What do you do there?"

I tried to dodge the query once again with a fib: "I work in the composing room." Indeed I did work there on makeup, if not typesetting.

But the agent, like a dogged prosecutor, was not to be evaded: "And you don't do editorial work."

"Nope," I lied again, but for nought. I did not get that apartment or any other, in months looking for a larger place.

Preferring to be accepted for my abilities as an editor and always fearful of exposure of my Communist Party connection, I always avoided any publicity about my race—unlike another white who followed me in black media. As the *Defender*'s national editor, I hired staff, and one of my hires was Earl Conrad, an overly earnest reporter from *PM*, the short-lived New York afternoon paper. He had written a biography of Harriet Tubman, the Underground Railroad heroine, and insisted that the very liberal *PM* was anti-Negro because it watered down his pieces on Negroes. The only way he could find full freedom to express himself, he believed, was by working on a Negro newspaper. I went to New York to hire him at a nominal salary, much below what he was earning at *PM*.

Having much in common, we spent a stimulating day together. As I was about to leave, he inquired: "Do you mind if I arrange to get a little publicity on my going to the *Defender*?"

"Of course not. Go right ahead."

"I have some friends on *Time* magazine and I think I can get a story in their press section."

"Sure, that's fine," I assured him.

A week after I returned to Chicago, my copy of *Time* arrived at the office with a story about Conrad plus his picture, announcing that Conrad was the "first white man ever to work for a Negro newspaper." Though bemused by Conrad's claim, I was not about to diminish his fancied glory or tangle with *Time*, especially since I did not want to draw attention to my own status as a Communist working for a Negro newspaper. I never mentioned the matter to Conrad, even though I knew he personally had staked the claim of priority. In actuality neither of us merited the distinction, since several other whites had worked on black publications before either of us. Probably the first was R. S. Elliot, who edited the *Colored American Magazine* for four years beginning in 1900. He was followed in the 1920s by at least two white reporters employed at black papers. In the early 1920s also the *Defender*'s mechanical department, from Linotypes to presses, was staffed almost entirely by whites, and later all its national advertising was handled by W. B. Ziff, who later became a principal in the Ziff-Davis publishing chain.

In the early days of *Negro Digest*, when we were able to obtain reprint permissions from magazines and books for virtually nothing, I did not correct the publishers' unspoken assumption that they were dealing with a Negro editor. A racial problem arose when we requested reprint rights from Dial Press for a chapter from Negro author Frank Yerby's first successful novel, *The Foxes of Harrow*. Yerby himself refused to answer our letters and phone calls, preferring to leave mundane business matters to his publisher and agent. Dial Press seemed anxious to keep Yerby's race a secret as part of the promotional build-up for the then unknown author and preferred not to have anything to do with a Negro publication. Our pleading letters to Yerby's agent, Helen Strauss, were ignored until finally she responded with a flat no.

Yerby's book, however, was too big a literary event for us simply to forget: he was the first black author since the days of Alexandre Dumas to write a best seller with a nonracial theme. After repeated attempts to reach his agent by phone, I managed to get through to Strauss and sought to explain to her the racial implications of the Yerby book and why we were so anxious to obtain reprint rights. "It's impossible since the rights have already been sold to *Omnibook*," she curtly informed me.

"Yes, I know that. The book is in the current issue of *Omnibook*. Surely they would not object to another sale if we came out with a single chapter several months after their issue. If you wish, I can phone *Omnibook* and clear it with them."

"No, that is not necessary," she said firmly. "Please don't bother them. I'm afraid the answer is still no. Dial Press does not want any further reprint rights." I had no option but to stoop to a ploy that never seemed to fail with self-described liberals.

"Well, Miss Strauss, I really can't understand your feelings. There's only one assumption I can make. If you give the book to a white magazine and refuse it to a colored magazine, then all I can think is that you are prejudiced against our people and won't let us have the book because we're colored."

An audible gasp was followed by an outraged, "Me, prejudiced!" Almost apologetically, she continued: "I'm the last person in the world you could call prejudiced. I've worked with Frank Yerby since the beginning, developing him as an author. He can tell you there isn't an ounce of prejudice in me. That's just ridiculous."

"What else can I believe, Miss Strauss? The facts are there and I can only go by the facts which are that *Negro Digest* can't have the book while a white magazine can."

"Well, I'll tell you what I'll do," she finally offered. "Just to show you that you're wrong, I'll talk to Dial Press and insist that they give you reprint rights. We'll make an exception in this case just because I want you to know how wrong you are in your judgment."

The next day a telegram from New York gave us full reprint rights for a chapter of *The Foxes of Harrow* for a ridiculously low fee.

Strauss did not forget the incident. When I met her some years later, she was clearly puzzled: was I Negro or white? In guarded conversation she finally learned that I was white and confessed that all the time she had thought that I was black. But white liberals were not the only ones who erred in thinking me Negro, as I later learned when I received a letter from a Negro editor asking for my biography for inclusion in *Who's Who in Colored America*.

Lillian Hellman coined the phrase "premature anti-fascist" in describing herself in testimony before the House Un-American Activities Committee. Although I have never heard the term "premature anti-racist" used, it well describes me and other committed whites who stood up staunchly for equal rights for Negroes long before the black revolution of the 1960s. It was a time when some Chicago Loop restaurants still refused to seat and serve Negroes, when Negroes could serve in the navy only in servile jobs, and when whites commonly used offensive derogatory terms to describe blacks. "Premature" we were, and precipitate we may well have been, but we were also prescient. I for one was convinced that in my lifetime I would witness dramatic progress toward equalizing the Negro's status in America— something I had never visualized for Communist goals. Dedicated to the principle of integration, I took heart in every breakthrough against racial barriers, while joining wholeheartedly in editorial protests against racial injustice.

The Negro press was a potent and effective instrument in chipping away at the most blatant aspects of Jim Crow, particularly in the armed services, and I took pride in being an editor of one of the foremost black protest organs. For all the vendetta against black newspapers by stand-pat Dixiecrats and often also by agonizing liberals who would bemoan its "shrillness" and militancy ("fire-breathing" is how *Time* once described black newspapers), the Negro press never retreated from its call for full racial equality in all spheres of American life. In my still youthful zeal, I agreed strongly with Rebecca West's exhortation that "a strong hatred is the best map to bear in our hands as we go over the dark places of life cutting away the dead things."

Regardless of its sometimes amateurish appearance, notwithstanding its occasional stridency in pillorying bigots, the Negro press was a significant influence in changing the racial pattern of America. I reveled in my small individual contribution to the effort in my role as an editor. In the war years black newspapers emerged from the hardscrabble 1930s, when they had struggled to survive with diminishing readership and curtailed advertising revenue, to attain new heights in influence and power by solidifying the mass of African Americans behind their vigilant watch over their rights at home and overseas at the fronts.

Bucking government pressures for wartime conformity, the black weeklies maintained an unrelenting drumbeat of exposure of racial injustices in military camps, on navy ships at sea, and then at the fronts in Europe and the south Pacific. Unlike World War I, when most Negro editors had caved in to federal threats and had muted their militant blasts against racist oppression, during World War II publishers did not surrender to federal threats to "close them down." The detailed story is told in Patrick S. Washburn's excellent book, *A Question of Sedition: The Federal Government's Investigation of the Black Press during World War II.*

The wartime role of the black press is one of the inspiring chapters in Negro history. To have been part of that turbulent, historic period in black journalism when the *Defender* lived up to its name in aggressively defending the rights and dignity of blacks in uniform as well as at home in defense jobs is a treasured chapter of my past.

II

1930–1940

4

Invisible Men and Communists

Paper will put up with anything that is written on it.
Joseph Stalin

While I was growing up my contact with Negroes—like that of most white youngsters in that era—had been minimal and superficial, practically nonexistent. In my teens, I never knew any blacks, and whatever awareness I had of racial problems came entirely from reading occasional newspaper reports about a Dixie lynching or some other racist atrocity. There were no Negroes in my high school, and if there were black students in my college years at New York University and Northwestern, I was unaware of their presence. The only book about Negroes I recall reading as a teenager was Carl Van Vechten's stereotyped *Nigger Heaven* with its pernicious portrait of what came to be known among whites as the Harlem "niggerati." I grew up in the same lily-white world as the majority of Americans of our ethnocentric generation, not knowing what it was to shake a black hand, to listen to black accents, to see a black slum, or to have a black chum. Negroes were truly the "invisible men" of novelist Ralph Ellison's perception. The gulf between the races seemed impenetrable. In the seltzer-bottling shop where I worked during my high school days, I heard the usual scurrilous calumnies about *schwarzers* (the Yiddish term for blacks), the repetition of the anti-Negro slanders that were standard back-alley talk. In those days, with rare exceptions, whites and blacks met only as "boss" and servile "flunky." My initial cagey association with Negroes came when I worked as the "straw boss" over a black crew unloading watermelons at a Chicago freight yard. It was not a setting to enhance understanding between me and the black common laborers who pitched melons out of freight cars. They were as crude and vacuous, as cloddish and indolent as any white crew of strong-arm roustabouts.

During my tenure at three Communist daily papers, my contact with "black comrades" was at best professional and political. The only blacks on the *Daily Worker* staff, Ben Davis and Richard Wright, were pretty much limited to covering racial news and issues, and that was the extent of my contacts with them. At the *Midwest Daily Record* I had a similar acquaintance with the only Negro on staff, William L. Patterson, who with his experience of living in Moscow became our political "commissar" in interpreting political right and wrong. At the *People's World* the only black was John Pittman, who as foreign editor rarely wrote on racial issues. For all the Communist Party's racial concern in those years, I—like most white party members—remained ignorant of black institutions and society, of black businesses and churches, of black universities and fraternal groups. Party policy viewed Negroes as an "oppressed" people, with excellent potential for recruitment, who were to be cautiously approached and specially treated because of their past persecution by white Americans. As I recall, we white "Reds" were overly guarded against committing a racial blunder, instead becoming excessively friendly—and inevitably patronizing—to blacks. Yet I must credit my years in the Communist Party for helping me to rid myself of much of the racist residue picked up in my youth at the seltzer shop and the watermelon track.

In time I found myself troubled by the party's racially distorted position and uneasy about what I saw as the contrived, fawning, tiptoe behavior of party people in relationships with Negroes, and I gave some blacks credit for sensing the inequality of this warped version of "equality." Yet for all its efforts, the Communist Party never succeeded in enlisting a substantial number of Negroes. FBI estimates, if they can be believed, credit the party with no more than fourteen hundred Negro members at one time. "The Communist the Negro sees as a rundown, underprivileged guy," observed Dr. Carlton Goodlett, publisher of a San Francisco black weekly. "The Negro just isn't interested in the underdog role. People, like myself, always protesting against injustice, wouldn't last ten seconds in Russia."

Once at a party unit meeting I suggested a shift to somewhat more even-handed association with Negroes, questioning the usual "bending over back-ward" tactics for interracial contacts. I was roundly berated as a "white chauvinist," the catchphrase employed by party zealots for dissenters from its racial shibboleths. I preferred to think of blacks as no better or worse than whites and had the temerity to maintain that the conclusive proof of racial equality was that perfidy no less than probity could be a black trait—a negative concept, no doubt, but projected to make an oversimplified point. The comrades roundly denounced such a "chauvinist" thought.

When I finally moved into the mainstream of black life and began asso-
ciating with Negroes on a day-to-day basis, I slowly overcame my long-time
party posture of up-tight toadying and began to relax in my social contacts
with Negroes as easily as with whites. I learned to ignore complexion, paying
no more attention to skin color than to the color of someone's eyes. My initial
adjustment was not without slips and stumbles, complicated by the need to
understand the black world's own prejudices. In the end I was able to function
smoothly in a succession of editing posts at black publications.

Writing became my prime interest in life while in high school when I won first
prize in the *New York World*'s weekly high school essay contest, "The Biggest
News of the Week." I had submitted my entries regularly but had never even
rated an honorable mention until the last week of my senior year, when I was
surprised and heartened to win the prize of $25. My essay on the Grundy
tariff bill, a piece of legislation long since forgotten, was printed in the *World*
and sparked my resolve to make journalism my career. Although my efforts at
writing were not encouraged at home, I began dreaming of becoming a foreign
correspondent for the *New York World*—or even a lowly reporter.

When I graduated from James Monroe High School in 1930 after the stock-
market crash, for me, as for all Americans, political and economic catastrophe
was at hand. Millions of Americans openly wondered whether the capitalist
system was approaching its doomsday, so desperate was the plight of so many
unable to find work or to see any hope for the future. President Franklin D.
Roosevelt warned: "The millions who are in want will not stand by silently
forever while the things to satisfy their needs are within reach."

Going to college seemed problematic for me after the 1929 crash. College
tuition then was about $350 a year, but in our family's circumstances that
$350 could have been $100,000. I found help, however, from an unexpected
source: my mother Frieda, who had divorced my father Alexander Bernstein
when I was only one year old and had married a Chicago produce dealer
named Nathan Denison. She was able to wheedle enough money out of him to
pay my college tuition. I applied to only one school, New York University, and
was accepted at a time when anyone who could afford tuition was welcome to
attend college. After a single semester of night school, I switched to daytime
classes, which gave me the chance to join the staff of the *NYU Daily News*.

I devoted a minimum of time to study and usually stayed late after classes
at the newspaper offices off Washington Square or in a shop on Third
Avenue where the paper was printed. I became intrigued with newspaper
technology—typefaces, layout, proofreading—and before many months was

supervising the *Daily News* makeup as night editor. "Working on the stone" (directing a printer in placement of columns of lead type in the page forms) became for me an intriguing game. The composing room—the world of ems and picas, Bodoni and Garamond, the smell of printer's ink, the clickety-clack sounds of the Linotypes, the feel of metal type in my hands—was particularly exciting. By my junior year I had become assignment editor, a post that traditionally would have led to appointment as editor-in-chief in my senior year.

Although New York was where I went to college, Chicago became home in 1931 when my father moved there after my high school graduation. In the summers after my freshman and sophomore years and during Christmas vacations, I would ride the bus back to Chicago. When my mother told me that her new husband was willing to give me a summer job on the watermelon track on the near South Side, at the then princely pay of sixty dollars a week, more than I had ever earned before, I quickly accepted the job. But that summer of 1931 I earned every cent of my pay. Still a scrawny youngster, I was put to work as the only white among a half-dozen Negroes. Our job was to line up side by side and pass watermelons from hand to hand onto trucks backed up to brick-red freight cars in which melons were shipped from Florida, Georgia, Texas, and Arkansas. Working hours on the watermelon track were from 6 A.M. to 6 P.M., or just about dawn to dusk, six days a week.

On the watermelon track, I found myself in a loathsome world I had never known before. It was a jungle of avaricious, well-heeled produce wholesalers, truculent and inhumane, fiercely competitive, fast with their fists and their dollars in the scramble for business. Fully as cutthroat as the "bosses" who exploited them were the overeager black workers, desperately waiting at the head of the track for pitching jobs at a dollar-fifty or two dollars a day. I had read much about the so-called "lumpen proletariat," and now for the first time I met them. For all my prejudices absorbed from the white "bosses," somehow I found more in common with the blacks than the whites I worked with. This was my initial close, continual contact with Negroes, working alongside them and becoming friendly with several, although I was in a sense, as the boss's stepson, their "straw boss" despite my young years.

Politically, I groped during my college years to find answers to Depression woes and the terrifying emergence of Adolf Hitler on the international scene. The neatly packaged litany of the Communists, as well as their role as the most stalwart opponents of the Nazis, began to appeal to me, but I kept on searching for an ideological refuge that seemed sound even if not entirely safe.

I also did not want to jeopardize, by political labeling, the likelihood of my being appointed editor-in-chief of the *NYU Daily News* in my senior year. Throughout my junior year I worked incessantly—to the detriment of my studies—to merit that honor.

In late winter of 1933, a months-long imbroglio between the senior editors and the faculty administration came to a boil and resulted in the suspension of the paper. A series of editorials in November 1932 charging that the university had been negligent in medical treatment of an injured boxer was angrily denounced by the chairman of the board of athletic control, who insisted on scuttling the college newspaper when the editors would not recant. On February 15 the *Daily News* was published for the last time. Leaflets soon were flying around campus, and a student strike was declared. Around Garibaldi's statue in Washington Square, there were exhortations to "rally around" the ousted editors. Students at the Square voted overwhelmingly to retain the paper, but to no avail.

For me the death of the *NYU Daily News* was a disaster. Dismayed by the turn of events, I lost my desire to return to NYU for my senior year. Disconsolate and distraught, I was ripe fruit for picking by Communist acquaintances. One of the first to contact me was the voluble Joseph Cohen, whom I had first met in 1932 at an antiwar congress in Chicago that I had covered for the *NYU Daily News*. He sought to enlist me as editor of a planned weekly newspaper being formulated by the National Student League, a leftist college organization. I readily agreed, seeking some avenue for my journalistic urge now that the college paper was but a memory.

The masthead of the short-lived *College News* included some future well-known Communist journalists, such as Theodore Draper and Adam Lapin, both of whom wound up on the *Daily Worker* staff. (Draper later became a nationally recognized authority on the Communist Party after turning antiparty.) A columnist in the first issue was Joseph Starobin, who later became the *Daily Worker*'s foreign editor and, like Draper, also broke with the party some twenty years later. There was I as well, with my name at the top of the masthead as an ad hoc editor-in-chief, though of the wrong publication! In actuality I did mostly mundane work on the *College News*, collecting and reading copy, writing headlines, doing the makeup always under the wary political eye of the Communist organizers. In all the *College News* survived just three weekly issues before succumbing to financial woes.

My New York farewell came in a letter in early June from Sidney Friedberg, *NYU Daily News* editor-in-chief, informing me I had been elected to Quill, the honorary journalism society, in recognition of my three years of "loyal and efficient service." It was by then a meaningless, bittersweet honor.

I returned home to Chicago dispirited and embittered, with hopes of finishing my college years as a transfer student at Northwestern University. Its journalism school courses proved a snap for me, despite the school's reputation for rigorous newspaper training; my experience working on the NYU paper paid off. Competition with other student journalists bolstered my self-confidence.

Journalism school, however, confirmed my disparaging notions about the media. Our News Reporting I class indoctrinated us in the principle of recording the unbiased truth with "fidelity to the public interest," in accordance with the "Canons of Journalism" of the American Society of Newspaper Editors, but I found surprisingly candid admissions in journalism textbooks that slanting the news was the way to keep a job. While the *Canons* upheld standards such as "News reports should be free from opinion or bias of any kind," an accepted classroom text, *News Reporting* by Carl Warren of the *New York News*, told us that "the observing reporter notes that the paper does attempt to sway opinion through the news columns. The owner or publisher, he discovers, has decided views upon certain public questions which are reflected daily in the news reports. . . . As he begins to handle the more important assignments, the reporter often finds himself deliberately cultivating the proper policy slant, confident that this sort of copy will please the boss." Warren gave frank advice to would-be journalists: "So far as the reporter is concerned, these questions of policy need not bother him greatly. He has little voice in the matter for, like any other employee, he is a salaried craftsman, receiving orders and not giving them. . . . He writes what his superiors instruct him to write, in a way that they want it written. If he is unwilling to do so, his only alternative is to look for another job."

In hindsight the formula sounds much like the kind of instructions that would have been given to an applicant for a job on *Pravda* during the Cold War. Albert F. Henning, in *Ethics and Practices in Journalism*, told us that "the newspaperman dissatisfied with his inability to say what he pleases when he wishes to say it will get considerable comfort by considering the plight of those in other walks of life." In 1934 that argument had much validity, especially to those journalism graduates among the millions of college alumni who since 1929 had been unable to find work.

Graduation day in June 1934 was a happy as well as sad experience. Delighted to have completed our college education, we graduates knew that jobs were next to impossible to find. At Dyche Stadium our graduation speaker was Harold L. Ickes, Roosevelt's secretary of the interior, none of whose words I can recall but whose theme was the despair of the Depression rather than any hopeful visions for the future. By then I had become so disheartened with Northwestern and the world at large that I hardly noticed the absence of any of my family or friends at the ceremonies, all too busy trying to earn a living. I collected my diploma, and changed from a cap and gown into painter's overalls the next day, going to work as a housepainter with my father.

I was well aware that I was just drifting after college, frustrated by my failure to break into journalism. As a result, I became absorbed in leftist activity, both political and social. I joined the Young Communist League sometime in 1935, a year after I had finished college and begun swinging a paintbrush, disenchanted with both my personal world and the world at large. Party membership came shortly after that. The arguments to sign up were overwhelming. Who was most outspoken against Hitler's anti-Jewish crimes? Who was the most antiwar and the most resounding in demanding help for the unemployed? The Communist Party seemed to me logical "compensation for a life of frustration," as Arthur Koestler described party enlistment.

Perhaps a significant factor in the party's recruitment of members—more important than any study of U.S. Communism has ever indicated—was the warm fellowship of likeminded individuals in convivial social activities. Party members held parties and picnics, dances and campouts, or just "hung out" together at streetcorners and bookstores. A West Side bookstore run by genial Bob Davis became a favored Communist social center in Chicago, a place where left-wing people met to socialize, to gossip, and even occasionally to buy a book, if they could afford it. There, inevitably, I met affable, solicitous party members.

Though I still disliked some aspects of the Communist Party—its doctrinaire discipline, the questionable personality of some of its leaders, and the shrill streetcorner soapbox oratory—finally I was able to rationalize some of these negatives as being necessary for organizational effectiveness. The media, after all, were closed to the party, and police harassment was common. Overthrow the government? Achieve world revolution and domination? Those possibilities, so often bandied about as Communist goals by various investigative bodies, rarely entered my mind. I simply wanted a change to give me a chance to succeed in the Depression-plagued America of the 1930s.

It might have been easy to become a Communist, but staying one was another matter. In the years that followed my enlistment in party ranks, I proved a dilatory, insouciant, ineffectual member. I despised unit meetings and avoided them whenever possible. I could not fully accept the glorified image of party leaders and was always instinctively restrained in my adulation of members of the party hierarchy, even though uninhibited hurrahs were an expected part of loyal party behavior. My study of Marxist theory was scant and cursory, and I was occasionally in hot water with party brass because of ingenuous expressions at variance with the official party line. Often I said not a word at the unit meetings I attended.

Yet for all my negative feelings about the Communist Party, I genuinely believed in and supported its avowed prime purpose: pursuit of a better world for the less privileged. Most of my friendships were soon restricted to devout party people, and the rich social fellowship of the left became stimulating and enjoyable enough for me to tolerate the dogmatic claptrap of party meetings. One of the few who has written of the 1930s and sensed the importance of this basic social impulse was Malcolm Cowley. "The party performed for its members the social and institutional functions of a church," he observed. "The comradeship in struggle . . . communism offered at least the possibility of being reborn into a new life." And so it was with me. However, I recognized in time—much too long a time—that in H. L. Mencken's words, Communism in practice amounted to nothing much more than "a transfer of capital from private owners to professional politicians."

Party life was not without hazards. There was always talk among Chicago "comrades" about who had been arrested of late by the Red Squad of the Chicago Police Department headed by Make Mills. Only once in my years in and around the Communist Party did I come close to being arrested. On a hot summer Sunday the Young Communist League, seeking to break the unwritten but rigid ban on Negroes at the Jackson Park beach (and incidentally to score some points with the black community), scheduled a multiracial beach party there. A large contingent from the West Side piled into battered old cars to add our numbers to the turnout, which included perhaps a half-dozen black Communists at most among the fifty or so people who attended. All day long we sunned ourselves, swam, or played volleyball while a police squad car stood by on the roadway adjoining the beach, with plainclothes cops eying us but not making any move to curb our integration "demonstration." Late in the afternoon, believing we had established our point for mixed bathing at Jackson Park, most of the West Siders headed for home. The next day we heard the news that after we had departed, police had moved in and hauled off to jail every one of the Communist group who remained on the beach.

Surprisingly, more than forty years later, I discovered that someone in our West Side party contingent had been an FBI informer and had reported my participation in that protest. A twelve-page confidential Federal Bureau of Investigation memorandum dated August 15, 1950, and sent to the Department of State, the Central Intelligence Agency, and four European embassies on the occasion of my application for a passport summarized the FBI's nine years of surveillance of me. Included was a reference to the Jackson Park incident: "XXXXXXXXX has advised that Burns has participated in West Side meetings broken up by police and in beach demonstrations in Jackson Park but that he had left before any arrests had been made."

Only party members knew of my presence at the beach demonstration. Up to the time of the wholesale arrests late in the day, police had no names of participants in the beach party. To this day I speculate who among my "comrades" was the informer: someone in our party unit, perhaps a supposed friend?

While earning my keep with paintbrushes, I never lost the desire to write, my idle typewriter haunting my conscience. I struggled to shape freelance articles and stories with what little energy I had after a hard day's work as a painter and paperhanger. But my efforts netted no more than an abundance of rejection slips. It was then that I first began using the name Ben Burns as a byline instead of Benjamin Bernstein, thinking that perhaps a non-Jewish name would change my fortunes—subconsciously blaming anti-Semitism for my lack of success. But the rejection slips kept coming. I had about given up all hope of ever breaking away from the painting trade.

My break came in late fall of 1936, when a long-time close friend in New York, knowing my ambitions for a newspaper job, sounded out a *Daily Worker* editor, Al Richmond, about the possibility of a job for me. This was a period when the "Popular Front" approach of the Communist Party had expanded its horizons to encompass "mass appeal" as never before. The party press was growing rapidly to reach out to non-party members, and a new weekend publication, *Sunday Worker*, was started. Additional staff were needed, and through Al Richmond I was offered a job as a reporter on the *Daily Worker*. The weekly pay was all of ten dollars.

I was unsure of my qualifications for the *Daily Worker* job. Had my college journalism training prepared me for professional work? Could I fit into the rigorous party discipline of formula writing? Did I know enough of Marxism to qualify as a Communist journalist? The main concern was whether I could manage to live in New York on my own on ten dollars a week. I recalled that I had done so as a college student and finally grabbed the opportunity of quitting housepainting, in spite of the steep drop in my earnings, which had been fifty dollars a week as a painter.

Soon I was installed at a desk in the *Worker* newsroom, an open clutter of desks and stacks of papers on the eighth floor of a block-long building, a veritable "propaganda factory" that the party occupied from ground level to roof between Twelfth and Thirteenth Streets east of University Place in lower Manhattan. Finally, I was a working journalist. All that I had learned in classes and textbooks now came into play—especially Carl Warren's textbook instructions on how to slant news stories.

As a cub on the *Daily Worker*, I initially covered the usual street assignments given beginners, such as strikes and fires. In a few short weeks I had my initial exposure to celebrities: Sinclair Lewis at a press conference before his play, *It Can't Happen Here*, opened on Broadway, and Ernest Hemingway and John Dos Passos explaining why they were going to Spain to cover the civil war. Before long the Ben Burns byline was appearing regularly over feature articles in the *Sunday Worker* magazine as well as in the *Daily*. After a five-part investigative series on neglect of patients in understaffed city hospitals, less than six months after joining the *Worker*, I was reassigned to the copy desk, where I was responsible for checking on stories of even veteran reporters. Except for writing occasional features in my spare time, I remained at the copy desk for the next year. I enjoyed the work, though it was generally seen as a dull journalistic chore.

The halcyon days of the "Popular Front" in the mid-1930s—when the Socialist government of Léon Blum in France welcomed Communist cooperation, setting an example for the world of the left with the blessings of the Comintern in Moscow—were a powerful stimulant for the U.S. Communists, who in 1938 attained a record membership of 82,000. To extend its propaganda far beyond its centralized apparatus in New York, the party decided to publish two new daily newspapers in addition to the *Daily Worker:* one in Chicago, the *Midwest Daily Record*, and the other in San Francisco, the *People's World*. Based on my knowledge of Chicago as well as my *Daily Worker* experience, I was asked to return to Chicago as city editor of the *Midwest Daily Record*, scheduled to begin publication in early 1938.

The timing of the projected move to Chicago was ideal since my new wife Esther was due to graduate from Hunter College in January. Esther and I had met for the first time on Washington's Birthday in February 1937 at the Bronx wedding of her aunt to my cousin, and we were married nine months later on Thanksgiving Day at her parents' apartment. We have celebrated our marriage on national holidays ever since.

Our first weeks in Chicago were a throwback to the past—living with my father and stepmother once again. Start-up of the new *Midwest Daily Record* kept me fully occupied at the second-floor offices of Adria Printing Company, a foreign language publishing firm located at 1838 N. Halsted Street. Now of somewhat higher party status than when I departed the city, I found that my initial days back in Chicago involved long hours of challenging work: planning and shaping the format, routines, and operations for the first months of the *Record*, as well as becoming acquainted with my new political bosses. Designated as editor-in-chief was Louis F. Budenz, a long-time party member who had been associated with the defecting Jay Lovestone wing of the party for almost a decade and had then returned to good graces when he confessed his "errors." I suspected that a cautious watch was posted on Budenz in the person of William L. Patterson, who was named to the associate editor's desk where he could monitor Budenz's behavior and report to the policy-making Communist bureaucracy. Patterson's years of living in Moscow beginning in the 1920s, followed by a long stint as top official of the International Labor Defense, the party's legal arm, qualified him to scrutinize the recidivist Budenz. When Budenz later proved irredeemable and became a turncoat, he emerged as one of the nation's foremost anti-Communist crusaders, embracing the Catholic Church, testifying repeatedly for congressional committees on Communist "sins," writing exposés of Communist "plots" in the Hearst press, and authoring several anti-party volumes.

The first issue of the *Record* was published on February 12, 1938, with greetings from Harold Laski and Langston Hughes. The debut followed a long fund-raising campaign that wound up $30,000 short of its $60,000 goal and, like so many such drives, spent excessively in soliciting funds. The six-page standard-sized *Daily Record* sold for only three cents while the weekend edition with an additional twelve tabloid pages was a nickel. Realistically, with such paltry newsstand revenue, giveaway two-dollar-a-year subscriptions, and minimal advertising in its pages, nothing could make the *Record* a break-even proposition unless the unceasing begging campaigns could cover the ever growing losses.

I recognized and observed my place in the party pecking order, rigidly keeping in line as the junior member of the editorial hierarchy; editorial mechanics were my province, but politically I was a nullity. Occasionally I would turn out *Daily Record* feature articles, given the urge to write and to gratify my ego with an infrequent byline. One such article got me in political hot water, and administering the blistering criticism was Budenz himself. Through a friend I had learned that John Steinbeck was in town incognito, staying under the name of Dr. Beckstein at the near North Side Cass Hotel. He had come to Chicago in connection with production of director Pare Lorentz's *Fight for Life*, a documentary film on a West Side maternity center that delivered babies at home for ghetto mothers. Actor Will Geer helped me arrange for a late-night interview with Steinbeck after I agreed to withhold publication until Steinbeck had left town.

In my article Steinbeck offered some mild criticism of Marxist literature as being concerned "too much with ideas, rather than people." Chicago to him was "a loathsome city," where "people have a downcast, starey look in their eyes. No one seems to be happy. No one seems to have anything to look forward to. They can't even get drunk to get happy. There's no transition between the first drink and final stupor." Steinbeck claimed he had never seen slums as miserable as Chicago's and had not met a happy person during his entire stay in the city. The day after the interview was published, Budenz summoned me to his office to berate me for writing a piece that he said was politically naive and veritable blasphemy.

Later, in print in the *Record*, Budenz attacked Steinbeck's statement and my interview with him. Prefacing his "Heart of America" column with a snide reference to me as "our gossip collector" and a prickly comment on my office reputation as a "very fast man . . . a little too fast," he excoriated my reportorial abilities, insisting that I did not ask questions that would have refuted what Steinbeck had said. "He did not give Steinbeck an opportunity to present a rounded-out view on the subject that was discussed," Budenz wrote. My interview was termed "an unfortunate conversation," with Budenz insisting that "the pictorializing of this city as a depressed community, where everyone goes around with his head in a sling, is simply not true. When that was said, the man who said it certainly did not know—and did not see—the people of Chicago. This great community is one of the great hopes of the United States." Using every stock party cliche about the "common people" of Chicago, writing like a flack for the Chamber of Commerce, Budenz tried to parry Steinbeck's truthful summary of the squalor and hopelessness of Chicago in the mid-1930s. Much as I resented the castigation by Budenz, I kept silent as I had learned to behave when confronted with criticism from the party's powers. I was determined to keep the best job I had ever had, at least in terms of status if not of salary.

The *Midwest Daily Record*, though an open party organ, sought broad labor appeal and for some time attained some success. Circulation rose to meet optimistic projections. But even if circulation had reached twice the figure it actually attained, the *Record* could not possibly have wound up in the black. Despite good intentions and ceaseless labors, the *Midwest Daily*

Record had a relatively short life span. By the fall of 1939 its coffers were nearly empty. Much of the staff was finally given notice of termination of publication, and a skeleton crew was retained to seek to continue the *Record* as a weekly. I left the *Record* with a glowing letter of recommendation from Budenz, which turned out to be empty praise indeed in later years. After becoming a weekly in mid-November of 1939, the *Record* folded forever with the issue of March 2, 1940.

Without a job, I found that wanderlust set in. With some $200 saved in the bank from our year in Chicago, Esther and I headed for Mexico as winter approached. Young in heart and without responsibilities, we decided impulsively to drive to Acapulco with my brother Milt and his wife Sonya in their old V-8 Ford. We had little more than $400 among the four of us. After some weeks in the sun, the inevitable day of reckoning arrived with our cash running low. We headed back to the United States, but in the direction of California, hopeful that perhaps we might find employment there. For me there was indeed a job in the Golden State. I contacted Al Richmond, who by then was managing editor of the *People's World*, which was thriving in the labor-conscious San Francisco of those years. Richmond was instrumental in my landing a job as a copy reader at twenty dollars a week. I remained in California while Esther returned to Chicago to her job with the packinghouse union until we could afford moving our household to the West Coast.

San Francisco was a feast for the eyes, the spirit, and, of course, the palate. I promptly fell in love with the city's natural beauties as well as the charm of its streets and buildings. My copy desk job at the *People's World* was a routine stint that left me with much time on my hands. I would tramp tirelessly up and down hills for hours, exploring the city. Once again, however, I fell into political trouble. On my desk one day I found a note from Harrison George, the venerable *World* editor, asking me to meet him at a nearby restaurant. There he related that he had just returned from a trip to Chicago where he had consulted with my old boss, Louis Budenz. "He told me you were a very good worker, but you lack political education," George related. "What are you going to do about it?" I swallowed hard and gave the expected answer to save my job once again: "I guess I'll have to go to Workers School." I never kept the promise to do penance.

For me March 9, 1940, was like a second wedding day: it was the day when Esther and I had a long-delayed reunion, ending the longest period of separation in our marriage. She arrived on the Union Pacific *Challenger* after a fifty-six-hour cross-country train trip, the cheapest way to travel in those years. To Esther fell the thankless task of locating a suitable, affordable flat for us, not an easy mission in the Bay area and one complicated by a vexing, unforeseen problem. Because of the epicanthic fold in her eyes, Esther was suspected of being either Chinese or Japanese and was flatly rejected for several promising apartments. We thus learned firsthand of the anti-Asian bias that then infected San Francisco. But finally, down a couple of blocks from Nob Hill on Sacramento Street at the corner of Leavenworth, she found an ideal small flat, two rooms with a Pullman-type kitchen and slide-away hidden bed, for twenty-two dollars a month. There we set up housekeeping once again, after I had used my housepainting skills to redecorate the place.

In the year that followed, we enjoyed a bustling life in San Francisco, discovering the offbeat delights of the city, making many new friends, and participating in the rich social life of Communist Party circles. Through party contacts Esther was able to land a twenty-five-dollar-a-week secretarial post at the San Francisco Housing Authority, which was then in the midst of a bitter controversy over a public housing project planned for Chinatown that was opposed by anti-Oriental bigots in the city.

Those years before World War II were a loony mix of puzzling politics the world over, and this was reflected in the Bay area—a foretaste of events of the 1960s and 1970s. While some of the residue of the "Popular Front" still prevailed to bolster the *People's World* readership, the Communists were reeling from the after-effects of the inexplicable German-Soviet pact and the Russian invasion of Finland. In the wake of the embarrassing Nazi-Soviet treaty, excuses for Stalin's political handsprings were difficult to come by. The party line stated that necessity was the mother of accommodation with Hitler, to give the Russians time for self-defense, and it was limply accepted by loyal, disciplined party members. Sadly, I fell into line, even though I gagged at the shocking Soviet about-face and at the thought of being part of a movement centered in the Communist power that had made peace with the world's worst anti-Semite.

The world as we had known it in the 1930s was coming to an end. How long until we would all be in the European inferno, I wondered. What were the prospects for Esther and me to improve our lot in San Francisco? Now married for more than three years, could we possibly think of having children? With tomorrow a question mark, we mulled over our dilemma and decided we had nothing to lose and perhaps a new perspective to gain in resolving to have a baby despite my lifelong aversion and objection to children. My opposition faded as we discussed the outlook for us if and when the United States went to war. Having a child would delay if not prevent my being drafted into the army, I sheepishly pointed out to Esther. It was perhaps a selfish, self-centered motivation, but it also arose from a lifetime of pre-Communist pacifism and then party-line antiwar tenets. There was another factor as well: an urge to perpetuate our love in a son or daughter no matter what the future brought for me, whether front-line combat or a labor camp for subversives. I had no need to convince Esther, who was family oriented from the start of our marriage. She more than readily agreed that we should start a family. Almost immediately, Esther became pregnant.

While the world we knew was collapsing around us, we were poised to start a new life. On my twenty-dollar weekly pay, we recognized that we could not possibly subsist as a family of three in San Francisco and that it was time to move on again. There seemed no choice except to return to Chicago, where somehow I felt I could more easily earn enough to feed three, even if it meant my returning to housepainting. Before leaving, we had the opportunity to indulge in a short Palm Springs vacation paid for by Esther's aunt and uncle, Dora and Jack Miller. We had no idea that the FBI, now in the midst of an anticipated wartime crackdown on Reds, was on my trail. But like bumbling Keystone Cops, the FBI investigators were thoroughly confused by my detour to Palm Springs, not exactly a hideout for Communist "agitators." A cross-fire of droll bulletins were circulated across the country in the attempt to locate me, as I learned years later when I obtained the FBI's voluminous reports on me under the Freedom of Information Act. One note from Washington even sought to track me to Oregon, where the FBI had me listed as a University of Oregon graduate, though I had never even visited that state.

Paradoxically, the FBI file on me commences precisely when I ceased to be a part of the Communist apparatus as a paid employee. Pursuing me as if I were a fugitive, the bungling FBI sleuths checked draft boards, WPA and relief offices, even the retail credit association in a futile effort to pick up our trail. Since we had left San Francisco, a message signed by J. Edgar Hoover authorized the FBI bureau there to forward our case to Chicago, making the Midwest the new tracking area to stalk us. Finally the FBI obtained a Chicago address for us from the Union Transfer Service, which had moved what few furnishings we had. However, an error in transmitting the address had the agents puzzled; the FBI report listed 391 West Nineteenth Street as my parent's home instead of No. 3914. What the FBI found at 391 was the vast railroad yards of the Santa Fe railroad! Their check of the local draft boards found no trace of my name, and by mid-November Washington was informed: "Therefore no other leads remain to be covered in this district, and the case is being closed." I do not know precisely when the FBI finally spotted me in Chicago, because the full reports on me withheld some fourteen pages that cover the next years. But the FBI once again embarked on a hunt for me after I became editor of *Ebony*.

III

1945–1954

5

Paris, Labor Skates, and Gertrude Stein

White men, whether they are in the majority or minority, must find
a way to purge themselves completely of racism, or face the ultimate
fateful confrontation of the races which will shake the very foundation
of civilization.

Ralph J. Bunche

Back in Chicago, my luck in starting a new career at the *Defender* was climaxed by a choice assignment at the end of the war. Considering the tight-fisted reluctance of its management to dole out expense dollars for out-of-town staff coverage, I was astounded in the fall of 1945 to merit approval for a European assignment: to cover the initial organizing sessions of the World Federation of Trade Unions (WFTU) in Paris. The suggestion for the *Defender* to report the leftist-nurtured conference in the wake of the wartime Allied unity of Washington and Moscow, I assumed, must have originated with my leftist sponsor, William L. Patterson (a belief reinforced by the jubilant *Daily Worker* headline, "Defender Sends Burns to Paris"), and was enthusiastically embraced by editor-in-chief "Doc" Lochard. It was hardly necessary to ask if I would be willing to go to Paris.

Boarding the *S.S. Argentina* in New York, I was surprised to find a small army of news photographers, cameras flashing, trained on a couple of familiar faces, those of the duke of Windsor and his wife, Wallis Simpson, who were our fellow passengers. I also discovered that I was not the only correspondent from a Negro newspaper going to cover the WFTU; on board was P. L. Prattis of the *Pittsburgh Courier*, the prime competitor of the *Defender*.

Cabins on the cruise ship normally were occupied by just two passengers, but as a troop ship the *Argentina* had been converted to accommodate twelve soldiers with bunks stacked four high to the ceiling. I was assigned to one of these cabins, along with eight labor skates, including the only black in the American delegation, the imposing, handsome Charles Collins of the AFL Negro Labor Victory Committee in Harlem. There was one bathroom

for the nine of us plus nine others in an adjoining cabin. On the other hand
Prattis, incredibly, was in a cabin with a private bathroom with only one other
passenger, Sidney Johnson, the Bahamian valet of the duke of Windsor. The
black "gentleman's gentleman" had initially been mistakenly assigned to a
cabin with women and then quickly switched to Prattis's cabin after his sex
and race were ascertained by the purser. Smilingly declaring in mock offense
that he and Johnson had been "Jim Crowed," Prattis invited Collins and me
to switch berths and join him. We readily assented, delighted to escape the
crowded CIO stateroom, and we moved in with Prattis and Johnson, joshing
about being relegated to the "Jim Crow" cabin aboard the *Argentina*. With all
the space we had, the four of us were the envy of the labor delegation. "Being
Jim Crowed" for once proved an advantage.

During the week's voyage, the duke's valet never suspected that I was not a
light-skinned Negro, and he helped Prattis and me arrange an interview with
the duke. Johnson slipped a note from us onto the table of "His Highness"
in the luxurious three-room suite he and the duchess occupied, and the duke
agreed to meet us on his private veranda. Seated overlooking the great waves
rolling by, the two of us addressed the former king of England with probing
queries about racial bias in the Bahamas where he had been governor-general
for five years. "There is no color bar in the Bahamas," the duke contended,
but during his tenure he had barred blacks from entering Government House
through the front door, an action that was in keeping with his thinly veiled Nazi
sympathies. In our thirty-five-minute interview the laconic duke with oblique
replies waltzed around our queries. He saw little hope for a proposed West
Indies federation, and based on that assertion the *Defender* front-paged my
story with the headline, "Duke of Windsor against Freedom of Islands: Indies
Not Ready for Self-Rule." Although my story was in general kindly disposed to
the duke, crediting him with speaking "more as a democratic official interested
in the common man's welfare than as a member of the reigning family of
the British empire," I was in truth unimpressed with the ex-king's limited
perception of Caribbean politics no less than of the broader world. My leftist
assessment of him was conveyed in my *Defender* summation: "His opinions
were not unlike any colonial-minded Briton but he has a slick and sometimes
demagogic manner of translating British imperialism into ostensible concern
for the lower classes."

My arrival in France was anything but auspicious. In my haste to leave the
States, I had neglected to get a tetanus shot, and after the heavy-handed ship's
doctor injected me with the vaccine, I developed a swollen arm and fever that
made the bumpy train ride from Le Havre to Gare St. Lazare torturous. Much

fanfare attended the kickoff of the WFTU conference, but I found little of substance in the oratorical circus by labor leaders from around the world. In my cabled dispatches to the *Defender* I concentrated instead on interviews with the black delegates from Africa and the West Indies. Soon after the opening session the black delegates exploded in anger over the seating of a white South African from an apartheid labor council on a key constitution committee. Their attempts at floor dissent were quashed by the chairman, Sidney Hillman, leader of the CIO delegation, who blandly responded to their protests against a white Afrikaner representing black unionists with a blunt confession that "I don't know anything about the geography of Africa." The black Africans related to me their frustration and fury over Hillman's ruling, and the *Defender* front-paged my story on their tangle with Hillman.

I was unaware then that key Communist functionaries in the CIO as well as aides to Hillman had advised a pro-white course to placate the bigger, recognized white unions from South Africa in the WFTU; in the mid-1940s the black South African unions represented only a small handful of members regulated and restricted by apartheid laws. For a Communist to question sacrosanct WFTU actions was a capital offense given the Comintern's blessings if not sponsorship of the world labor body, and in New York and Chicago the party brass was infuriated at my *Defender* story. CIO leaders back home, touchy on the issue of racial bias, cabled Paris questioning the veracity of my *Defender* report, and Hillman claimed in a cabled response to New York: "No contest was made regarding seating of such [South African] representative," which was an outright falsehood. At the Palais de Chaillot I was collared by John Abt, an aide to Hillman, who growled, "What are you trying to do to us?" Another top CIO aide, Lee Pressman, also passed along his extreme displeasure at my news report. Hillman himself confronted me and denied he was guilty of any "racial discrimination" but openly admitted he was ignorant of the color situation in South Africa. "There are some things you don't know about labor," he challenged me. "This race discrimination in South Africa is something I did not know about."

Small fry as I was in the Communist Party, I did not realize that both Abt and Pressman were actually fellow party members, so described some years later in hearings in Washington, and both were obviously unaware of my party affiliation or else they could have insisted that I retract my accusations against Hillman, their boss. I had been guilty of a serious transgression against the party in my "slanders" against the WFTU leadership, but because I was in effect standing firm for Negro rights—as inviolable as the WFTU—I could not readily be challenged openly by the party strategists on my return home. Undeniable fact was my defense to what criticism I heard, and I had enthusiastic letters from colonial delegates to support my version of what had occurred in Paris. When in response to his request I sent copies of my *Defender* reports to *CIO News* editor Len DeCaux, he responded, "I think you did a remarkable job of reporting the conference and brought out many angles that I wasn't too familiar with myself. Speaking personally, and not for publication, I think that colonial questions were underestimated and inadequately handled at the conference, and that you have rendered a great service by bringing them up so sharply and eloquently to the fore. But, even so, I think you were unduly rough with Mr. Hillman." More than fifty years after the letter was written, perhaps the "not for publication" proviso can now be set aside (years later I heard reports that DeCaux, too, was described as a fellow party member).

Paris during my first visit was not all cables and controversies. To me the Old World was a new world, and I fell in love at first sight with the great city. Every moment I could spare from the conference sessions, I stole away to marvel at its wonders, from museums and churches to boulevards and squares. Strolling down the Champs Elysées one afternoon, I accidentally encountered some black GIs, one of whom was a friend of Charles Collins, my shipboard roommate. He was a staff writer for *Stars and Stripes*, Allan Morrison, whom I had never met but who was known to me as the past editor of an ill-fated version of *Negro Digest* that had published several issues almost simultaneously with John Johnson's magazine before dying for lack of funds.

Drafted into the army, Morrison became one of the very few Negro staffers on the military daily, and I spotted him as a magazine writer whose talents could be a valuable addition to our staff if and when we were able to afford an editorial payroll. *Negro Digest* had reprinted several of Morrison's pieces from *Stars and Stripes*, and in our meeting in Paris I immediately established a rapport with the equable, astute writer, whom I urged to contact me for a job when he was out of service. The soft-spoken but highly articulate Montreal-born Morrison (whose parents were from Jamaica) later came to be a close friend. He was one of the most gifted and conscientious black journalists I have known, a dependable, forthright intellectual who showed great acuity in the many articles he later wrote for me as New York bureau chief of *Ebony* magazine. I often turned to him for guidance and comfort when faced with perplexing editorial decisions, and he could always be depended on for judicious sagacity, especially on sensitive racial issues.

Before leaving Paris, I had one unfulfilled editorial assignment to complete: Lochard, before my hurried departure from Chicago, had urged me to try to get an interview with Gertrude Stein, who had become interested in black soldiers on the return from her wartime refuge in the south of France. I had no personal contacts to enable me to reach her, so I used the most obvious stratagem to find her—the 1938 telephone book, the only one available in Paris in the days after VE Day. Sure enough, there was the name of Gertrude Stein at 5 Rue Christine, and I phoned to try to make an appointment. To my clumsy "Est Mademoiselle Stein ici?" a voice responded knowingly, "Oh, you can talk English. This is Alice Toklas." Ill prepared to recognize how significant Alice B. Toklas was in the renowned literary duo (I had never read any of Stein's work), I did not even acknowledge her name, but rather brusquely insisted on speaking to Stein, explaining who I was and what was my purpose. Toklas groused that their Rue Christine flat was invaded constantly by GIs and officers (who had heard that Stein was writing about U.S. soldiers) and told me I might as well join the parade. "Why don't you just come right over" was her invitation.

In the typical shimmering grayness of a Paris dusk in autumn, I was on my way to Rue Christine for one of the most unforgettable interviews of my journalistic years. Stein was then writing a book on U.S. soldiers in Europe called *Brewsie and Willie*, and in her brash, uninhibited way she would stop a GI at random, often a black soldier, and conduct "research" by asking probing questions designed to elicit the thinking of young Americans abroad. Such was her common touch that the most unlettered felt comfortable in her presence. Finding Rue Christine on the Left Bank, I soon was seated before the Picasso painting of Stein over the mantel and the living Gertrude Stein on the sofa. I was awed by both. The remarkable room we met in, covered from floor to ceiling with celebrated impressionist works, a miniature museum of modern art with canvases by her painter "friends," was enough to intimidate me into silence while I admired the collection. I sat and listened as her words poured out with little pause about the Negro and "the problem." It was as if she had herded her thoughts for years and must suddenly release them. Finally I was able to inquire about the book she was writing about U.S. soldiers and how Negroes fitted into it. "They're hard to pick up" was her comment about black soldiers. "They're always on the defensive, always trying to cover up when they have nothing to hide because of their color. I'm afraid they take offense as if I'm trying to patronize them."

I am not the most persistent interviewer, but Stein needed no prompting once she began speaking her mind. She spoke almost nonstop with her own dissonant approach on race and color, unlike anything I have ever heard before or since. She was more concerned for white Americans than for the

Negro, "the persecutor, more than the persecuted," she insisted. "The white man is sinking deeper into the mire trying to hold the Negro by the leg. The Negro can take care of himself. I'm worried about the white man. Don't worry about the Negroes. They holler a little but they take care of themselves. Being pushed around makes them strong. It's the whites who suffer spiritually."

To her the "nonsense of race" was incomprehensible, an abomination: the Negro sensitivity, about his color, and his dodges to escape race labels, as well as the white notion of racial superiority, the fear of miscegenation or even simple interracial socializing, the brutish vendettas to keep the Negro in his place. Concerning attempts by Negroes to cover up their identity by shunning the word, Stein once wrote:

> I knew that they do not want you to say Negro but I do want to say Negro. I dislike it when instead of saying Jew they say Hebrew or Israelite or Semitic. I do not like it and why should a Negro want to be called colored. He may not want to be one that is all right but as long as he cannot change that why should he mind the real name of them . . . I have stated that a noun is to me a stupid thing, if you know a thing and its name why bother about it but you have to know its name to talk about it. Well, its name is Negro if it is a Negro and Jew if it is a Jew and both of them are nice strong solid names so let us keep them.

As on anything she spoke about, there was a certainty, a sweeping generalization in her assertive pronouncements on racial concepts: "The Anglo-Saxon is the weakest of all racial types. Mix a Saxon with a Latin and the Saxon disappears. That's what makes him nervous. However, mix a Latin with a Negro and the Latin doesn't have to worry. The weakest of races are the Germans because they are pure Anglo-Saxons. The Russians on the other hand don't have race on their mind because they mix without losing their Slav identity."

She related to me the story of her friendship with a French doctor during the war years in a small town where some white American troops were quartered. There had been a report that Negro troops were to arrive in the town, and she had expressed apprehension that there might be trouble. The doctor asked why. She explained the usual feelings of American whites toward Negroes. Though familiar with U.S. racist attitudes, the doctor was puzzled by the complexions of many American Negroes he had seen, who seemed no darker than some tanned Frenchmen and yet were still considered colored, in contrast to French Africans who were so much blacker and yet supposedly not the object of prejudice.

"You see everyone is considered a Negro in America who has a single drop of Negro blood," she had explained.

"But doesn't that show a singular lack of racial pride? Certainly the French would not admit that 10 percent of Negro blood was better than 90 percent of French blood," the doctor declared.

Stein considered racial pride as an attribute, to be recognized not as an arrogant notion for belaboring others, but rather as those particular ethnic characteristics that distinguish a racial group and provide a cultural heritage that can be learned from and passed on to others (and no race enjoyed a monopoly in this regard, she felt). Her own version of racial pride was related in her stereotypical story, still relevant today: "A single Negro family will move into a white street where 100 white families live. Immediately the 100 white families will rush to move out. Doesn't it show a lack of racial pride to have 100 white families driven out by one Negro family?"

Assessing the Negro's invasion in the block where he is the stranger, pushing in where he is unwanted, Stein viewed him as the close counterpart of the earliest Americans breaking new frontiers.

> The Negro has the advantage over the whites. They are the only people in America who are still pioneering. In the last 50 years they have pioneered up from the South. In a kind of way the Negro is much more lively minded than the white. If you pioneer, you're alive. The mass of white Americans have forgotten how to pioneer. Jews because they are also persecuted keep on pioneering. Persecuted races have to pioneer. That's poverty. It's a very urgent matter. Americans have to get to do something about it. I'm ashamed of them, ashamed that the only people who pioneer are Negroes and not whites. The more whites persecute Negroes, the more Negroes have to pioneer to live. They have lost their own liberty in holding down the Negro.

Gertrude Stein was not uncritical of some Negroes—and strangely Paul Robeson for one. Her attitude toward him set him in the perspective of the early 1930s, when she wrote of him as a Negro who "knew American values and American life as only one in it but not of it," claiming he was always "playing the role of Negro." At a time when Robeson was not yet fully identified with the left, she expressed impatience and dismay over his inclinations: "I find a new lot of Negroes coming along. They're different than Robeson generally. They're not so pious, they're not Uncle Tom's children." Although I disagreed with her assessment of Robeson, since I admired him greatly, I did not offer any dissent, not wanting to break off her train of thought.

In contrast, Stein was an unrestrained enthusiast for Richard Wright, who by 1945 had emerged from the lowly status of a Harlem staffer for the *Daily*

Worker, when I knew him in the late 1930s, and was being hailed as the bright new Negro star of the literary world for his *Native Son* and *Black Boy*. Stein's appraisal of Wright was in keeping with her pontifical pronouncements on every subject she discussed. "The best American writer today," she called Wright. "Every time he says something, it is a distinctive revelation. He tells something never told before in a perfectly distinctive way. He is a Negro who writes about Negroes but he writes like a man rather than a Negro. The theme is the Negro but the treatment is that of a creative white. The material is within him but he is outside of the material. The ordinary Negro isn't outside of his material. Wright's material doesn't dominate him. With most Negro writers, the Negro is on top of him." With customary vanity, she added, "He is without question the best master of English prose since myself. Only one or two creative writers like him come along in a generation. Wright follows in the tradition of creative writers like Twain, Henry James, Howells, Walt Whitman and Gertrude Stein."

A coincidental follow-up to our conversation occurred later when Wright wrote Stein a desperate letter. He had had an ugly bout with racial bias and decided to leave the United States after he was rejected by a New Hampshire realty broker when trying to buy a home out in the countryside. Returning to New York, he informed his wife of his decision to leave for Paris within a month. But when Wright applied for a passport, the State Department turned him down. The official excuse was that postwar European conditions were such that a U.S. citizen might become stranded there. He turned to Gertrude Stein, with whom he had been corresponding, and she succeeded in convincing the French government to issue an official invitation to Wright to visit France. The U.S. passport was finally granted, and when Wright descended from the boat-train in Paris, Gertrude Stein was there at the Gare St. Lazare to greet him.

Once they had met, however, the two highly opinionated, self-centered writers found little common ground. In the few months before Gertrude Stein died at the American Hospital in Paris, they were continually in battle, Wright later told me: "We were wonderful friends until we met. But then our relations were just one long argument. And then she up and died on me in the middle of the argument."

That they should squabble was inevitable since they were both spirited and tenacious in their views. Their concepts on the Negro were far apart. On the one hand, Gertrude Stein was still immersed in the perceptions of her early book, *Melanctha*, admiring what was primitive and uninhibited in the Negro. In a letter to her friend Mabel Weeks (published in 1991 in the book *Gertrude and Alice* by Diana Souhami), she complained that she was limited in her early writing "to content myself with niggers and servant girls. Dey is very simple and vulgar and I don't think they will interest the great American public." Wright, on the other hand, was playing Bigger Thomas on an intellectual level, striking out angrily at racism and its ills. Yet their underlying analysis of Negro character was basically along parallel lines. It added up to what Wright called "emptiness" and Stein "nothingness." Neither saw any anomaly, however, in their belligerence on behalf of racial equality, their insistence on the Negro's rights, in contrast to their disparaging appraisal of what they described as the Negro's ever simple, natural character. More analytical than Stein, who simply accepted the "nothingness" of the Negro as a fact of his life, Wright ascribed "emptiness" to the denials the Negro faced from the moment he was born. Stein rather saw the deficiencies in terms of his African background. She concluded in our interview that Negroes "were not suffering from persecution, they were suffering from nothingness . . . the African is not primitive, he has a very ancient and a very narrow culture and there it remains. Consequently nothing does or can happen."

The "nothingness" discerned by Gertrude Stein was expressed even more strongly by Wright in his *Black Boy*. He gloomily spoke of "the essential bleakness of life in America" and detailed his dour outlook. He wrote of "the strange absence of real kindness in Negroes, how unstable was our tenderness, how lacking in genuine passion we were, how void of great hope, how timid our joy, how bare our traditions, how hollow our memories, how lacking we were in these intangible sentiments that bind man to man, and how shallow was even our despair . . . I knew that Negroes had never been allowed to catch the full spirit of Western civilization, that they lived somehow in it but not of it [the exact term used by Gertrude Stein to describe Paul Robeson]."

When I had earlier reviewed *Black Boy* in my *Defender* book column from my orthodox leftist perspective that rejected any reflection upon Negro characteristics, I particularly criticized Wright's negativism in picturing blacks and ventured to upbraid him for his departure from Communist Party ranks. Terming him a "self-centered, anti-social rebel" as a result of his childhood trauma in Dixie, I chided Wright as being "without feelings of solidarity with the Negro people . . . a lone wolf, wily and wise to the ways of the white man, yet still so suspicious and wary of his own that he cannot bring himself into common struggle with them. This inner, subconscious distrust of all men perhaps explains his failure to find any genuine identity with the Communists." Such was the party line of criticism of *Black Boy*, which I echoed.

The sweeping extremity of Wright's views was typical of his sense of the dramatic. Yet in my Communist Party days I believed in the validity of much of what he and Gertrude Stein maintained, even though their captious appraisal of Negro character would today no doubt be rightly refuted by most race-proud leaders, who have advanced far from "the cultural barrenness of black life," as Wright described it. Wright saw "cultural backwardness" as just another burden the Negro was forced to bear by white Americans; to Gertrude Stein, though it was a part of his African heritage, it was also a challenge, a phase of pioneering, another frontier to cross after the Negro had broken racial barriers to achieve freedom.

6

The Happier Side of Negro Life

*I'm so goddamn sick and tired of the white man telling us about us.
He can't.*

Dick Gregory

After having worked for three years at war's end with two black publications, I still could only see my status as transitional. I had no idea what these jobs might lead to and no notion even of where I wished to go, what I wanted my anomalous journalistic work to develop into. I did sometimes speculate that making my mark on the *Defender*'s circulation and launching *Negro Digest* successfully might lead to other newspaper or magazine work, perhaps even to a position in mainstream, "respectable" white journalism, but my radical pretensions, wavering though they often were, rejected such a possible future. Yet I well knew that as a white, I would have limited opportunities at any Negro periodical. I never even dreamed of becoming a top editor, recognizing that such an outcome was, to say the least, unlikely. Black resentment against a would-be interloper and the need for black self-assertion had been reflected in the very first issue of a black newspaper, *Freedom's Journal*, which insisted, "We want to plead our own causes. Too long have others spoken for us." An even more important factor limiting my long-range prospects for a career in the Negro press was my "shady" Communist connections, which I feared were bound to surface someday. My anxiety about possible exposure never ceased, always preventing me from embarking on any decisive, steadfast course of action I might consider later in life. As Victor Hugo wrote in *Les Miserables*, "A man trying to escape never thinks himself sufficiently concealed," and always for me there was a fear of exposure to bedevil my thoughts and planning.

My gradual drift away from the party had begun not long after I began working full time at the *Defender* and was accelerated in the months after I returned from Paris. Appearing more and more frequently at my office desk was a South Side Communist Party official, the surreptitious monitor of my editorial work, who sought to place the Communist stamp on my editorials. He would slyly "suggest" stories as well as critique the paper's contents. I deeply resented him and his attempts to meddle with *Defender* policy making, but I did not dare to communicate my feelings to him. At this point I was still subject to leftist domination, even in some cases agreeing with his comments and continuing to collaborate with party dictates. The party still influenced me, and through me the *Defender* news and editorial content.

The more hours I began to devote to the *Defender* and to *Negro Digest*, the less contact I had with the Communist Party at unit meetings and social events. Lack of time and fear of party identification were not the sole reasons; I also increasingly questioned some of the party's disciplinary tactics, its cruel trashing of anyone who challenged party policy, its never-ending round of recantations and expulsions, its continual feuds and splits, its seeming tendency to self-destruct. More and more I was able to shed longtime straitjacket Communist views on economics, politics, and especially racial problems. Unlike the Communist party line, the new "cause" I had embraced involved no detours and about-faces like the Nazi-Soviet pact; racial equality was an inviolable principle.

Still, I had no illusions about my new bosses, the black publishers. Black journalism I quickly recognized as having a dual raison d'être, serving a cause and at the same time profiting from it. Early in my years of working for the Negro press, I accepted that black publishers—like other American publishing companies—were in business to make money, although the fight for racial equality was their vehicle for financial success.

While working for the *Daily Worker*, I could and did write opinionated copy without compunction. I had learned well the tricks of angling news stories to the left to savage "reactionaries" and writing headlines to play up protest stories. My Communist apprenticeship served me well in Negro journalism. In some cases there was more angling of news coverage in black publications than in the leftist press. The news was truly black and white editorially as well as on the printed page. I did not hesitate to accept the pro-black "angle," since I saw the scales tilted so unfairly against Negroes and believed strongly in the goals of racial integration.

Soon after my return from the merchant marine, I was delighted to hear John Johnson propose an idea for a new magazine. Since the Negro version of the most popular white magazine, *Reader's Digest*, had been so successful, he wanted to publish a black version of the second most read white publication, *Life* magazine. Even though I was already working long hours on two publications, I nevertheless readily agreed to assemble and edit the projected monthly, which Johnson decided to name *Ebony*. Whatever worries and confusion I still had about where I was headed soon ended; my future course was firmly fixed when *Ebony* magazine was born.

The first issue of *Ebony* magazine was produced with a Royal portable typewriter, a pica ruler, a stack of copy pencils, scissors, and a bottle of rubber cement on the kitchen table of our Jackson Boulevard apartment in spring of 1945. Over a three-month period, I had solicited pictures from photo agencies and articles from freelance writers on black and interracial themes. Our target date for the new magazine's debut was early summer. It was to be a *Life*-size magazine, printed on glossy paper and featuring outstanding pictorial essays. As with *Negro Digest*, I was the entire editorial staff of *Ebony*. At home each night I slowly pieced together the magazine, writing much of the text and all the photo captions and headline titles, doing photo layouts, selecting typefaces for body copy and article titles, scaling photographs, proofreading galleys, stripping galley proofs, and laying out the final dummy-page pasteup of the fifty-two-page initial issue. Although I lacked experience in photo journalism and picture magazine editing, I had copies of *Life* constantly in front of me to emulate, and I did so religiously, replicating entire page layouts and seeking to match title types and writing styles as much as possible. The *Ebony* logo in a bold gothic typeface was a copycat of the logo of *Life*.

But the first issue of *Ebony* almost proved stillborn. For all Johnson's business acumen, he had failed to consider one vital factor in publishing a new periodical during wartime. With rigid wartime restriction on all materials still in effect, paper use was controlled by the War Production Board (WPB), and magazines were allowed only a limited allotment. New magazines were not granted any paper at all. *Ebony* fell victim to this unbreakable rule in spite of Johnson's desperate pleas to the WPB, based on the usual ruse of the projected importance of the new magazine in buoying wartime Negro morale. I was able to complete every detail of the first issue, all its contents in metal type ready for press, and there *Ebony* remained for almost six months.

Although the first issue of *Ebony* was shelved, it was not scuttled. Finally, in the fall of 1945, the WPB relented after Johnson once again appealed for a paper allotment, and 25,000 copies came off the slow flatbed presses of Progress Printing Company between regular issues of *Negro Digest*. In spite of the delay, few editorial changes were necessary in any of the pages of *Ebony*. A new, current dateline was inserted, and volume 1, number 1 of *Ebony*, priced at twenty-five cents a copy, was distributed on newsstands early in October with an issue date of November 1945.

My first sight of the issue came while I was still in Paris; Johnson had airmailed a copy, along with clippings from *Time* and *Newsweek* commenting on the new magazine's debut. The *Time* notice read almost like a paid puff, but *Newsweek* was more critical, commenting on "lax editing, loose writing and inaccuracies." The copy from Johnson was followed by an agitated cable urging me to return home immediately: "Editorial work on *Ebony* and *Negro Digest* piling up. Why not come home by plane. We will pay difference in cost." But at a time when even military officers and wounded soldiers found it difficult to arrange plane transportation, I could not book a flight and had to settle for another Atlantic voyage after several days of waiting at a military compound for homebound GIs appropriately named Camp Home Run.

My assessment of the first issue of *Ebony*, as I perused the finished product in my Paris hotel room, was mostly groans and grimaces over the inferior quality of the printing; obviously Progress Printing was not up to the production of an acceptable imitation of *Life*. Like most imitations, *Ebony* was far distant from the high editorial standards of the prime picture magazine, even though *Time* had reported that *Ebony* "imitates *Life*'s format." Most of the photos were pallid washed-out grays, as if the printer had stinted on ink. The editorial content seemed threadbare, as I sat reading articles written months earlier. I found glaring problems not only in the helter-skelter choice of some of the subject material and my own uninspired writing but also in the less than imaginative photographs. Much of the issue consisted of a mélange of stock photo agency packages (at a cost of no more than $100 each) and publicity pictures, around which I had improvised lengthy text; few of the picture essays involved original photo assignments. That debut issue showed an obvious lack of direction, of editorial cohesiveness, of thematic substance.

For our first cover of *Ebony* we had chosen a black-and-white photo by a New York photographer, Marian Palfi, of an interracial group of youngsters at the Henry Street Settlement, only one of whom was black. The shot illustrated an article on eliminating racial prejudice among children, written by a white minister and illustrated with photos from the New York daily, *PM*. That cover photo violated just about every rule later laid down by Johnson for selection of *Ebony* covers: (1) no group pictures; (2) no unknown people; (3) no children.

The advance billing for the first issue had proclaimed that *Ebony* would portray "the happier side of Negro life." But for all the "happiness" touted in that first issue, the brightest notes came in my introductory message proclaiming Johnson's aims and in the warm reception the issue received from *Time* magazine, which lauded its "cheeriness." Aside from two lighthearted cartoons on the back cover by E. Simms Campbell, then a popular contributor to *Esquire* magazine, and six gag cartoon panels on an inside double spread by Jay Jackson, then a *Chicago Defender* comic strip artist, the mostly dour contents did not live up to the promotional claims. Most articles had a bookish approach, such as one piece on African art put together with publicity photos of plaster reproductions from the University of Pennsylvania museum shop—the kind of serious high-toned subject that Johnson refused to tolerate in later issues. Another batch of publicity photos from Warner Bros. studios of a strobe jazz movie filmed by Gjon Mili was used to illustrate a manufactured article on supposed interracial "good will" between white and black musicians. But in actuality black faces were rare indeed in name orchestras in the mid-1940s. *Time* magazine chose to illustrate its puff piece with a publicity studio shot of singer Sheila Guys, but even that story had a sad theme: the Broadway show she was to star in, a swing version of *HMS Pinafore* called *Memphis Bound*, was a flop. "Starving Negroes Can't Eat Racial Equality" was the headline on a picture story on allegedly integrated Brazil, which as *Time* noted was a reminder to *Ebony*'s readers of the "unpleasantness" in Negro life overseas.

The masthead of that first issue listed John Johnson as publisher and myself as editor, with Jay Jackson as the art editor (though his sole contribution was his cartoon panels). Only two first-rate photographers were represented: Gordon Parks, who continued freelancing for *Ebony* until he became a full-time *Life* photographer, and Gordon Coster, who was regularly sent on assignment for *Life*. Coster had assembled an impressive photomontage to accompany an editorial I wrote called "Sixty Million Jobs or Else," on the specter of Negro unemployment with millions of servicemen returning home—yet another phase of *Ebony*'s contents that was anything but positive.

In many ways crude and amateurish, the first issue of *Ebony* justified *Newsweek*'s carping assessment. My lack of magazine experience—in article composition, photo selection and layout, caption and title formulation—was evident, and I wondered if I had not attempted more than I was capable of doing. I had assembled the first issue of *Ebony* over a period of months. Could I produce a similar package in a single month, and then keep it up month after month? I agonized over that question on the voyage home, preparing myself to confront the editorial mess I would have to face. Recognizing that I had substantially to improve the standards of a publication that, unlike *Negro Digest*, was not based on reprinted materials, I returned home determined to learn much more about magazine editing.

Despite almost a decade of experience as journalist and editor, I had to acknowledge that I knew next to nothing about photo journalism. My knowledge of photography was limited to bathtub development of Brownie-class snapshots. My editorial approach was still attuned to words rather than pictures, yet the visual aspect was the essence of the *Life* formula. I felt anxiety over my ability to judge photographs, to assess picture placement, to weigh the relative merits of photos as related to copy. But I never admitted my doubts either to Johnson or to the early editorial recruits to the *Ebony* staff. Instead I plunged in, jaunty if not confident. Under the pressure of impending deadlines after my dire assessment of the initial issue of *Ebony*, there was no time for doubt or hesitation. My concern over my inexperience was soon forgotten as I recklessly plunged into the enormous task of assembling and refining the mountain of material needed to keep the magazine going from month to month.

If Johnson was apprehensive about my editing ability based on my initial performance with *Ebony*, he did not say so. He seemed jubilant over the praise *Ebony* had received "in the street," as he put it. In truth he had full reason to rejoice at black readers' reception of the first attempt at a popular Negro picture magazine. Not surprisingly, black readers remained the magazine's main audience over the years despite favorable notices in the white media; for some half-century, whites did not constitute a significant portion of *Ebony*'s readership. As an innovative concept in black journalism, *Ebony* drew immediate attention from the white media, but far more critical to its health and survival was the lavish praise from black readers. The magazine had been almost casually placed on sale on newsstands, mainly in black neighborhoods, with almost no fanfare or promotion, minimal advertising in black weeklies, and very little publicity. Nonetheless, the first issue sold out almost completely, proof that an excellent potential market existed that was far larger than the 25,000 copies of the introductory issue of *Ebony*.

What was most innovative in *Ebony* magazine in its early years was its daring (for the period) editorial approach. For the first time, a national black periodical openly rejected negativism and advocacy of a cause: the persistent theme of the Negro press from the start. Black journalism had always been synonymous with racial militancy, and newspapers bore such names as *Whip* and *Defender*. In contrast, *Ebony* in its opening editorial proclaimed: "*Ebony* will try to mirror the happier side of Negro life—the positive, everyday accomplishments from Harlem to Hollywood." The words were mine, but the thought was Johnson's. He and I had had long discussions about this new, untried approach before I ever began putting words on paper. In contrast to my hard-hitting editorial blasts in the *Defender*, I wrote: "We're rather jolly folks, we *Ebony* editors." (This was a blatant misstatement to start with since the total number of *Ebony* editors added up to one; it was not until the fifth issue that any staff additions to *Ebony* were listed.) "We like to look at the zesty side of life," the editorial continued. "Sure you can get all hot and bothered about the race question (and don't think we don't) but not enough is said about all the swell things we Negroes do." Here I was obviously writing down to my audience in a patronizing fashion, yet that upbeat approach is what caught the eye of *Time*, which headlined its story on *Ebony* "The Brighter Side."

Spotlighting what was best in Negro life, the superlatives in black accomplishments, was Johnson's credo for *Ebony*. Although I had reservations about this approach, which has remained controversial among journalists and black intellectuals to this day, I was coopted, perhaps too well, in my years at *Ebony*, though I always expressed my doubts to Johnson. Aiming to entertain and educate, to foster black pride, *Ebony*'s pages were assiduously shaped to shun traditional polemics and politics, so that the most critical of the white media, even in the deep South, had good reason to welcome *Ebony*'s debut.

The changed wartime status of the Negro was the essential base of Johnson's affirmative formula. *Ebony* in his view was to be a kind of escapist publication for Negroes who sought some spark of felicity in a world of suffering and sorrow. Sensing that an improved racial climate was coming, Johnson delegated me to synthesize in *Ebony*'s pages the changes in the everyday life of blacks. Negroes were now working at more and better jobs than ever before, enjoying wartime prosperity. Color barriers were falling in some areas of American life, and blacks' push toward greater racial equality was progressing. Most important, black people had more money now than ever before, and they were willing to spend it. Johnson himself exemplified this trend: a few years before he had had to scrounge funds to launch *Negro Digest*, and now he was a prosperous publisher. Knowing that he himself was too busy enjoying life—going to nightclubs, parties, and movies—to read as much as he once had, Johnson came up with the idea that a picture magazine was the best way to portray the new hedonism among black Americans. "We try to present the good things that Negroes are doing, with emphasis on what can be done, not on the handicaps," Johnson described the editorial aims of *Ebony* in a *Business Week* interview. "We try to emphasize and play up points on which Negroes and whites can agree rather than stress points on which they disagree, We try to avoid too much pressure," he said in the pages of the *Christian Science Monitor*. "We're not the NAACP. We're a business," he declared on another occasion. Even on *Ebony*'s fortieth anniversary, at a time of political regression for blacks under the Reagan administration, Johnson was still singing the same tune, declaring in a special anniversary issue of *Ebony*: "We try to seek out good things, even when everything seems bad."

In the postwar period a new black middle class was evolving, even in the midst of race riots. With new money, new goals, and new concerns beyond racial parameters, black Americans, having once tasted the good things in life, had learned what they had been missing and now aimed for even better, Johnson contended. Even as rebellious a novelist as Ralph Ellison could note: "After a man makes $10,000 or $20,000 [then excellent income], the magic fades. He is just another man with his problems." Money in this view was seen as an escape from racism that would confront middle-class blacks with the same personal headaches that faced white Americans in higher income brackets. In *Ebony*'s pages, however, the forgotten man was the Negro without money, still in the ghetto and still facing bias in so many areas of American life.

Although I could see the virtue of playing up black pride, I was too well schooled in the language and tactics of dissent to swallow Johnson's approach whole. The flame of racial militancy kindled in me by Metz Lochard and expounded in the *Defender*'s pages in editorials I wrote could not be easily extinguished at *Ebony* by Johnson's position of benign passivity in print (though he privately professed to be as racially aware and defiant as any other Negro publisher). My Communist and *Defender* training in protest proved a source of continual acrimony between Johnson and me for almost all the years I worked for him. My never-ending arguments for balance to report some of the worst of racism along with the most significant advances for the Negro went unheeded as *Ebony* increased in circulation.

Johnson saw increasing circulation as proof of the success of his formula, and no amount of disagreement on my part could dissuade him from his determination to maintain the sunshine-and-roses spirit. But for all my objections to *Ebony*'s racial "happy talk," the journalistic challenge of editing the blossoming magazine was too much of a temptation to resist. So I stayed on, often disputatious or sulky, but always in the end following Johnson's prerogative as publisher. I rationalized that I, as a white, could not persistently challenge Johnson's judgment on racial matters. "I've been a Negro all my life and you're still new at it," he would say to me when we disagreed. How many times was I reminded that a white person can never really know how blacks feel and think. Mostly I had to agree, but sometimes I rebelled. After all, ideological and political differences among Negroes, as among whites, ran the full gamut of opinion, and I could always find some black support for my views.

I could salve what conscience I had by recalling the advice to would-be journalists in my old college textbook: the reporter "writes what his superiors instruct him to write, in a way that they want it written. If he is unwilling to do so, his only alternative is to look for another job." For me, after I was later ousted from the *Defender*, there seemed no other jobs to look for. Once again, anxiety over my Communist connections was a persuasive factor in my decision to accept Johnson's approach.

When I began appearing less and less at Communist functions, I knew that I was sure to hear about it from the party. Sure enough, a hard-line party official arrived at the *Defender* office one afternoon. Well did he match the sage observation of playwright Clifford Odets that "Communist organizers and workers are often as unfeeling and brutal as their opponents." Grim-faced, he marched into my office unannounced. His presence would have been highly embarrassing if his identity as a Communist leader had been known. But if any of my colleagues at the *Defender* were aware of my Communist connections, none ever uttered a word of it to me, and I was never aware of any whispers circulating in the office about my leftist politics.

"You haven't been to any meetings lately," he complained and began to lecture me on "Marxist-Leninist responsibility," He then offered me a way to expiate my transgressions, demanding "a substantial contribution to the cause." I should have shown him the door, but angry as I was, I still did not have the courage to act on my less than loyal feelings for the party. He railed on about how much money I was making on my job (then all of $125 weekly at the *Defender*) and how I owed it "to the people" to share my salary. Finally he demanded, "Well, how much are you going to give?"

For some moments I remained silent, considering my wisest course. Fearful of the possible consequences—party disciplinary action and public expulsion and/or exposure to the *Defender* publisher of my Communist affiliation—if I rejected what amounted to a shakedown, I agreed to give him fifty dollars.

He instantly took offense: "That's insulting to your comrades! I won't accept that little!"

Fists clenched, I fought to regain my composure. "In that case just forget it," I told him.

Red-faced he rose from his chair. "You'll be hearing from us," he warned as he walked out. It turned out to be an empty threat. I suspected that in my key editorial post at the *Defender*, I had become too important a "mole" in penetrating the Negro press for the party to risk losing me. As the *Defender*'s national editor, I was in control of much of one of the most widely circulated black weekly newspapers. I also edited the magazine that had the biggest monthly circulation among blacks. I was too valuable an asset to lose over my playing "hooky" from unit meetings and refusing to kick in "substantial contributions" to the party coffers.

I was less and less concerned with deviating from the official party line. Though I remained grateful that the Communists through William L. Patterson had provided me with my initial introduction to the black press, I no longer felt beholden to the Communist Party. I reasoned that my journalistic abilities rather than any political considerations had enabled me to attain my current status. And had I not "paid my dues" in full in my beginning years at the *Defender*, when subject to the watchful eye of the party's hard-line monitors? The moment had come when I was ready and willing, if not altogether able, to break the chains that bound me to the Communist Party.

But no one could make an easy or clean exit from the Communist Party. This was one party that a member did not simply walk out of; rather a member had to be publicly expelled as an example to the faithful. Continual anxiety over the possible exposure of my Communist ties caused me to stay on despite my changing views. My troubles with the party continued to simmer through the mid-1940s.

Meanwhile, at the *Defender* I became embroiled in a union dispute with party overtones. As a longtime Newspaper Guild member since my early employment at the *Daily Worker*, I continued in the Guild even though I was now classified in the management category. I attended meetings of the small Communist Party "fraction" in the Guild, which numbered at most a half-dozen reporters working at downtown papers and wire services. When I first went to work at the *Defender*, it had no Guild unit. I helped to recruit a handful of members into the union, even though I myself was ineligible to function openly in the Guild because I was in "management." When an attempt was made to win union recognition, publisher John Sengstacke balked, and for months negotiations went nowhere. The Guild did not have sufficient numbers to call a strike, and nothing was resolved while talks continued. Despite my "management" status, I encouraged Guild members to be steadfast to the union and to their demands for recognition as well as for higher wages.

Some years later I learned from editor-in-chief Metz Lochard, after he himself had been ousted from the *Defender*, that one of the Guild negotiators, a *Sun-Times* editor, had informed Sengstacke that I was a Communist and the "stumbling block" in reaching an agreement. "Get rid of Burns and we can reach a settlement right away," Lochard quoted the Guild official as saying. Sengstacke did indeed get rid of me, but not over the Guild issue (and the *Defender* never did sign a Guild contract). He had always resented my editorial work with Johnson on *Negro Digest*, and publication of *Ebony* was the last straw. Sengstacke became increasingly incensed, if not envious, over the growing success of the magazine edited by one of his staff. There was whispered talk at the *Defender* that I had purloined editorial material from its files and its news sources to put together the initial issue of *Ebony*, which was untrue. I was much too wary and worried about that possible accusation to attempt such easily detected larceny, but I was even more conscious that such a journalistic practice would be unethical. Sengstacke was correct in at least one aspect of his belief that I had "borrowed" from the *Defender* to shape *Ebony*: much of my knowledge of the Negro world did indeed come from my *Defender* experience.

When I found a dismissal notice with my paycheck at the end of March 1946, I was not at all surprised. To Doc Lochard as editor-in-chief had fallen the unwelcome task of firing me. With his usual fine hand he softened the impact with his formal memo: "We regret to inform you that we are in the process of reorganizing the editorial department, and we find that your services are no longer needed. This is to notify you officially that you are relieved of responsibility and are hereby dismissed from the *Chicago Defender* organization." It was the first time I had ever been fired from a job; I had always before left on my own or been a casualty of a paper folding. In one way I was relieved, since once again I would now be working only one job, editing *Negro Digest* and *Ebony*. Another aspect of the situation was more problematic: as a boss the easy-going Sengstacke had been the antithesis of my new boss, John Johnson. A hands-off publisher who rarely voiced any comment or criticism of his editors, Sengstacke differed vastly from the domineering, hard-driving Johnson, who insistently checked and censored every last word before stamping his personal imprimatur on his magazines. Both men were to become outstanding figures in black journalism. Sengstacke at one time controlled more newspapers than any black publisher ever had before, and Johnson became the dominant publisher of black magazines—and also perhaps the richest black businessman in the United States.

7

The First, the Only, the Biggest

*White was not a favorite complexion with God. There is nothing
important, nothing essential, about a complexion. I mean to me. But
with the Deity it is different. He doesn't think much of white people. He
prefers the colored.*

Mark Twain

Ebony succeeded immediately in escaping the negative "radical"
stigma of the Negro press, but in so doing it angered black militants
who vilified its "happy talk" approach as "Uncle Tomming." They
did not hesitate to accuse *Ebony* of "sellout" journalism in letters to the editor
as well as in street talk. The "moderate" label was permanently fixed on
its editorial policy as Johnson from the outset unabashedly rejected racial
belligerence in its pages. In his view an editorial comment in *Tide*, the
advertising trade organ, praising *Ebony* for "taste and restraint to avoid the
taint that afflicts so much of the Negro press" precisely reflected how he
wanted the magazine to appear to the white media and particularly advertising
agencies.

Once the "positive" tone was set in early issues, *Ebony* had to find appropriately bland features to fit—not an easy task given that racism still prevailed
in so many aspects of American life. In searching for black achievements
to crow about, *Ebony* struck a sure-fire formula that it continued to follow
for decades: first, only, biggest. With Negroes breaking into many new fields
in postwar years, *Ebony* could rely on a "first" in almost every issue. One
month it was the first black entertainer to play a Miami Beach nightclub:
Miami Beach in the 1940s still would not allow a Negro to stay overnight, and
singer Joyce Bryant had to return to a hotel in Miami's black neighborhood
after each night's performance. I, too, stayed there while covering her debut
for the magazine. In the next issue it would be the first Negro to pilot a
Navy plane, and so on. The "only" Negro was much the same story; in one
issue it was the only black man living in a small New York town. In a quaint

twist, another month it was the only white living in Harlem's Theresa Hotel. "Biggest" usually applied to money and business. We featured a succession of articles on the biggest landowner, the biggest beauty parlor, and so on. Once we ran an article on the Negro with the "biggest" number of wives, perhaps linguistically questionable but fitting *Ebony*'s editorial packaging.

The "first-only-biggest" formula of *Ebony* stressing black accomplishment was in Johnson's eyes the needed antidote to so much negative news and a whiff of cheer and inspiration in the lives and dreams of ordinary African Americans. While I agreed in part with that spur to young blacks, I still wanted the magazine's editorial content to reflect somewhat the still deleterious U.S. racial climate. Johnson's determination to be always affirmative sometimes proved bewildering, if not futile, when negative racial headlines predominated in white as well as black newspapers. Again and again a race riot or a grievous instance of discrimination would occur—significant developments that lay outside *Ebony*'s purview, but that I felt we could not ignore. In these instances Johnson and I would tangle about the need for such coverage.

Occasionally in the first year of *Ebony* I might catch Johnson in a weak moment and persuade him to approve an article that reflected the harsher reality of black life, but such personal triumphs were rare. One such clash took place after I was able to obtain some exclusive bloody photographs of a Tennessee race riot taken by Edward Clark. I won Johnson's grudging approval and ran these gruesome shots of whites with hunting rifles stalking blacks as a five-page lead story in May 1946. I had obtained the shocking pictures from *Life* magazine while on a short visit to its Manhattan offices to meet with the magazine's sole Negro editor, Earl Brown, in order to learn more about photo journalism. In his office Brown pointed to a three-foot-high stack of rejected picture stories on Negro subjects to emphasize what a very small percentage of photographs shot by *Life* were actually used in the magazine. Thumbing through one pile of Harlem pictures taken by ace photographer Herbert Gehr, I told Brown, "You know, I could keep *Ebony* going for a year with these pictures."

Surprisingly, Brown offered, as a goodwill gesture to *Ebony*, to give me a couple of the rejected photo packages. I did not hesitate in selecting the grisly race riot shots and another set of photographs of Rep. Adam Clayton Powell and his new wife, singer Hazel Scott. Returning to Chicago, I proudly showed off my prize to Johnson, but he immediately questioned why *Life* had not published the riot photos: if the shots were too shocking for *Life* to print, were they not also too strong for *Ebony*? But I argued that rejection of the photographs by a white magazine was the best reason for *Ebony* as a black publication to print them. Reluctantly he finally dropped his objections. Once the photos appeared, however, several advertisers complained about them. Johnson laid down an ironclad rule: never again. Coverage of race riots never again appeared in *Ebony*'s pages.

The seminal years of *Ebony* were not easy ones financially despite all the "success story" publicity about the magazine that appeared in white media. Often paydays were uncertain as the still green publisher learned that circulation revenue was very slow in arriving from distributors and often was not quite enough to meet the mounting printing bills. But the agile Johnson ducked and dodged deftly as creditors closed in on him like sharks.

The slight addition of some advertising that *Ebony* was able to solicit was not enough for the magazine to turn a profit. Rumors in the office frequently foretold disaster, and one Friday staffers gossiped that their pay was in kited checks. Outwardly Johnson maintained his chipper demeanor, seemingly confident that somehow his printers, engravers, and paper suppliers would carry him until the tide turned. Although I was not privy to company account books, I still sought to reassure staffers that the Johnson magazines were not about to fold, even while uncertain myself about *Ebony*'s ability to survive. In those first few months competent writers were so scarce that we could ill afford to lose those few I was able to enlist.

By the spring of 1946 the entire two-magazine operation had moved to a two-story red-brick building at 5125 South Calumet Avenue off the rear courtyard of what was then the South Parkway Community Center (later to become the Chicago Baptist Institute). South Parkway (now Martin Luther King, Jr. Drive) was in effect the "main street" of the "Black Belt," as the South Side was then termed. Located behind the main community center building, the offices of *Ebony* and *Negro Digest* had a separate entrance on Calumet Avenue in what may have been at one time a school building. The large high-ceilinged offices off long corridors seemed like classrooms, and I was relegated to one of these away from the vision of routine visitors, just as I had been at the *Chicago Defender*. Although I had been working for Johnson for more than three years, this was the first time that I actually spent full time at a desk in one of his offices.

Staffing was a thorny problem from the start of *Ebony* since there was no existing pool of available Negro talent with magazine experience. In the mid-1940s there were no other popular black monthlies, only organization publications such as *Crisis*, the NAACP organ, and several church magazines.

When I edited the first issue of *Negro Digest* in 1942, I knew of not a single black editor or photographer on the staff of any recognized national magazine. At the time *Ebony* began publication, only *Life* magazine had a black staff editor, Earl Brown.

One of the first black writers I was able to recruit for *Ebony* was a former *Stars and Stripes* reporter, Allan Morrison, one of the very few Negro journalists who had some magazine experience. When I had first met Allan in uniform on the Champs Elysées in Paris some months previously, I had spoken to him about joining the staff of *Negro Digest*, not fully anticipating the speedy success of *Ebony*. Six months after our Paris meeting he became one of the first two editorial additions to *Ebony*'s masthead. The other was a white writer, Kay Cremin, a Wheaton College graduate, who had won honorable mention in a *Negro Digest* college essay contest. Allan turned out to be a choice find indeed, but unhappily he was unwilling to stay in Chicago, in spite of all I could say to persuade him to give up Harlem. One of those urbane New Yorkers to whom the rest of the United States is the boondocks, Morrison was morose on the South Side, missing the hectic Harlem life and the rich theater and nightclub scene of Broadway. Even though he was paid more at *Ebony* than he could possibly make working for any Negro newspaper, he still could not tolerate Chicago. His unhappiness, however, was not reflected in his lucid, incisive prose. Despite my frantic appeals, Allan left *Ebony* in the spring of 1947 to return to New York as a freelancer. Several years later, when *Ebony* was able to open a New York bureau, I prevailed upon Allan to rejoin our staff. Allan was not only a fine writer but also a scintillating personality.

The other initial editorial recruit had come to our office based on her outstanding essay in *Negro Digest*'s writing competition, "Should Negro Students Attend Mixed or Negro Colleges?" I personally thought Kay Cremin's piece arguing in favor of mixed colleges was the best entry and should have won first prize, but I agreed with Johnson that our winner should be from a black college, so Cremin received only an honorable mention. I sounded her out, however, on whether she would be interested in working for *Negro Digest* when she graduated. She readily assented to become an editorial assistant at *Negro Digest*, and this willowy, chestnut-haired college graduate surprisingly demonstrated a racial awareness that belied her privileged background growing up in New York's upper-class Westchester County. Her writing talents more than measured up to all that I could ask when she switched to writing *Ebony* copy. However, the winsome Kay just could not manage to get to her desk on time mornings. For all her unquestioned talents, her captivating personality, her total commitment to interracialism, and her willingness to work late, in Johnson's eyes Kay was a bad example. Obdurate, he fired her, initiating the revolving-door employment policy that eventually earned him a citation from *Fortune* magazine as one of America's "Toughest Bosses."

Another white writer who joined our editorial staff was the youthful, slight Mark Harris. I had excerpted for *Negro Digest* part of his successful first novel about racial discrimination in the army, *Trumpet to the World*, and after he had written several freelance pieces for *Negro Digest*, I offered him a job. I was surprised when he accepted the offer, consenting, like other white liberals, to take a relatively paltry salary to help "the cause." But the highly talented Mark never adjusted to disciplined desk writing and after a few months departed for a career in academia. He later wrote several best selling novels, including *Bang the Drum Slowly*.

Skin color made no particular difference when I began lining up photographers who could shoot magazine-quality photographs for *Ebony*. Since in the late 1940s not a single Negro worked as a staff photographer at *Life, Look*, or any other nationally circulated magazine or metropolitan newspaper, I had to turn mostly to outstanding white freelancers in the Chicago area, as well as to photo agencies. I was able to line up a small constellation of stellar talents, among them Wayne Miller, who had been schooled by Edward Steichen in the navy during the war and who later with Steichen edited the classic *Family of Man* collection at the Museum of Modern Art in New York; Mike Shea, who regularly did freelance assignments for *Life*; and Archie Lieberman, who was *Look*'s prime photo source in the Midwest.

Nationally our prize find was a Negro photographer, the charismatic, multitalented Gordon Parks, who was undoubtedly among the top-ranking photographers in the nation but at the time still was receiving very few magazine assignments. His photographs appeared in most issues of *Ebony* our first year. Later he began to receive well-deserved recognition, and he stopped taking *Ebony* jobs when he was hired as a full-time staff photographer at *Life*. He later became a Hollywood movie director and acclaimed author.

Whenever feasible, I sought to use staff photographers working for Negro newspapers in New York, Los Angeles, and other big cities but was usually disappointed to find their pictures geared to newspapers rather than to a feature magazine. After several years *Ebony* was able to afford its first full-time staff photographer, Griffith Davis, a young, clean-cut ex-GI who had made photography his hobby while attending Morehouse College. Recommended by Langston Hughes, Davis had no professional experience before arriving at our office but rapidly learned his craft. Sometimes a single issue of *Ebony* would have as many as three or four of his photo layouts. With a case of wanderlust not unlike my own in later life, Davis moved on to other ventures before long, joining the Black Star photo agency and eventually winding up in Liberia with the State Department.

The problem of finding additional competent staff to keep producing the expanding monthly magazine became a continual crisis. In desperation I turned to my leftist contacts in journalism, particularly photographers. Johnson knowingly agreed to my suggestions to retain or employ some of my radical friends, even if my own Communist background made these people suspect and even though all of them were white.

One of the first of these conscripts was top-ranking photographer Gordon Coster, whose work appeared regularly in *Life* magazine and whose acquaintance I had made at fellow-traveler social affairs. He readily agreed to provide monthly pictorial montages to accompany editorials that I wrote. In *Ebony*'s first issue Coster's photomontage portrayed a forlorn black itinerant tramping down a railroad track, a symbol of the growing army of unemployed blacks in a job market flooded by returning GIs. Coster's fee for the montage was only a fraction of what he would normally bill and amounted to his making a financial contribution to *Ebony*.

In almost all the first year's issues, the photo credits included the ever youthful idealist Phil Stern, who turned up creative features on black movie actors and nightclub entertainers from his base in Hollywood, where he was often on assignment for *Look* magazine. Phil gave *Ebony* a long lead on other publications with its spread on Sammy Davis, Jr., the first to appear in any national magazine. Phil had accompanied me in 1937 on an assignment for the *Daily Worker*, when I took my first plane flight for an article on the International Workers Order Flying Club, a leftist offshoot of the party. Like Coster, he agreed to shoot photos for *Ebony* at a meager fee since the magazine was a "worthy cause."

No doubt my most significant catch was one of Chicago's premier studio photographers for advertising agencies, the versatile Hungarian-born Stephen Deutch. Deutch's photos were featured often in national media campaigns, and he produced many of the illustrations used in Marshall Field & Co. store advertising. I had not known him in Communist Party circles, but I had heard that he was a "close sympathizer." When I called upon him for whatever material he might have in his files that *Ebony* could use, all he could find was a shot of a "Whites Only" sign on a southern restaurant, since he rarely photographed Negro subjects. But we were able to use the photograph in our

August 1946 issue, the first of hundreds of his pictures that appeared in future pages of *Ebony*. With Old World graciousness, Steve also offered to work for a reduced fee. At first he produced fashion layouts, but he soon turned to more serious subjects that resulted in a succession of outstanding photo spreads and color covers.

Six months after *Ebony*'s debut another leftist friend, Irwin J. Stein, was listed as the magazine's advertising manager. He was retained by Johnson at my suggestion when the need became apparent after *Ebony* began soliciting advertising. In addition to the technical business of handling engravers' plates, checking them and sending them to the printer with insertion orders, and then billing for the space, the job involved the critical task of soliciting for new accounts. I had known Stein as an official of the International Workers Order in the 1930s before he became associated with the advertising department of a Chicago Jewish weekly. When Johnson could find no advertising staff members at Negro newspapers who were willing to give up their jobs to join his still shaky, untried magazine, he agreed to meet with Stein and then offered him a job. Johnson kept Stein on the payroll for several years, eventually replacing him with Negro personnel recruited mainly from the National Urban League.

In those early months and years, *Ebony*'s masthead changed as often as a weather vane, a gauge of Johnson's splenetic temperament no less than of the unwillingness of some newly hired editors and writers to put up with the pressures and demands of *Ebony*'s editorial pace. Even though we were always shorthanded in every department, Johnson was trigger-quick with dismissal letters, so that from week to week sometimes I would hardly know what to expect. But Johnson was not solely responsible for the staff turnover; sometimes editors left of their own volition after a few months on the job for other reasons, including lack of respect for Johnson's blinders on racial issues.

Although at *Ebony*'s inception the staff was multiracial, gradually both the staff and freelancers became predominantly black as more writers, editors, and photographers were recruited from the ranks of the Negro press. The writers we enlisted in the first decade of *Ebony* ranked among the most outstanding black journalists of the times, but few remained on staff for more than a few years. Their personalities varied from the traditional old-style "hustlers" of black journalism, always on the lookout for payoffs when out on assignment, to the overly sincere intellectuals immersed in black culture and history. Some were highly talented writers who knew little about magazine writing, while others were routine craftspeople, able to perform the mechanics of assembling a magazine speedily under deadline pressure. Few among the staff believed in the publisher's carefully calibrated racial positivism, but like me, they were compelled to follow the "party line" as set forth by Johnson, just as I had done in my Communist Party years.

One of the first black editors hired at *Ebony* who was able to cling to the job through successive waves of ruthless firings by Johnson was Era Bell Thompson, the North Dakota author of an excellent autobiography, *American Daughter*. Era Bell eased her way to an *Ebony* office desk in the fall of 1947 on the basis of having written a book, even though she had never held a job as a writer before. She became a fixture on the staff, compensating for her diminutive stature with a combination of chip-on-the-shoulder bravado and super-sharp wit that was a plus in her writing style. Era Bell eventually became international editor before her death in 1986. Another black editor hired in those early days became *Ebony*'s longest survivor on its masthead and my editorial surrogate. Bronzed Indian-appearing Herbert Nipson walked into our offices one day in 1949 when as usual *Ebony* was hard put for editorial help. He was on a job hunt after postgraduate courses at the University of Iowa, and was promptly assigned to a typewriter. Nipson was able to hang on through every one of Johnson's periodic "economy" layoffs. He learned enough of magazine techniques finally to move into supervisory posts and eventually, by sheer seniority, achieved the top editorship. He remained on the *Ebony* staff for some thirty-eight years. Nipson was executive editor at the time of his retirement in 1987.

The surest indication of success in the magazine business is to be sued. At *Ebony* this litigious initiation came very early, when heavyweight champion Joe Louis filed a $100,000 libel suit in May 1946 after we belatedly published a rehash of what sports columnists in white dailies had been reporting for some months about his financial woes. What mainly angered the champion was the title *Ebony* used on its picture story: "How Joe Louis Spent $2,000,000." The article related how the spendthrift fighter had squandered his money on unwise investments, camp followers, and "slick chicks," as *Ebony* wrote in ghetto vernacular. *Ebony*'s article actually contained little that was new, printing what was being said about Joe in the street. Still, the pairing of a dramatic four-color head shot of Louis on the cover and an article repeating the cumulative reports of his wastrel ways was enough to push *Ebony*'s circulation to a new high—cause for joy at a time when the magazine was still being produced in limited numbers on flatbed presses. However, our early rejoicing over sales reports ended abruptly when Louis decided to sue following the brash prompting of a sports writer for a Negro newspaper, who confronted him with *Ebony*'s story and challenged him: "Say, Joe, is all that stuff in the *Ebony* article true?"

Louis denied the reports, and as we later heard from the Louis camp, the sports writer goaded him, "Then why don't you sue them?" So he did. For a magazine six months old to be slapped with a libel suit was very nearly a knockout blow. It came when *Ebony*'s finances were still so shaky that Johnson had retained a new business manager, Charles Beckett, a cautious accountant who, he hoped, would somehow untangle his accounts. Summoning Beckett and me to a crisis meeting, Johnson sought our views on how to proceed: should we assuage Joe Louis with a retraction or stand behind our article? Beckett counseled surrender, but as editor I had to insist on the accuracy of our report and urge that *Ebony* stand by its factual account. If we gave in, I felt that our apology might encourage future threats and intimidation from other public figures anxious to keep their indiscretions out of our pages. Beckett's recommendation of prudence won out, however, and our apology to the champion was printed in the October 1946 issue—the last to be printed on flatbed presses.

One aspect of my work at *Ebony* was quite difficult to accept: I served as a convenient scapegoat for militant black critics, who could attribute to me *Ebony*'s "Oreo" orientation—brown on the outside but white inside. As the editorial deputy for Johnson's policy of racial timidity, I was compelled to defend it outside office confines, even while within the office I continued my opposition to Johnson's conservatism.

For all my problems with Johnson over *Ebony*'s editorial confections, I still felt much exhilaration and excitement in assembling each issue, buoyed by the magazine's growing acceptance and acclaim, and by its rocketing circulation figures. The pursuit of new readers impelled me, like any other editor, to continually search out a new exclusive or exposé, find some special angle to present an intriguing subject in a new light, turn up outstanding photography to dramatize a significant story. I was caught up in the fever of creation of an entirely new Negro medium, even if *Ebony* did choose to neglect the more serious side of the rapidly changing postwar racial scene, which reached its climax in the 1960s. *Ebony* was never even close to the forefront of the movement and paid only lip service to the achievements of the militants who were challenging the racial status quo. Their heroic deeds went unsung in our pages. At best *Ebony* editorially tagged along after the pioneer activists who were beginning to break down color barriers in endeavors ranging from the military to the movie industry, from politics to literature, and then finally in the streets. But despite *Ebony*'s pussyfoot reporting and my continual vexation at being confined to the sidelines, I still exulted to be at least a minor player in this fascinating drama that eventually rocked the nation.

I soon discovered that as an editor I had to contend with more than just Johnson's retreats on fundamental racial issues. I quickly learned how far raw racism could affect even the mechanical phase of the magazine business. An unexpected tangle with bigoted printers posed a predicament in *Ebony*'s early days. The problem arose after it became apparent that the Progress Printing flatbed presses could neither keep up with *Ebony*'s fast growth nor provide adequate reproduction quality. Even after a move to a larger downtown shop, M. Kallis & Co., which had more flatbed capacity, copies of one issue were rolling off the presses while plates for a new issue sat idly for a week or more waiting to go on press. We did no better with our next printer, the John Maher firm, and as a result our circulation potential was sorely restricted. Shopping desperately for a printer with rotary equipment, Johnson was spurned repeatedly, in part because open press time was still at a premium as a result of postwar shortages. Telephoning one of the biggest printing houses in Chicago, W. F. Hall, Johnson insisted that the company at least do him the courtesy of sending a sales representative to see him, implying that Hall might have turned him down initially because *Ebony* was a Negro publication.

The sales rep was a chipper Irishman named Vincent McMahon, who defensively came to our South Side office to say no once again. Proffering regrets with charm and grace, McMahon explained that as a good Catholic he did not have the slightest prejudice against Negroes, but that the truth was that Hall's presses were being used to capacity. Johnson, however, was a better salesman than McMahon. Having ascertained from the Chicago Urban League that Hall was having personnel problems with its Negro workers—lateness on the job and a high rate of absenteeism—Johnson perceived an opening and convinced McMahon that Hall's production of a Negro magazine would give its black workers a sense of pride that could change their working habits. McMahon bought the argument and proceeded to sell it to his superiors. *Ebony* was ready to go big-time—but not before a major tangle with Hall's white engravers and press operators was resolved.

Early in 1946 I assigned a French photographer, Ilya Gregory, to go from Paris to Berlin to cover the many news reports circulating about Negro soldiers dating white girls in conquered Germany. Whether Gregory could set up a photo story was highly doubtful, given that racial mixing was so objectionable to white army officers. But as a calculated risk that involved only paying

Gregory's expenses if he could not obtain the pictures, I thought it was a worthwhile attempt and obtained Johnson's approval for the project. Many weeks later word came from the local customs office that they were holding for clearance a set of photographs from Paris. Sensing trouble, Johnson and I went over to the Canal Street customs office. The inspectors glowered as we examined the photographs of Negro GIs at parties, on the beach, and in private necking sessions with German women. One shot, showing a blonde stripper performing barebreasted before a dozen black soldiers, provided the customs officials with a pretext to stop the entire shipment as "salacious." Despite our contention that many similar photos were being circulated in the United States, the customs inspectors refused to budge until we hinted at a charge of discrimination. Johnson intimated, not too subtly, that perhaps the shipment was being held because the prejudiced customs officers did not approve of Negro men consorting with white women. Immediately, all the pictures were cleared, but only after we promised not to publish the shot of the partially nude dancer, which Johnson had never had any intention of printing.

As it turned out, however, the trouble with the German story layout was just beginning. Censorship from our new printer was something we had not anticipated, especially in the first issue to be printed by the Hall firm. Several days after the layout and copy for the story had been completed and dispatched to Hall for processing, Johnson received a call from a Hall executive.

"Mr. Johnson, I've got a ticklish problem I'd like you to help me with," he began, as Johnson recounted to me later.

"Sure, I'd be glad to," Johnson assured him.

"Well, you know when you start printing a new magazine at our shop, there are always minor problems with the first couple of issues and it takes time to make adjustments. You have to sit tight and be patient."

"Yes, I understand. What seems to be the trouble?"

"You know we've never printed a colored magazine before, and our men haven't seen the kind of stuff you're publishing. We've got to go slow for a while."

"Sure, sure, but what seems to be the trouble?"

"That German story. There are some pictures some of the fellows are hot about. And you know with the unions and everything, well, we've got to be careful."

"You mean they won't print the pictures."

"I wouldn't put it that way. It's just that they don't like them, and we figured it would be best at the beginning to take it easy until they get used to the job."

"What do you suggest we do?"

"It's nothing serious, understand me. It can be taken care of easily. It's just that we'd like to start slow. If you take out the pictures that the fellows object to, that'll be it."

"That's a strange request from a printer to a publisher. But I can see where there might be objections to some of those pictures."

"Oh, there's nothing wrong with them. But you know how some people are, and we have to work with these fellows and the unions every day. We've just got to be careful."

"Why don't you send back those pictures and let me think about it," Johnson slowly retreated, in his typical backdown when confronted with controversial material. Hall sent back the "objectionable" photographs—mostly shots of mixed couples embracing on a beach. "Thinking about it" for Johnson usually meant caving in when a racial principle was involved, despite his later reputation for toughness. The offending photographs were deleted and "milder" pictures substituted to appease the engravers. Although I was infuriated by Johnson's retreat, I had to accept his surrender—after expressing the strongest scruples against censorship by printers.

Several issues later printers once again became *Ebony*'s unofficial censors. This time the offending photograph was submitted in a letter from a reader who had spotted—and photographed—the uncommon sight of a white woman shining a Negro's shoes (she was the wife of a Negro bootblack). I included this unique inversion of the shoeshine stereotype in our letters to the editor column. But the Hall printers vetoed that picture, too. Once again Johnson knuckled under and agreed not to run the offending photo—though he did run it later, when he was a more substantial Hall account.

In time the printers' attempts to censor *Ebony*'s contents diminished somewhat, no doubt influenced by the fact that the monthly check from Johnson to Hall had risen to more than $100,000. *Ebony* became too big an account for the printer to risk losing. Still, attempts to censor the magazine continued, but now they came from advertisers rather than printers.

8

Finally in the Big Time

Skin and hair. It has mattered more than anything else in the world.
Nadine Gordimer

While John Johnson's "positive approach" to racial issues was frustrating for me personally, it also put me into hot water with the Communist Party, of which I was still a member, though I had long ceased to function in party ranks in any organized fashion. Early in 1948 I received notification from the party to report to a kangaroo court trial—my own. The charges ran the full gamut from "selling out to the enemy" to the even more heinous accusation of "white chauvinism." Here I was, editor of the most widely read black publication in America—and accused of "white chauvinism"!

What had precipitated this final decision to expel me was an editorial that appeared in *Ebony* in November 1947 as part of the "positive approach." A stereotypical Thanksgiving-type essay listing what gains blacks had been able to achieve despite the still existing inequalities of the American way, "Time to Count Your Blessings" was based on one of my regular discussions with Johnson, whose thinking I reflected in all the editorials I wrote. What particularly distressed the doctrinaire "comrades" was the contention that "around the world there are countless people who are fighting and dying to win a measure of the American Negro's standard of living, his civil rights, his everyday enjoyment of life. Yes, the Negro is deprived of his vote and sometimes his life in many southern states, but where else in the world can a person yell as loud and long about it except in America?"

Of course, I had personal doubts and reservations about some of this twaddle, but I knew it was of no avail at that point to resist the "positive" outlook to which Johnson was fully committed. I was resigned to the blunt truth that if I stated my opinions rather than Johnson's in an editorial, I would not survive long at *Ebony*. I was a white editor working for a black publisher, and as such I recognized that I had not only to accept but also to express his views, not mine. If ever I did not reflect his opinions and insisted on mine, I would have only one choice—resign. Though I argued often and loudly with Johnson over his conservatism, in the final analysis I had to write what he wished: he was the boss and I was his employee, and he was black while I was white.

The Thanksgiving editorial I wrote at his bidding was perhaps too good, too convincing to some. *Reader's Digest* decided to reprint it along with lavish praise for its assumptions from NAACP executive secretary Walter White. For my efforts I received a $500 check from *Reader's Digest*, half the total payment to *Ebony*, and I also received a firestorm of criticism from the Communist Party. In a two-page, single-spaced "indictment," the Garfield Park neighborhood unit to which I had been transferred accused me of engaging in a "betrayal of the Negro people," "helping to keep the Negro people tied to the parties of Wall Street," being a "turncoat who for a few pieces of silver takes his place with many other traitors," and "keeping a job that pays him something like $200 per week rather than fight growing fascism." To increase the humiliation, I was offered a chance to attend party proceedings and defend myself before the party curia. Presumably I would in true Western frontier tradition have been "given a fair trial and then hanged," as the old story goes. I chose not to attend. I later heard that there was a show hearing with testimony presented against me by one-time friends who had been pressured to speak out against my "sellout." I was formally expelled from the party in absentia. Finally, I had escaped the quicksand of Communist Party membership.

If I had not been sufficiently "punished" for my political straying by the staging of a show trial, further punishment came in the form of a resolution of expulsion printed in the *Daily Worker* in the spring of 1949. If anyone did not already know that I had been a Communist Party member, here was a half-page "advertisement" to that effect, a vindictive attack under a damning three-column headline: "No Compromise with White Chauvinism." The resolution was signed by a party spokesman, one Frank Mucci, whom I knew by reputation only, as chairman of the review commission of the Communist Party.

Although I was distressed by the open disclosure of my party membership in the *Daily Worker*—a move seemingly calculated not only to embarrass me but also to cost me my job and friends—I was relieved that my links to the party had been completely severed. Naively, I believed that I now no longer had the baggage of Communist taint to burden me—an illusion that soon faded. Soon the vengeful party apparatus began working to cut me off from my old friends of the left, threatening to discipline anyone who spoke to or associated with me. In effect, I was declared a nonperson. I was accused of "actively helping the forces of reaction and fascism in America," furthering "Nazi-like ideas of white supremacy," and writing "words welcome to American imperialism." The *Daily Worker* reported that several party members had been "censured for fraternizing" with me, and to the party's horror "in one instance a comrade invited Ben Burns to a social affair, which was attended by a number of party members." Readers were told that "fraternizing with Ben Burns means condoning the white chauvinism of a renegade, and therefore is actually an expression of white chauvinism itself. Any comrade who continues to fraternize with Burns will immediately be brought up on charges before the party."

"Guilt by association," which was so bitterly condemned by the Communists, was precisely what the "comrades" were professing and practicing. But our longtime circle of radical friends did not see the obvious parallel, and they swiftly fell into line with party dictates lest they face the wrath of their party units. A few ignored, even defied, the party edict and remained close friends, eventually themselves dropping out of party ranks. But mostly even the closest of friends turned on me. I could then well understand Arthur Koestler's trenchant observation that "friendship can transcend politics, but not when politics means commitment to a totalitarian ideology, be it Nazi or Stalinist."

If Johnson saw the *Daily Worker* report—and undoubtedly he did—to his credit he did not comment to me about the public announcement of my expulsion from the Communist Party. After all, he knew of my political past, so there would have been nothing new to him in the disclosure of my Communist ties. He could have seen the *Daily Worker* denunciation of myself and *Ebony* as an indirect testimonial from the left to his racial moderation, an impression he was intent on selling. Yet to have a former Communist as editor of *Ebony* was not entirely a judicious sales pitch, and I naturally worried that the *Daily Worker* announcement might result in my dismissal. How long would Johnson be able to resist outside pressure to get rid of me? Could my merits as an editor outweigh the "Red scare" of the late 1940s? Public anti-Communist hysteria was fueled by sensational newspaper headlines on the espionage charges against former State Department aide Alger Hiss, the conviction and imprisonment of Communist Party leaders (including my former sponsor at the *Daily Worker* and later boss at the *People's World*, Al Richmond), the outbreak of the Korean War, and the trial and scheduled execution of Julius and Ethel Rosenberg as Soviet spies. I awaited the worst in the wake of the *Daily Worker*'s exposure of my Communist past. But I was able to weather yet another crisis, since for Johnson my contribution as an editorial workhorse apparently outweighed my liability as an ex-Red.

In the unequal conflict between publisher and editor, I came to acknowledge there could be but one outcome. Belatedly I recognized the painful, undeniable truth of publisher M. Lincoln Schuster's delineation of their roles and relationship: "An editor selects manuscripts; a publisher selects editors." Gradually I lowered my resistance to Johnson's entrepreneurial commercialism, coming around to the conclusion that having entered the tawdry, avaricious business world, I now had to adjust to it. The survival and profits of *Ebony* had to be my prime goal.

After our initial issues, I sensed that launching a periodical successfully in the mid-1940s in the nation's Negro communities, where no popular mass-circulation magazine had ever succeeded before, required more than the cream-puff contents dictated by Johnson or the standard promotional devices employed by white magazines. I was convinced that persuading Negro readers to pay more for a publication, new and untried, than they ever had before for a black newspaper or magazine would necessitate some novel features and presentation to stimulate the word of mouth that is the most effective of all media sales strategies. Since *Ebony* had been denied the racial militancy that had always been the prime ingredient of Negro publications, we had to search out some other compensatory element to lure readers to our pages. Once the impact of *Ebony*'s introduction as a picture magazine had diminished, the realities of the magazine business necessitated new dimensions to move copies constantly off newsstands. (Unlike white magazines, which depended on subscriptions, *Ebony* for more than a decade depended on newsstands as its circulation base.) In my view, what was needed was an eye-catching "cover" article with a cleverly worded title to attract the eye of the newsstand browser—what *Ebony* staffers came to designate as a "hot story" conceived, written, and displayed primarily to grasp the transient reader and achieve maximum sales, just like a newspaper's front-page banner headline.

The "first-only-biggest" formula would not suffice; such stories were already being exploited by the Negro press at large, and as a monthly *Ebony* could only embellish pictorially what often had already been reported in black weeklies. To solve that dilemma, I turned to old-fashioned journalistic techniques that I had learned not only in my newspaper training but also by observation of the best selling white magazines, such as *Reader's Digest* and *Life*. I opted for the creation of cover articles quite off the beaten path and either neglected or shunned by Negro as well as white media.

Examples of such sales-promoting cover articles included the earliest private-life coverage of Lena Horne (which I wrote myself after spending hours talking to her backstage at the old Chez Paree nightclub in Chicago) to a withering broadside, "What's Wrong with Negro Baseball," by Jackie Robinson (ghostwritten by A. S. "Doc" Young) that lambasted Jim Crow in the major leagues while describing the crude, makeshift conditions players had to live with in the Negro leagues. Other controversial articles followed. Never before covered in Negro media were such daring (for the times) picture stories as photographer Wayne Miller's revealing series on the birth of a baby, depicting an actual delivery in a ghetto home by a doctor from a Maxwell Street clinic. Long before marijuana became a national addiction for so many of the younger generation, Miller produced a remarkable "close-up" layout covering its effects on participants at a "tea party." For most black publications at that time, syphilis was a taboo subject; photographer Stephen Deutch's revealing photographs taken in a venereal disease clinic in Chicago—though frowned upon by many readers as reflecting on Negroes by daring even to suggest that venereal disease was a dire problem in the black community— was a journalistic breakthrough. Month after month I labored to create such provocative articles to stimulate street talk about *Ebony*.

One unusually explosive article that resulted in an unexpected kickback was an exposé by bandleader Earl Hines titled "How Gangsters Ran the Band Business." In his account of night life in the Roaring Twenties and early Thirties, Hines detailed names, orchestras, and nightclubs involved in gangland control of the thriving entertainment business. Not long after the issue appeared on the stands, Johnson nervously summoned me to his office and ordered me to "lay off gangster stories from now on."

"Why, what's wrong? The Hines story is selling pretty well, I hear."

"Sure, too well. You know who was just in here to see me?"

"No—not one of those gangsters Hines mentioned?"

"No, not a gangster. They sent someone. And he let me know in no uncertain terms that they didn't like the Hines story!"

"Aw, there's nothing to be scared about. They don't shoot newspapermen."

"That's what you think. I don't know whether they do or don't—and I don't ever want to find out."

Hines himself had a siege of fright when he first saw the article in print. As with most of *Ebony*'s bylined pieces, his story had been ghostwritten, and Hines had given his approval by long-distance telephone, not quite comprehending that the story was to appear under his byline. When he saw a copy of the magazine, he was astounded to see his name flaunted in large type over the article and was shaken up by the photos of gangsters he had named, including the likes of the Capone brothers and Owney Madden. Meeting staffer Allan Morrison in a New York club, Hines grabbed him by the coat and muttered angrily: "I'm afraid to go back to Chicago now. But I'll tell you one thing—if any of those hoodlums ever catches me and asks me about the story, I'm going to break my mother-fucking finger pointing at *Ebony*'s office."

Beyond the threats by proxy, there were no casualties following Hines's revelations or any of the many articles *Ebony* published on the numbers rackets. However, we did turn to safer subjects and bylines, such as Marva Louis revealing her marital problems with her heavyweight champion husband in an article titled "Why I Quit Joe" and popular singer Johnny Ray admitting that "Negroes Taught Me to Sing."

After four years of publishing *Ebony*, our commonplace back-street address on Calumet Avenue and our makeshift offices no longer fit Johnson's dreams of publishing glory, and now that he could afford it, he resolutely commenced a search for an exceptional building that would suit *Ebony*'s vaunted status as the nation's foremost black publication. Determined to break out of the "Black Belt," he retained a shrewd white real estate agent who specialized in buying white-owned property for Negroes by deluding sellers into the belief that they were selling to white buyers. Soon the agent spotted for sale a showy funeral parlor at 1820 South Michigan Avenue close to downtown, a location that matched Johnson's notions of a distinguished home for his expanding ventures, which now included a new cosmetics business as well as publishing.

From the exterior, as first viewed by Johnson and myself, the green tile-bricked structure was impressive indeed, and Johnson was immediately disposed to negotiate a speedy purchase at the asking price of $52,000. The structure had been built as a fashionable art gallery when Michigan Avenue south of the Loop was a prime business area. It was later converted to an ornate mortuary, the Hursen funeral parlor, where one of Chicago's colorful political characters, ward boss Michael "Hinky Dink" Kenna, had his glittering wake. When white residents began moving out of the surrounding neighborhood and white funerals became fewer (Negro funerals were never booked by any but black undertakers), the funeral parlor moved to a white community. But the mortician was reluctant to sell to a "colored" buyer and shunned Negro offers of as much as $60,000.

Even though he had never been inside the building to inspect its condition, Johnson was set on acquiring the property and turned to the kind of subterfuge for which he seemed to have a natural aptitude. Our white advertising manager, Irwin Stein, and I became bit players in Johnson's maneuvering; we rather than Johnson himself became the prospective buyers, supposedly representing a white publishing syndicate that wanted to keep its planned expansion hush-hush. The Hursen people were informed that Stein and I wished to have our building maintenance worker inspect the heating and air-conditioning system, and Johnson dressed for the occasion. Despite higher bids from Negro would-be buyers, Johnson's rock-bottom offer of $52,000 was finally accepted because he was presumed to be the "white buyer." It was characteristic of him to employ whatever trickery was required to achieve his goals. "I stooped all the time to get what I wanted," he admitted unabashedly in later years. "If I had to do it over again, I would."

Moving day on April 4, 1949, was a momentous occasion for Johnson, for the staff, who now numbered more than twenty, and also for me personally: I felt that I had finally reached the "big time" after more than a dozen years on the journalistic fringe. Certainly the imposing headquarters we now occupied matched those of many a top-rank magazine, even if on a smaller scale. Johnson had spared no expense in remodeling the three-story structure, particularly in his private office, a spacious spread with paneled walls and indirect cove-ceiling lighting.

My opaque glass-enclosed office, an ample if unembellished workplace, was located a dozen paces from Johnson's door on a balcony level overlooking the wide-open general editorial offices, which had once been the display room for Hursen's top-of-the-line caskets and which now in paneled arches displayed blown-up prints of some of the best photographs from the pages of *Ebony*. As in the past, I was relegated to a spot not readily seen by outside visitors. I fretted over my location, not because I was hidden, but rather because by looming atop a stairway to summon a staff writer to discuss his copy, I found myself in the embarrassing position of literally talking down to the staff like an overseer. I welcomed a move some years later to a wood-paneled office in an adjoining building, when Johnson expanded the facilities yet again.

Whatever social intercourse I participated in with writers took place mainly in the third-floor lunchroom. Johnson had ostensibly installed the lunchroom for the staff, but as he candidly admitted to me, it was as much for himself since he was uncomfortable eating out, especially with whites. Often invited to downtown luncheons with business executives, he would be disinclined to go.

When he could not conveniently decline the invitation, he would sometimes eat his fill in the *Ebony* dining room before heading for his Loop luncheon. On other occasions, in the middle of a luncheon with a white person, he would provide himself with some excuse to bolt and would appear late in our lunchroom to wolf down some leftovers. In eating with white business executives, he invariably would cross off certain items on a restaurant menu that he would not order. He was convinced that if he selected some of his favorite foods, such as pork chops or watermelon, whites would think: "It's just as they say—all Negroes like pork chops and watermelon!"

"I just don't feel comfortable eating with white people," he once bluntly told me. "I can't relax."

"But I'm white," I responded.

"Aw, but you're not a real white man. I can even eat spare ribs when you're around."

I was to hear that "not a real white man" many times during my years at *Ebony*. At first it seemed to me a symbol of my acceptance in the Negro orbit, and I accepted it as a racial badge of honor. Later, however, the designation was turned on me repeatedly by Johnson in my acrimonious encounters with him over *Ebony*'s policies.

Some of the best *Ebony* story ideas were born in the lunchroom interplay rather than in editorial conferences. In the course of conversation, secretaries, librarians, and editors would discuss unusual happenings on the South Side or in cities they had visited. Always scouting for story material, I would see a possible article and pursue further details, exclaiming, "Hey, that'll make a good *Ebony* piece." My ability to perceive a story when other editors failed to recognize one disturbed me; I worried that it reflected my inadequacies as a boss in training my staff. I tried to remedy this by alternating between closer guidance for editors in their writing or allowing for individual initiative through less rigid direction, but I never was satisfied with my administrative role; I always disliked playing the boss.

The Johnson Publishing Company complex, with one of the publisher's three family Cadillacs (one each for himself, his wife Eunice, and his mother) often parked in its covered driveway, became a Michigan Avenue showpiece. In an unending series of lavish catered receptions for advertising agency executives, city movers and shakers, black celebrities, and high society, the exultant publisher displayed his jewel. In time a tour of *Ebony*'s headquarters became a required stopover for black visitors to Chicago from across the country, a recognized tourist attraction like a historical landmark. I was constantly amazed by the unceasing parade of "pilgrims" who trooped through our offices. Teachers would bring entire classes of tots and teenagers to cast eyes on what seemingly had become a wonder of the Negro world; religious and business conventions would arrange special visits.

The spectacle of the publisher's Cadillac rolling up to the building's entrance each morning inspired an *Ebony* editorial—as usual, one that Johnson suggested and that I had to write, tongue in cheek and hat in hand. In "Why Negroes Buy Cadillacs," I followed Johnson's catechism in defense of his Cadillacs:

> Granted that the man who owns a Cadillac has his obligations to give to race organizations that strive to better the good and welfare of the Negro, it is also nevertheless true that investment in a Cadillac has its points, too, as a weapon in the war for racial equality. The fact is that a Cadillac is an instrument of aggression, a solid substantial symbol for many a Negro that he is as good as any white man. To be able to buy the most expensive car made in America is as graphic a demonstration of equality as can be found.
>
> To deny the pleasure of driving a Cadillac to Negro well-to-do because there are still other Negroes who live in slums and shotgun shacks is as ill-advised and illogical as demanding that white millionaires voluntarily surrender their estates and Park Avenue penthouses to the unemployed. The world never has and never will work that way despite the idealism of utopians. To berate colored Cadillac owners for not spending their money instead for good causes is to deny Negroes the right to reach for equality on every level of U.S. life. As long as there are rich and poor in this country, there will always be rich and poor Negroes. And that means there will always be Negroes with Cadillacs.

The editorial was much quoted and understandably much berated in the Negro community. For militants the Cadillac polemic was a summary self-indictment by *Ebony*, setting forth Johnson's doctrine as bluntly as a Chinese Communist wall proclamation. Much as I had sought to distance myself from the politics of my past, I still bridled at this spurious defense of Cadillac ownership by rich Negroes.

Early on, the articles that did the most to boost *Ebony*'s sales had proven to be in four basic subject areas: interracial marriage, Negroes passing as whites, sex, and anatomical freaks. Our experience with the phenomenal sales of *Ebony*'s issue spotlighting romances of GIs with German girls showed the degree of reader interest in this sensitive subject. Despite threats of subscription cancellations when *Ebony* featured articles such as "Famous Negroes Who Married Whites," those issues usually increased our circulation by as many as 50,000 copies. One of the most controversial and successful of these cover articles was "Life with Father" by Mother Divine, a ghostwritten article by the white Canadian wife of Father Divine, the wealthy charismatic Harlem preacher who called himself God.

Shrewd, perceptive author Roi Ottley, who had become a staff writer, did the prodigious research to document *Ebony*'s best selling feature, "Five Million U.S. White Negroes." This was a popularized chronicle of race mixing over the centuries that had resulted in so many light-skinned Negroes who could pass for white, as indeed many did in the 1940s to find employment. Ottley's numbers were hard to believe but his facts were solid, and I played his article to the hilt, illustrating the piece with an eye-catching cover photo of a teenage platinum blonde Negro girl from Los Angeles. Perhaps even more intriguing than the text was the collection of more than a dozen photographs of both light-skinned Negroes who could pass for white as well as some whites, displayed as a quiz challenging readers to guess their racial identities. Among the whites in the pictorial layout were my wife Esther and my son Richard, both of whom might appear to be Negro in some of their photos.

Ottley stated in his article that "between 40,000 and 50,000 Negroes 'pass' into the white community yearly and between 5,000,000 and 8,000,000 persons in the United States, supposed to be white, actually possess a determinable part of Negro blood." To reinforce his figures, Ottley noted that "nearly 82 per cent of the Negro community have some white blood." A further argument for his statistics was "the anthropological fact that every living man today can count more than a billion ancestors. Somewhere in that billion there indisputably was colored blood."

Ottley's article had a surprising sequel. Candidly outspoken in his personal relationships and conversation, at a dinner party one evening at our apartment he engaged in a verbal tangle with his wife Alice. Discussion in our mixed gathering turned to his *Ebony* article and then to skin coloring of marital partners in the Negro community. When Ottley bluntly declared that lighter skinned women married darker Negroes only if they were prominent individuals, his light-skinned New Orleans wife protested, "Oh, that just isn't so!"

But Ottley stubbornly stood his ground, and to the astonishment of all his white listeners he told his wife: "I know most people don't like to hear it said, but it's true. Now let's take us as an example. Would you have married me if I wasn't a well-known author? Of course not, I'm too dark, but I also have a name."

Everyone gasped as he continued: "Sure, I know you love me, baby, and I'm very much in love with you. But let's face it, in the Negro community color is a big thing. No light-skinned woman marries a dark-skinned man unless he's a somebody." Unsaid was the corollary: that dark-skinned Negro women were shunned by black celebrities, who chose light-skinned wives.

Visibly mortified, Alice hotly denied Roi's assertion, while our white friends, who were not usually privy to such frank racial discussions, were embarrassed and remained silent as the argument continued between husband and wife, becoming so heated that Alice suggested that they leave. They walked out still arguing.

Ottley's article caused some office controversy as well, when in the process of selecting photographs, I sought to learn if they would be identified as colored or white by staff members. A part-time artist to whom I showed the layout unhesitatingly picked out Esther's photo as one of the Negroes. He was told by a writer, "That's a laugh. She's Burns's wife!"

"So what," was his response. "I still say she's colored. And if she says she isn't, then I say she's just fooling Burns!" His comment was typical of the kind of racial self-disparagement that was common in office talk among many of our staff at a time before "black pride" was popularized. To our artist, to be colored was something shameful, to be hidden, something that called for "fooling" me.

Another who was "fooled" by Esther's appearance in another racial miscue was Truman Gibson, an official of the International Boxing Club whom I had known since his wartime days as a token Negro aide to the secretary of war. At one of the frequent social gatherings at *Ebony*'s offices, he was introduced to Esther. Later approaching Johnson, he whispered to him, "Say, I didn't know Burns had gotten married again."

"Married again? Where did you get that idea?"

"Sure, I was just introduced to his new wife."

"New wife? That's crazy. He's only been married once."

"But I always thought his wife was white."

"She was and still is," Johnson told him.

How mistaken even staff members could be about racial presumptions was graphically illustrated in a comedy of racial errors in which all our self-professed "color experts" were completely hoodwinked. At a time when many public places in Chicago, particularly restaurants and hotels, still excluded Negroes, a staff member's suggestion to spotlight the restrictive racial barriers seemed a clever article idea: a photo layout showing how a light-skinned Negro woman could pass in public places that tabooed blacks. Finding the right fair-complexioned Negro woman became a problem, however, since few light-skinned women were willing to risk such a problematic assignment.

Weeks went by while we scouted in vain for the "star" in the drama we planned to enact. Finally one day an eager volunteer showed up in the office, having heard about our search for a woman who could pass for white. She declared that she was willing to risk the embarrassment of being ejected from a discriminatory establishment. She fitted the bill perfectly for the projected story, being as pale-skinned as any white woman and willing to work at regular model's rates. Our enterprising white photographer, Wayne Miller, began shooting pictures of our model having her hair done at exclusive beauty salons, attending all-white dance schools, dining at exclusive restaurants, and checking into top downtown hotels—all places that were known to bar Negro guests. When published, the *Ebony* story was much talked about in the black community—and especially in our offices after we discovered that the model we had booked for the job was really white and had deceived all of us. *Ebony* never acknowledged the mistake in its pages.

There was frequent, seemingly innocent banter about black-white relations in our offices. While I joined in the spirited repartee, I sometimes sensed that much of the levity reflected the self-derision and disdain that was inscribed into the thinking of too many Negroes in those years. On one occasion white advertising executive Allan Marin, who placed *Ebony* promotional advertisements in white media, happened out of past habit to let the word *boy* slip in referring to *Jet* managing editor Ed Clayton. He promptly apologized when Clayton remonstrated in his usual brusque fashion. Relating the incident the next day, Clayton relished his triumph until a colleague asked, "Nigger, did he call you 'boy'?"

The irrepressible Al Duckett, who delighted in reciting racial witticisms, once confided to me that a visiting publicist to our office had mistaken me for colored. How? "He called you 'boy.'"

Johnson himself enjoyed playing the derisive race game, and often I was the butt of the mirth. Once watching a couple of white carpenters accurately estimating just where to break through a wall to build a passageway to an adjoining building of different height, I wondered out loud, "How did they figure that out?"

"That's white folk's business. We're not supposed to know," Johnson caustically remarked. Then he added, "Now I know you're not a real white man."

When some disorderly, badly composed advertising copy would arrive in the mail, some wiseacre might comment, "Now, that ad has a Negro look." A common expression to describe something amateurish was "mammy-made." The stock expression for why somebody was late to work or to dinner was, "He's operating on CP time," that is, "colored people's time." I remained unconvinced when Johnson sought to persuade me that the color brown should not be used on a magazine cover, because Negroes subconsciously disliked it as the root cause of all their problems. Johnson himself carried the hypothesis to the ultimate in his tastes: he said he liked every flavor of ice cream except chocolate.

His convoluted racial rationale resulted in a confrontation on one occasion when I complained about working too hard and expressed my dream of a leave of absence for an extended vacation in Paris, a trip I had promised Esther on my return in 1945. Johnson looked at me in wonderment, shook his head as if I had committed some unpardonable faux pas and said, "You know, Burns, you talk just like a Negro. As soon as he gets some money, he wants to spend it. I never feel that way. I get a lot of fun just out of making money. When I go on vacation, I'm sort of lost and can't wait until I get back at my desk."

"Yes, I understand," I could not resist parrying. "I talk like a Negro and you talk like a Jew!" Disconcerted that in my quick retort I had blurted an anti-Semitic banality, I was ashamed of stooping to a stereotype, yet still exultant to have spoken out for once and turned the tables on the money-minded Johnson.

In spite of my discontent with Johnson's policies, I basked in the heartening accolades *Ebony* received from literary lights and journalists for the magazine's editorial excellence. Less than two years after its debut, *Ebony* was a recognized success, a significant journalistic achievement for which I could take much personal credit. Yet I had to recognize that for me its success represented a pyrrhic victory: creation of the first acclaimed, profitable mass-circulation black magazine, but one that failed to uphold the racial principles I espoused. I consoled myself with the reflection that I had finally been able to demonstrate my mastery of the journalistic craft. I speculated about where one might find an unsullied publishing venture: certainly not the Communist press with its party-line rigidity, not the Negro newspapers with their highly questionable standards, and definitely not the metropolitan dailies where a reporter is no more independent than a factory employee on an assembly line. The *New Yorker*'s A. J. Liebling best summed up the situation: "Freedom of the press is guaranteed to those who own one."

Out of my unsettling self-analysis, I irresolutely retreated to the comforts I could enjoy: the material benefits of a regular paycheck and the increasingly glowing praise for my role in shaping the best of *Ebony*'s features. I was particularly gratified by the commendation I received from Sinclair Lewis for a pictorial condensation of his best seller, *Kingsblood Royal*. Lewis had objected strenuously to the proposed picture reenactment of the book's story when I first proposed the idea to his publisher, Random House. Finally he relented, and I worked with creative photographer Wayne Miller for three days setting up the photographs, using a white male model for the hero of the story about a Minnesota family besieged by their neighbors when their partial Negro ancestry is uncovered in their small-town, all-white community. I enjoyed playing director as if on a Hollywood movie set, then laying out the photos and writing the story and captions, borrowing liberally from Lewis's crackling prose. When the article was published, I awaited Lewis's reaction to my taking liberties with his book. But to my surprise the article met with his approval: "I was excited about it. I thought it was a magnificent job." *Life* magazine agreed and borrowed Miller's pictures to illustrate their story about the book.

Increasingly *Ebony*'s features were being picked up in white publications. *Time* magazine had reprinted some of the photos from Roi Ottley's article on white Negroes. (Among the photographs was the one of my wife Esther, which surprised some of her Los Angeles relatives. Several years later even Johnson admitted he had had his doubts about Esther's true racial background until he met her parents, both of whom were unmistakably eastern European Jews, if only for their accents.) From publisher Bennett Cerf came a flattering tribute in his *Saturday Review of Literature* column: "*Ebony* is edited with taste, intelligence and a shrewd understanding of what its public wants."

By the time of the magazine's fifth anniversary in 1950, *Ebony*'s circulation pattern was well established, easing close to the half-million mark. If there were any doubts remaining about *Ebony*'s racial stance, I once again synthesized and defended Johnson's go-slow approach editorially in our anniversary issue: "There are some who have accused *Ebony* of fence sitting. If being a middle-of-the-roader who refuses to carry either a chip on the shoulder or a hat in hand is fence sitting, we plead guilty. Frankly we are firm believers in carrying both a big stick and soft glove when approaching white folks on the race question." The pallid restatement with its overused metaphors was aimed more at wooing prospective advertisers than at beguiling readers; for all our success in attracting the latter, we were still struggling to win the former.

Unusually for a popular magazine, *Ebony* began publication without any advertising whatsoever and did not solicit any ads until six months after its debut. Then with inexperienced personnel a desultory sales campaign began, seeking accounts with a rigid policy against accepting any advertisements for hair-straightening and skin-whitening products. Determined to steer away from the kind of questionable ads that constituted much of the advertising in Negro weeklies, Johnson gambled that such a stand would attract better accounts from agencies. I detailed our high-minded standards in the May 1946 issue, the first that included advertising: "We will accept advertisements only of products of use, interest and benefit to your comfort and well-being. For this issue we have rejected fifteen accounts, because the products did not measure up to our standards."

This approach elicited expected and welcome praise from advertising trade organs, but resulted in few space orders from accepted advertisers in white magazines. The advertising world's praise for *Ebony*'s principled stand was cheering, but Johnson would much have preferred blue-chip advertisements. The full-color advertisements that appeared in *Ebony* that year were mostly for whiskey, sanitary napkin, and cigarette accounts—Seagram's, Schenley, Chesterfield, and Kotex, among others. In all of 1946 *Ebony*'s gross advertising revenue totaled only $27,000, far less than a single-page ad costs in *Ebony* today.

Despite all my earnest hopes and intentions of keeping our advertising columns "clean," slowly objectionable luck charms and skin bleaches were cleared by Johnson and eased their way into our pages as the discouraged Johnson opted to glean whatever revenue he could. For all their claims that they shunned the Negro press because of its sleazy ads, agency account executives were not about to break precedent with space orders for *Ebony*.

Ebony's newsstand sales, about 90 percent of our total circulation, were primarily in big urban areas where Negroes had better jobs and more money to spend. Although seven out of ten Negroes still lived in the South, most of our readers were in the North. Not only did we find rural blacks unlikely to spend thirty cents (a five-cent increase since *Ebony*'s beginnings) from their limited income to buy a magazine, but it was almost impossible to locate sales outlets in the southern countryside. Yet even without reaching that substantial black population, *Ebony* was still able to achieve the highest readership ever attained by a Negro periodical. Nonetheless, for all our success in realizing that goal, our advertising remained sparse and insignificant.

Finally Johnson, hard pressed to pay printing bills, not only partially lifted his taboo on offensive ads but also decided to enter the skin and hair business himself. Contacting a beauty products firm, he arranged to place his Beauty Star company labels on their jars and bottles and market his skin whiteners and hair straighteners through the pages of *Ebony*. Raveen "for the thrilling beauty of lovelier, more lustrous hair" and Star Glow "for lighter, brighter skin appearance" were his introductory entries in a highly competitive field, but one in which he had the edge of his own advertising medium. Soon our pages began to resemble the rest of the Negro press. Ignorant as I was of the black beauty world and convinced that hair straighteners and skin bleaches represented acceptance of white racial notions, I questioned not only Johnson's surrender of our lofty principles but also the inflated advertising claims for Raveen, such as that it helped hair grow longer. "Well, it really doesn't," Johnson admitted. "But women have to comb it into their hair and it's the combing that does the trick. It must work because even some of the women in the office are using it." Both Raveen and Star Glow flourished, developing into a successful business for Johnson, with Fashion Fair cosmetics becoming a top-of-the-line merchandising bellwether.

Beauty Star products as marketed in *Ebony* proved the pulling power of the magazine as an advertising medium, as did mail-order accounts. Response to mail-order ads was so strong that soon *Ebony* was overwhelmed with these accounts, and in one issue more than fifty ads were omitted for lack of space in our fifty-two pages. Even with the omissions, it appeared from the ads in many an issue of *Ebony* that Negroes consisted of only skin and hair. Even though so many readers patronized our advertisers, there were also happily some who were sensitive enough to protest against *Ebony*'s deterioration. In response, Johnson agreed to call a halt. I drafted a letter to cancel the most obnoxious ads, some twenty in all:

> Our readers are insisting that the calibre of our advertising match the quality of our editorial matter. Their special ire is directed against sex books, skin lighteners, hair straighteners, longer hair and wig advertisements. As a consequence we are establishing a policy of not accepting any more advertisements in those categories unless the layout is attractive, the copy is written with subtlety and the advertisement as a whole is in the best of taste.

Although the clean-up gratified our readers, the big blue-chip ads were still not forthcoming. Our advertising sales representatives received cordial receptions at top advertising agencies, but the cordiality did not extend to placing ads in *Ebony*.

For most account executives of advertising agencies in the 1940s, the Negro market was still an unexplored wilderness, and nobody seemed willing to be the first to explore it. In many agonizing sessions with Johnson and our skimpy, low-pressure advertising staff, we would discuss how to break through the seemingly impenetrable barrier of white account executives who resisted any Negro incursion. All we could devise were the same promotional strategies the white media employed: compiling statistics to demonstrate that *Ebony* exceeded sales of ten leading white magazines combined at some twenty sampled newsstands in black communities and producing a slick brochure to proclaim our circulation superiority. To spotlight further our self-professed leadership in coverage of the Negro market, the brochure, which I drafted, proudly pointed to the reprinting of *Ebony* features by *Life* and *Reader's Digest* and cited quotations from our pages in *Time* and *Newsweek*.

> *Life* knows it. *Look* knows it. Do you know it? In one week, *Life* and *Look*, the nation's leading picture magazines, reprinted stories from the leading Negro publication in America today, *Ebony*, because they know *Ebony* is the door to Negro America. When *Life*, *Look* and other magazines want to catch the pulse of America's 14 Million Negroes, they turn to *Ebony* as the authority in the field. Advertisers who want to catch the 10 billion dollar Negro market also turn to *Ebony*, which is read by more Negroes than any other publication in the world.

The reaction to the brochure was swift—not from agencies but from other magazines, which were affronted by our upstart circulation claims. Long having the entry to agency executives, white magazine representatives derided our brochure with the argument that a *Life* ad covered all races and nationalities. Why spend money on fringe, special advertising? Agency executives echoed this contention: why prepare special copy with black models for *Ebony* when Negroes read all the white magazines? The *Ebony* advertising staff found that agencies now scoffed at and ignored them, while white media representatives confronted them in competing for advertising space.

For decades circulation rather than advertising had been the lifeblood of the Negro press, and *Ebony* was expected to thrive likewise. But it was readily apparent after the first couple of years of publication that because of its higher costs the magazine could not continue to publish without a breakthrough to substantial advertising revenue. A blitz to land blue-chip accounts was critical for our survival. I became convinced that the crusty, conservative executives in command of advertising agencies could never be induced to change their attitude toward the Negro market. Instead, we had to come up with a fresh, unconventional, daring scheme to crack their racially grounded obduracy or else circumvent them entirely.

I mulled over this dilemma for months. Finally, perceiving that most blue-chip advertising originated from the largest corporations and that the only way to bypass advertising agencies was to reach top company executives directly with our specialized market approach, I suggested a scheme that seemed far-fetched but at least had the virtue of novelty. Since top executives could break precedent and change advertising policy, why not send a top Negro executive to sell the Negro market? A *Life* sales representative could not possibly get in to see the president of Procter & Gamble, but Henry Luce could. Why not John Johnson as publisher of *Ebony?*

"You know who's got to start selling advertising? You," I told Johnson. "You're the only one who can get to the top guys who make policy. You don't have to tell them you're selling advertising—anything but that. All you want to talk about is company policy—yours and theirs. Once inside the door, you're halfway there."

But how to gain entry to corporate executive suites? I pondered over what stratagem would enable Johnson to penetrate the inner sanctum of company presidents. With my innate cynicism toward corporate executives, a hangover from my leftist years, I suggested to Johnson a desperate, shoddy ploy that corresponded with Johnson's gospel, if not mine: wave the American flag.

"The way businessmen feel about Negro militants, talk about how America is doing so much for Negroes with full employment and jobs for everyone," I told Johnson. "Tell them what they want to hear, how loyal most Negroes are to the American way of life. Explain to them how *Ebony* shows the brighter side of Negro life. Talk about how Negroes are the greatest barrier against Communism." From the patriotic pitch, it was a short step for Johnson to elicit an expression from business executives of their avowed nondiscriminatory policies. As I projected Johnson's sales routine, he would never solicit advertising space: "Just ask that they make their policy clear to sales executives—that as a corporation they do not discriminate and consider a sale to the Negro as important as a sale to a white man."

Johnson was not enthusiastic about adopting the role of a salesman, yet he acknowledged that my suggestion merited a trial. I drafted a letter to incorporate the executive-to-executive approach and the patriotic "loyalty" theme, and on impressively engraved stationery the letters from Johnson were dispatched with requests for meetings to discuss corporate policy.

The cynical ploy worked almost immediately. At Elgin Watch Johnson was ushered into the sumptuous office of T. Albert Potter, who listened with interest as Johnson related how he had started *Ebony* with just five hundred dollars and how much the magazine was seeking to promote American ideals. Potter then recounted how he himself had started in business as an immigrant youth. Johnson did not have to be subtle in seeking to translate goodwill into advertising; Potter summoned his advertising manager and instructed him to assign some of Elgin Watch's ad budget to "this boy," as he put it.

In response to his letter to Zenith Radio, its hard-driving president, Commander Eugene F. McDonald, declined to see Johnson, suspecting he was soliciting advertising and pointing out that as corporate chief he handled only policy, not ads. Policy was exactly what he wished to discuss with McDonald, responded Johnson. McDonald agreed to see him. With a bit of digging into McDonald's background, we learned that as an Arctic explorer with Admiral Robert E. Perry, he had become friendly with Matthew Henson, the Negro aide who accompanied Perry to the North Pole in 1909. Coincidentally, *Ebony* had published an article on Henson and his newly published autobiography, and with these in hand Johnson made his call on McDonald. In his office McDonald had a pair of Henson's snowshoes hanging on the wall, and for fifteen minutes the discussion was only of Henson and Arctic exploration rather than of corporate policy or *Ebony*. Johnson recalled that McDonald lectured him: "Young man, those snowshoes were given to me by Henson. He is worth any two white men I have ever known and if you're smart enough, you will emulate him." Then, after leafing through the magazine, McDonald summoned his advertising director and asked him why Zenith was not advertising in *Ebony*. Told that "we're considering it"—for more than a year *Ebony* had been "considered," the ad director admitted—McDonald ordered, "We should be in it." Zenith has been "in it" ever since, and Johnson many years later became a member of the board of directors of Zenith. In gratitude for that initial breakthrough, Johnson at one time had only Zenith television sets in his home and in *Ebony*'s offices.

When Quaker Oats agreed to listen to Johnson's presentation, he was faced with an exasperating dilemma: he was asked if *Ebony* would publish ads for Aunt Jemima pancake flour, the name itself and the fat, black mammy depicted on the package representing the most objectionable of brand-name advertising. Rationalizing that beggars cannot be choosers, when the Quaker Oats president asked if *Ebony* would agree to publish Aunt Jemima ads despite years of Negro protests against the name and packaging, Johnson readily assented. "After all, Negroes are buying plenty of Aunt Jemima flour no matter how much they protest," he excused his decision in a conversation with me. Ironically, the first Aunt Jemima ads in *Ebony* opened the door for leading Negro newspapers to drop their objections to the "handkerchief head" mammy and also run Aunt Jemima ads in their pages. (By the 1960s Quaker Oats had recognized the persistent Negro objections to the demeaning "slave image" of the original Aunt Jemima and turned the bandanna headdress into a narrow headband. Since the original "mammy" portrait, there have been six makeovers of Aunt Jemima, gradually altering her into the present acceptable figure wearing pearl earrings and an elegant lace collar. Gone entirely is any trace of the "handkerchief head" portrayal.)

Having initiated the letter-writing scheme to break the ice with blue-chip advertisers, I was intrigued to hear Johnson's accounts of his adventures in what amounted to a white wonderland for him, the executive suites of corporate America. Many of these business leaders had never before confronted a well-groomed, articulate black corporate president. So enthusiastic was Johnson about his reception and successful sales technique that he told *Business Week*, "It's sort of like the Army. There a little general can always talk to a bigger general. As president of the Johnson Publishing Company, I can get to see the president of a big company."

Reactions to Johnson's intrusion into the white corporate top level ranged from guarded apprehension to naive curiosity, from graceless hostility to polished affability. Johnson would return to our offices to relate to me some of the uncertainty and disquietude he encountered in his sessions; many of the executives seemed genuinely frightened about radicalism among Negroes and particularly in the Negro press. Many would pointedly ask him, "What do you think about Paul Robeson?" These were the days after the famous singer in a Paris speech had shocked Americans by asserting that U.S. blacks "won't fight Russia." Johnson would wriggle out of that embarrassing question by assuring potential advertisers that Robeson was wrong, that much as Negroes admired Robeson as a performer, they disagreed with his "pro-Communist views."

With the coveted blue-chip advertisements finally rolling in, by the time of our fifth anniversary Johnson was confident enough to flaunt in print his "positive philosophy" and rejection of the traditional protest role of the Negro press. In what amounted to an open challenge to Negro newspapers with which *Ebony* had maintained an uneasy peace, competing hotly with them for advertising but observing a quiet editorial truce in other respects, Johnson decided to draw a sharp line between *Ebony* and the black press. To mark our fifth year, *Ebony* took out full-page ads in the *New York Times* and *Chicago Tribune*—the first time a Negro publication had run such ads in the major white dailies—to proclaim its independence from the rest of the Negro publishing world. As usual, I wrote the advertising copy, which trumpeted, "At long last the Negro has a national publication of force and stature"—implying that Negro newspapers did not fit that description. In a blatant pitch to the advertising world, I spelled out Johnson's appeal, which by now had become routine in his calls on business executives:

From the beginning, the publishers of *Ebony* were convinced that Negroes needed and wanted more than a 'protest' organ. They sensed the desire for a publication to chronicle in a positive, informative and entertaining way the remarkable story of Negro progress as solid citizens in all income levels. *Ebony* attained its uncontested editorial leadership in its field by graphic reporting of the story of Brown Americans who have helped make the United States the glorious democracy it is. In the Negro community it is considered much as *Life* and *Look* in white neighborhoods.

Believing *Ebony* to be strong enough finally to divorce itself from Negro weeklies and the "radical" tag stamped on them by big advertising agencies, the ad crowed about "new postwar Negroes with more jobs, more money and more to spend than any Negro generation in American history," an undisguised pitch for advertising. By 1952 advertising revenue for *Ebony* topped $1 million annually, the highest ever attained by a black publication.

As the model of a black business executive, Johnson always tried to say what he anticipated that business leaders wanted to hear, and he proved himself an excellent advertising salesman. On occasion he sold himself so well, so completely impressing white executives with his patriotic credo, that they would sometimes summon him when confronted with a racial problem. He willingly played the "expert's" role. "Just make believe you know everything and they'll believe you know everything," he once told me. As he moved around more and more in business circles, acceptance came not only for *Ebony* but also for Johnson as the "leading Negro authority" on racial relations. Soon he was writing ghosted articles for advertising trade papers and addressing regional and national conferences. From there he became a civic leader, too, being called upon to serve in important groups that had nothing to do with race—such as the Chicago Council on Foreign Relations—but where he could rub elbows with corporate executives who were potential advertisers.

Always an immaculate dresser, Johnson became even more so to impress white business executives, telling me in confidence how much he had to spend on clothing, such as his custom-made white initialed shirts bought by the dozen. His buying habits were sometimes the subject of his speeches to advertising conventions to illustrate the potential of the Negro market. His favorite yarn recounted how he bought his first three-hundred-dollar suit when a salesman at Marshall Field's doubted the ability of a Negro to buy a high-priced suit. When shown a forty-dollar suit, Johnson asked for something better. Asked how high he wanted to go, Johnson felt he had to play the racial drama to its ultimate and grandiosely said he wanted "the best in the house," whereupon the salesman brought forth a three-hundred-dollar suit. Racial pride being at stake, Johnson had to buy the suit to prove his point, and the moral for advertisers was that they should not talk down to Negro customers.

One of Johnson's earliest and most significant triumphs in business recognition also proved one of his most disconcerting. The U.S. Junior Chamber of Commerce selected him in 1951 as one of the ten most outstanding young men of the year. He was only the second Negro ever selected for the award, the other being Joe Louis. But the banquet for the honorees was to be held in Dayton, Ohio, then a notorious Jim Crow town, at the Dayton-Biltmore Hotel, which had never admitted a Negro. Well aware of the ban, Johnson was initially reluctant to attend even though the Junior Chamber assured him that special arrangements had been made to allow him and his wife to become the first blacks to stay at the hotel. Our irrepressible white public relations manager at the time, Al Weisman, had been instrumental in having Johnson nominated for the award. Staggered to see his carefully laid plans thwarted, he finally with much salesmanship convinced Johnson to go to Dayton accompanied by himself. But annoyed and uncomfortable despite their warm reception, the moment the banquet was over Johnson rushed to catch the last train for Chicago, refusing to stay at the hotel overnight.

Weisman had come to *Ebony* from the United Fund; I had persuaded Johnson to hire him as part of the campaign to attract major advertisers. He had never worked closely with Negroes before, and he became embroiled in racial difficulties when he flunked his introductory course in race relations in our offices. His first dereliction occurred when, in a typical glad-handing publicist's approach, he called everyone by their first names in an initial meeting. He innocently followed this practice with Negroes as he had with whites, not realizing that it was considered disparaging (in the South for generations blacks were always called by their first name by whites, as a way to avoid using "mister"). When he made the mistake of calling the publisher "Johnny," he was summoned to Johnson's office, caustically told that he was too familiar, and bluntly ordered, "Call me Mister from now on."

The most virulently anti-white Negro in our office—at least so he assessed himself, although we quickly became friends—was Milton Smith, who always spoke of whites as "the enemy." He sensed in Weisman an easy, tempting target and went after him with relish the moment he came to work at *Ebony*. Al had made his usual daily entrance with hail-fellow-well-met greetings to all when Milton cracked, "Hmm, do I smell a white man in the office?" Al had his own office, and Milton would tell visiting friends, "This is where we Jim Crow our white employee." On days when fried chicken was on our lunchroom menu, he would rib Al, "No lunch for you today. We got colored folk's food—fried chicken." Finally Al in desperation came to me and begged, "Tell that clown to quit it, will you? Enough is enough. I can take just so much. One of these days I'm going to swing on him." It was Johnson who finally called a halt to the intense racial cross-fire when in one of his economy binges he dismissed Weisman, who then became public relations director for one of the nation's biggest national advertising agencies, Foote, Cone & Belding.

Beneath the staid, serene exterior he displayed for prospective advertisers, Johnson burned inwardly with resentment of how he had to demean himself for business ends. His ability to play a role, to cover up the racial rage ingrained from his Arkansas childhood and his early years of struggle to overcome Chicago racism, grew out of his consummate determination to escape the past, to make his magazine business a success. This negative side of Johnson—his frustration and bitterness, his abiding wrath and hatred for what America had inflicted on blacks from its beginnings up to his generation—was deeply buried and became evident only under extreme stress. Only to the closest of black friends and unguardedly to me on occasion did his true rage emerge. I can recall him returning disconsolately from a meeting with a shampoo company executive who had openly stated his biased doubts about the cleanliness of Negroes, questioning any possible sales prospects for shampoo among blacks. Many blacks would have felt insulted and taken offense at such disparagement, but Johnson to sell the account swallowed his pride and laughingly informed the white businessman, "I take a shower every day and wash my hair with shampoo."

Although he seldom betrayed his real inner feelings, except in instances where some unknowing bigot such as the shampoo man had rubbed a raw nerve, I can never forget my one glimpse of the depths of his rancor when after a particularly frustrating experience he exploded: "Sometimes I wish they'd drop an H-bomb on this country and wipe out every white man! Sure, they'd kill all us Negroes but it would be worth it!"

9

That White Man at *Ebony*

If America in actual practice could show the world [that] the Negro became fully integrated into modern democracy, all mankind would be given faith again.

Gunnar Myrdal

The hazards of a black backlash against a white editor were evident from the beginnings of *Ebony*, especially since persistent rumors of covert white ownership of the magazine circulated widely in the Negro community. One version was that *Life* publisher Henry Luce was secretly financing the magazine, while another credited the Hearst publications with being the actual owner of *Ebony*.

"It's too good to be Negro" was the usual line of tavern talk. "There must be whites behind it." The rumors gained credence when *Ebony* published photos I had obtained from *Life* magazine on Tennessee race rioting and pictures of Rep. Adam Clayton Powell and singer Hazel Scott at a Washington party. So many people at the party had been told the pictures had been taken for *Life* that upon seeing them turn up in *Ebony*, they were convinced that this confirmed the rumors of *Life*'s ownership of *Ebony*. Another seeming clue was the repeated publicity puffs for *Ebony* that appeared in *Time* magazine, which always referred to *Ebony* as "a frank imitation of *Life*" or "a *Life*-sized Negro magazine." Sometimes *Ebony* pictures were reprinted in *Life*, which made the relationship even more suspect. In actuality Luce was friendly to *Ebony* from its inception and frequently expressed to publisher John Johnson his unreserved admiration for the magazine's quality. The two men occasionally met at dinners of the National Urban League in which Luce was quite active. But that was as far as Luce's interest in *Ebony* extended.

Our sole competitor, *Our World*, which had begun publishing several months after *Ebony*, sought to capitalize on the rumors and stir anti-white feeling based on my role as editor. In a malicious interview with a Negro weekly, the

Los Angeles Tribune, its publisher John P. Davis, like me a one-time leftist, scornfully badmouthed us: "*Ebony* reads like a white man's idea of what Negroes want in a publication." He then derisively noted that *Ebony* "has a white man high on its staff, one Ben Burns." It was the kind of reverse racism that could have but one intent: to arouse black readers of *Ebony* against its white editor. This was the kind of bias Davis ostensibly had so long battled while heading the National Negro Congress, a left-oriented organization of the 1930s. I was outraged to be the target of such an attack by a one-time black radical despite my past years of commitment to the left and the black cause. Ironically, the quotation from Davis appeared not many months after an emissary of *Our World* had contacted me to offer me the editorship of the New York–based magazine—an offer that was hastily withdrawn when I asked for higher pay than I was receiving at *Ebony*.

The rumors gained enough credence that Johnson finally agreed to my proposal to confront the falsehoods head on. With his photograph printed especially dark to lead off our "Backstage" column, I wrote a blunt denial:

> Every so often some person who refuses to believe that Negroes are capable of publishing a first-rate magazine will drop us a 'love letter' to charge that *Ebony* is really white owned. This month's statement of ownership required by the U.S. Post Office printed in the next column might be a good occasion to note just who does own *Ebony* and even let readers see what he looks like. He is Arkansas-born Johnson, who together with his wife and mother hold 100 percent of the stock of *Ebony* and *Negro Digest* magazines. He is the brains and money behind this enterprise with no strings attached.
>
> Johnson is a Negro, as anyone with eyes can see. But we here at *Ebony* like to think that the color of the publisher is important only insofar as it emphasizes his interest in the good and welfare of the Negro people. Because of that concern for the Negro, because we believe in practicing as well as preaching about fair employment practices, *Ebony*'s staff is interracial though necessarily predominantly Negro. The staff is hired on ability not color.

The forthright last words of the statement sought to cover my status as editor as well as that of the few other whites then on the staff, but the presence of even a few whites among the black staff members was enough to keep the rumors surfacing periodically. They continued to circulate until the day I left *Ebony*. It remained for the white publisher of several Negro magazines in Texas, including *Sepia*, to embellish what had by then become more than a "little white lie." Still a publishing novice, George Levitan, looking like a Hollywood version of an oil millionaire, visited our Chicago offices and was shown through the building by Johnson. Introduced to me perfunctorily and told by Johnson that I was white, Levitan volunteered that as a Jew he was concerned with minority problems. Johnson then casually noted that I, too, was Jewish.

"I knew it, I knew it!" Levitan exclaimed. "I knew there must be a Jew somewhere behind this setup!"

For all my relative affluence once *Ebony*'s success was assured, the continuing housing shortage in the years after the war still thwarted all my attempts to break out of our cramped four-room West Side apartment. Our family of five was elbowing and tripping over each other in our restricted quarters. However, housing of any kind was not to be had in those years as returning servicemen had priority and besieged any landlord with a flat to let. Complicating our search was my transformed "racial identity," since applying for an apartment required that I list my place of employment: a Negro magazine. I had to decide first whether and then how to conceal my racial "taint," as seen by the real-estate world, if I was to find a large enough home for my family. Yet I was reluctant to hide my *Ebony* editorship, as if it were something to be ashamed of.

Esther and I at first toyed with the notion of buying a house, even though we had only modest savings. My income in the late 1940s seemed enough to afford a moderate mortgage, and we decided to take the plunge. Our tentative first venture into house hunting, however, terminated soon after it started. We were discouraged by tiresome plodding through houses we either did not like or could not afford, and we feared possible racial problems because of my *Ebony* job. A new development then cut short our search. In the spring of 1950 photographer Steve Deutch, who had purchased a home in the suburb of Wilmette, was vacating his spacious six-room apartment on the North Side. I immediately went to his landlord, a gracious, convivial Greek who studied philosophy as a hobby. I was certain I would pass muster with Mr. Pappas, but here as elsewhere "the problem" quickly arose. In recommending me as a possible tenant when he moved out, Deutch had disclosed my "secret," so that Mr. Pappas knew just what I did for a living. When I returned several days after our initial meeting to learn what he had decided, he cagily inquired: "Do I understand correctly that you work for a Negro magazine?"

"That's right," I admitted.

"Now understand me, I'm not in the least prejudiced. I'm Greek and I know what prejudice means. But we have to face these things in this country."

"Uh-huh," I nodded, fearing the worst.

"I'd like to give you the apartment, but I can't ignore my wife and daughter in making a decision. I have to consult them and so we talked about it. My wife asked whether you will have many Negro friends visiting you. Let me make clear that I don't object, but I've got to consider my wife's wishes, too."

Nonplussed, I didn't know what to say. An outright fib would not do since we would have to live just one flight above the Pappases, who occupied the ground floor. They would see our visitors. I had to level with him. "I don't want to lie to you even though I admit that I'm very anxious to get the apartment," I told him. "I've got Negro friends and they visit us quite often. But my wife and I are not social butterflies; we don't entertain that often."

"Yes, yes," he encouraged me.

"We may have some friends over every couple of weeks or so and when we do, they're all colors, not just Negro. I can assure you there won't be a Negro invasion. We don't pick our friends because they're Negro. They're all mixed, and if and when we do have a party, we have Negroes as well as whites, and they're all well behaved. I don't want to give you a wrong impression and I hope you'll understand."

"Well, let me talk to my wife and think it over. I'll let you know."

For days I was on tenterhooks, awaiting his decision, and I was not comforted when I related to Johnson the gist of my meetings with the landlord. He chuckled and said, "Goodbye apartment." And I agreed with his assessment. But both of us were proved wrong when Pappas agreed to a lease. The Pappases never said a word about the Negro friends who visited with us. After a half-dozen years of vainly searching for an apartment, it was gratifying to discover at least one landlord who was willing to give more than lip service to racial tolerance.

As a white editor of a black publication, I was inevitably caught in a no man's land between the races. Black readers generally rated me either as a devout interracial activist or as an unwelcome meddler. I was seen either as a well-meaning but less than knowledgeable champion of the black cause (since many blacks felt that no white liberal could ever truly know or feel the evils of racism) or else as a perfidious newsmonger depriving a black editor of a job. Most white readers considered me a radical flake, an ardent ideologue dedicated to racial equality, or a frustrated journalist unable to succeed in mainstream journalism. In my years of working for half a dozen black publications, I do not believe that I ever fit precisely into any of these formula characterizations, but I was invariably labeled with one or another of them, depending on who was judging me.

My own feelings about my role in the forefront of Negro journalism after my short roller-coaster career on radical dailies were somewhat like those of a refugee finding comfort in a new homeland. So I was able to shrug off most of the negative critique originating particularly with black militants, who usually attributed to its white editor both *Ebony*'s moderation and any gaffes in the magazine.

Many of *Ebony*'s readers fell back on convenient scapegoating to explain away *Ebony*'s controversial features or editorials not to their fancy. "Oh, it's that white man" would be the street talk. "Johnson's okay, that white man's putting all that stuff in there." One such instance involved me in a tangle with a dynamic South Side preacher, Rev. Clarence Cobbs. He was worthy of an *Ebony* story for his exploits both in and out of church, but when a staff writer and photographer were assigned to the story, the suspicious minister balked, wary of what might be reported about the rumored gambling propensities of his well-heeled flock. When on assignment at the racetrack to shoot a story on a Negro jockey, an *Ebony* photographer spotted Cobbs at a betting booth and attempted to photograph him. But one of Cobbs's aides blocked his camera lens. Thereupon Cobbs became convinced that *Ebony* was "out to get" him and informed some of his parishioners, "That white man, Burns, is behind it."

Cobbs and his large church were too powerful and important to antagonize, so I sought to make peace with him by suggesting that Johnson invite him to lunch at our offices. I sat uneasily with him in our lunchroom anticipating the worst. Cobbs readily conceded that he had ascribed to me personally what he angrily denounced as *Ebony*'s underhanded attempt to embarrass him and his church. I sought to assure him that the imagined *Ebony* "plot" was not my doing, since I knew little of South Side church matters and even less about Cobbs personally. I had had nothing to do with our photographer trying to grab his photo at the racetrack, I told him; I had been out of town at the time. But Cobbs remained angry and fearful of what *Ebony* might print about him, convinced that as its white editor I must be guilty of targeting him.

Unlike Reverend Cobbs, some others acknowledged and praised my role in shaping *Ebony*, ascribing to me the noblest motives and crediting its success to my editorial guidance. Most flattering was the praise I received from singer Lena Horne one evening when I was chauffeuring her back to the Blackstone Hotel to perform at the Mayfair Room after a dinner at Johnson's home on Drexel Boulevard. Originally I had invited Lena to my house for dinner, presuming that she would welcome a home-cooked meal instead of the usual bland hotel fare. In my several interviews with her in her nightclub dressing room for an *Ebony* article, we had established a cordial rapport. I was a

staunch admirer not only of Lena the beautiful performer but also of Lena
the glowing inner person with her worldly awareness and everyday common
sense, her racial consciousness and stout-hearted militancy. I discerned that
she enjoyed and wanted to continue our discussions, and I thought one of
Esther's savory dinners at our home would provide the right setting for relaxed
conversation. But Johnson insisted on arranging something more formal at his
house, and I had no choice but to accede. The dinner menu and society were
excellent, but the conviviality was less free and easy than I would have hoped
for at my home.

On the way to her hotel, we talked about her problems getting a break in
Hollywood. Suddenly she turned the tables on me to ask about my professional
background: "How come you went to work for a Negro magazine, Ben? Why
are you working with Negroes when you probably could be making more
money with a white magazine?"

Taken aback, I hesitated, not quite sure whether to level with her about
my disenchangment with *Ebony*'s editorial policies. Finally I simply said, "I
don't know about white magazines. I had very little real experience when I
started with Johnson. I had never worked on a magazine before."

"But now you've got the experience. I'm sure you could get another job
making more money."

"Yes, but I like my job. Why should I change?"

"That's what I'm getting at. Is it that you're working with Negroes because
you have a feeling that you're doing something worthwhile? Don't you get a
special feeling of pride in what you're doing?"

There was no further evading the issue. I had to reply, "Of course I do. My
job's more interesting than most, and more gratifying in many ways." But I
could not comfortably play the righteous pure in heart with Lena; having deep
respect for her, I had to disclose how negatively I felt at this point about my
Ebony career and about the new black world in which I moved. I continued,
"But—and there are a lot of buts—I've gotten over the idea that I'm something
special, that I'm some kind of hero in the front lines fighting for racial equality.
I once had that cause feeling but half a dozen years of working with hard-
headed, hard-fisted Negroes in this publishing business have convinced me
I'm on the wrong track."

"What do you mean?" she asked.

Emboldened by her interest, I was now wound up and unstoppable. Believing Lena a sympathetic audience for my confessional, I could not resist
expressing disdain for some of the seamy side of black life that I had ex-
perienced. "I've seen too many selfish, money-grabbing black guys around

who are all too willing to cash in on race prejudice. I've come across too many hustlers and con men whose only concern with the fight against race discrimination is how much they could make out of it. I'm sure you know what I mean. Sure, I get a big bang out of what I'm doing. But I have no illusions about too many black politicians and phony promoters. And so I feel more and more that what I'm doing is mainly just a job, even if it's the most exciting job I've ever had. But I'm afraid I've grown up and don't swallow that cause stuff anymore."

"Yeah, you have a point there," Lena nodded in approval.

"In many ways I'm in the same shoes you're in," I claimed. "Maybe I shouldn't say this, and maybe I'm stupid to bring it up. If I asked what was your work, you'd say singing. Everyone thinks you're absolutely wonderful and so do I. You really know how to sell a song, but there's something else you're selling, too. I hate to mention the word but since I'm in this deep, I might as well go all the way. It's sex. All those glassy-eyed guys sitting there at ringside tables and drooling in their Scotch don't pay the tab just to hear you sing. They flip for what they're seeing. It's sex—and you're packaging it just like I'm packaging my ability to put together a saleable magazine."

I regretted my indiscreet words almost as soon as I uttered them, but I had been carried away by my desire and need to find a kindred soul in my predicament at *Ebony*. Instead of showing empathy, Lena looked at me in flinty annoyance. I knew I had gone too far and hurriedly tried to retreat: "If I said something to offend you, I hereby apologize. I guess I just talk too much."

"You certainly do," snapped Lena. Clearly, I had touched a sore spot with her, and she was extremely piqued, refusing to say a word the rest of our ride back to the hotel and stepping out of my car without even responding to my "Good night." Driving home I chided myself for my misplaced candor and assumed I had made yet another enemy in the black community. Of all people, Lena Horne, whom I admired and respected, was certainly the last one I wished to affront! But if I believed that my faux pas had made me another enemy like Reverend Cobbs, the gracious Lena proved me mistaken. She forgot this contretemps and was her usual convivial self the next time we met, as friendly as in our first encounter.

If my knotty problem of winning acceptance by the black community was not complex enough, my troubles were complicated when the question frequently arose of whether I was Negro or white. Visitors to *Ebony* who assumed its editor was Negro were not the only ones who were confused about my identity; on occasion, so too were new office personnel. The range of skin shadings among *Ebony*'s personnel extended from very dark to white, so that although I was in the light-skinned minority, I was still somewhere on the darker side of light, particularly in the summer months when I spent weekends on the beach. I was darker than half a dozen others, all of whom were Negro.

My dark complexion as against the pale skin of two Negro women who worked in our library could be particularly confusing to first-time visitors, Negro as well as white. Both women could not possibly be identified by outsiders as anything but white, so fair were their skins. After *Ebony* became recognized as the leading black periodical in the nation, the State Department would often dispatch foreign journalists and academics to our offices, presenting *Ebony* as an example of smooth-functioning democracy. These overseas visitors would invariably ask, "Do you have an interracial staff?" Told that *Ebony*'s staff was indeed racially mixed, the visitors, whether white or black, would usually pick "the two girls in the library" as whites. Informed that they were mistaken, they would ask, "Then who is white on your staff?" When they learned that I was white, the foreigners were left wondering at the perverseness of America's race problem, which could identify a dark-hued person as white and a fair-skinned one as black. Even white executives whom I consulted with constantly were confused about my racial identity. The general sales manager of the big printing firm that handled *Ebony*'s production, Carl Braun, summoned enough courage after I had been working with him for some years to ask at a small office party, "Say, Burns, what are you anyway, Negro or white?"

I accepted his query in the jocular spirit in which it was asked and responded lightly, "Neither—I'm Jewish."

On one occasion a friend of mine who worked at a downtown advertising agency recounted a conversation he had had with a colleague about *Ebony*. The executive informed my acquaintance that he had been at lunch with Johnson and me to familiarize himself with the Negro market. "Oh, then you've met Burns. He's a good friend of mine," my friend said.

"Sure, he's that light-skinned Negro down there. He's one of their top editors."

"No, you must have him mixed up with someone else. He's white."

"Not the Burns I met," insisted the executive. "I'm certain he's colored."

When the story was repeated to me, I found myself unable to remember the executive as described by my friend, and to cover my faulty memory I retreated into the favored black take-off on an old white stereotype: "Well, I've been working with Negroes so long that all whites look alike to me."

Another time, musician Glover Hampton on a visit to my office related his racial troubles. When I offered him my sympathies, he assured me: "Oh, you don't have any problems with this thing. You can pass for white easily!"

The ultimate symbolic token of my racial metamorphosis was a bit of doggerel written by a discerning *Ebony* writer, Kenneth Campbell, for an office Valentine's Day party. At the time the Mau Mau revolt in Kenya was at its height, and in their hearts most American blacks secretly admired the guerrilla tactics of native Africans in resisting English colonial rule. In *Ebony*'s offices there was a mock Mau Mau chapter, which posted fanciful reports on our bulletin board about imagined Chicago Mau Mau doings or plans. With all this talk circulating, Carter penned the following rhyme:

> Germany had Einstein,
> England had Shaw,
> And *Ebony* has
> The world's only white Mau Mau.

My racial identity was anomalous enough to confuse a southern U.S. senator, who described me on a national network radio program as "an able Negro writer." After *Ebony*'s Thanksgiving editorial, "Time to Count Your Blessings," which had so incensed my former "comrades," was reprinted in *Reader's Digest*, Senator John Sparkman of Alabama in a "Town Meeting of the Air" broadcast quoted substantially from its text to bolster his opposition to President Truman's proposed civil rights program. It was disconcerting to hear him repeat *Ebony*'s contention that with all the many evils blacks suffered in America, they were still better off than most of the world's population. Even worse was his reference to me as the author of the editorial, which I viewed about as favorably as if some Klansman had asked me to wear his hood. Sparkman maintained that admission of black "contentment" by a black writer in a black publication was an argument against Truman's rights plan.

Although I never sought to correct Sparkman's erroneous racial categorization of me, hearing a traditional Dixiecrat cite *Ebony* to oppose civil rights prompted me to write an irate editorial rejoinder titled "When Bouquets Are Brickbats." I pointed out that Sparkman had cited one positive sentence in my editorial to affirm that Negroes were so well off that there was no need for civil rights legislation. In my anger I referred to Sparkman in my editorial as "a Claghorn congressman popping off with Bilboisms." Normally the skittish Johnson would have red-penciled such harsh terms, but hearing *Ebony* used against civil rights was mortifying enough for him to indulge my gruff words.

When Sparkman later was slated as a candidate for vice president on the Democratic ticket with Adlai Stevenson in 1952, *Ebony* and the vast majority of black voters had no choice but to support him if they wished to back Stevenson. I once again found myself flip-flopping as I wrote *Ebony*'s endorsement of Stevenson. (This was a rare political endorsement by *Ebony* when Johnson was still a Democrat, and one he regretted when Stevenson lost the election. Johnson then informed me, "I'll never again make an election endorsement.") In my editorial I appealed to black voters to forgive Sparkman his past trespasses and expressed the hope that he would change his thinking in the future.

Eleanor Roosevelt believed that Sparkman was a covert liberal, a view she expressed on a luncheon visit to *Ebony* during the Stevenson campaign. When asked about Sparkman and the fears of black voters based on his segregationist record, the former First Lady assured us that the Alabama senator was far more intelligent on the race problem than he seemed in public. She then revealed a private chapter in Sparkman's days as a United Nations delegate, which she pledged us to keep secret lest Sparkman lose the southern white vote. During his tenure there he had become friends with another delegate, Edith Sampson, an ebullient black lawyer from Chicago, and Mrs. Roosevelt was surprised to see the two of them dancing together at a social affair she had arranged for U.N. delegates at her Manhattan apartment. When she unobtrusively cornered Sparkman and congratulated him for dancing with Sampson, he told her, "I find her most stimulating company. But I know I don't have to tell you to keep our secret. If the voters of Alabama ever learned that their senator was dancing with a Negro woman in New York, I would be the ex-senator from Alabama."

Frequently during my years at *Ebony* instances of racial folly caused more amusement than anger. One occasion involving Eleanor Roosevelt in a preposterous episode demonstrated that racial foolishness can be perpetrated by Negroes no less than whites. When the former first lady agreed to lunch at our offices on a stopover during her world travels, Johnson was in a tizzy over the choice of a menu. Enterprising editor Milton Smith, who had arranged for her visit, had been informed that Mrs. Roosevelt's food preference was fried chicken. But Johnson immediately balked. "Fried chicken! No way!" he exclaimed, and everyone knew what he was thinking.

Ever since our guest dining room had been set up at *Ebony*, fried chicken had been a ticklish problem: to serve it to white guests would confirm all the white legends about Negro eating habits. Although fried chicken was on the menu once a week for staff, when white guests were scheduled the regular staff dining room was closed off so visitors would not observe what staff members were eating. During the watermelon season the same rule was in force, for the same reason. Instead, white guests were usually served filet mignon or else some exotic dish like East Indian chicken with a dessert of rose-petal pudding, a tasty specialty of our capable food editor, Freda DeKnight.

On this occasion, when Johnson vetoed fried chicken, Milton Smith still insisted, "But I was told she's really partial to good fried chicken and Freda makes the best. Why not serve her what she likes?"

"No, we just can't do that," Johnson said.

"Aw, Mrs. Roosevelt's okay. You don't have to worry about her getting ideas."

"Sure, she's okay. But we just can't serve fried chicken."

And so Eleanor Roosevelt had to eat steak at our lunch, in spite of her preference for chicken.

The photograph of a Negro kissing a white British woman lay on my cluttered desk. It was the kind of graphic shot never seen in any conventional magazine or newspaper in the America of the late 1940s, what the staff of *Ebony* called a "hot" photo. Seated around my office were Johnson and assistant editors Era Bell Thompson and Herbert Nipson, both of them on the unofficial editorial board of *Ebony*. The delicate question before us: should we publish the picture?

"It's just the kind of thing white folks always think Negro men dream about—to have a white woman. I know it'll get us circulation but I don't like it," Era Bell said sullenly. As the only female executive at *Ebony*, her opinion regarding any story on mixed marriage carried much weight. She was a formidable antagonist in any wrangling over articles concerning sex or interracial romance, and we crossed swords frequently.

Nipson, cautious to the extreme, usually opted for prudence in any controversy, and on the British photo he chimed in as usual: "Most Negroes won't like it. They get angry when they see pictures of Negro men chasing after white women, as if there's something wrong with black women. I'm against using it."

With my now devout belief in total integration in every facet of everyday living, I was the recurrent spoiler in our repeated policy discord over racial-mixing themes. I now spoke up in favor of the disputed picture: "I can't see anything wrong with it. Sure, there may be some people who won't like it. And maybe some southern distributors won't want to handle the magazine. But for every sale you lose there will be two people who will buy the magazine because of street talk about it."

"But what about our advertisers?" spoke up Johnson. "We have been getting all kinds of complaints from agencies and advertisers about our mixed-marriage stories. This thing could be the last straw for some of them. We got a letter the other day from one of them telling us to send the magazine to his office instead of his home because he didn't want his wife and kids to see all that mixed-marriage stuff."

I sought to counter by protesting that we could not "edit *Ebony* to please advertisers." I added, "Maybe some white folks will squawk but perhaps we could once forget what white people think."

Knowing full well that advertising was a key consideration, I realized I had lost the argument when Johnson declared: "I kind of like to worry about what white folks will think. And I can't take your word for what white people will think. You're not a real white man!"

There it was again: I wasn't a real white man! The others joined in laughing at Johnson's pointed jibe and returned to their offices while I mulled over once again that repeated phrase. Johnson was using it more and more frequently whenever we disagreed. While I could take it as a compliment that I was accused of forgetting my white skin, I still recognized that it was a cover-up for Johnson's own waffling on racial issues. Whenever he wanted the opinion of "a real white man" on some doubtful editorial decision, he would refuse to rely on my judgment and instead turn to his white lawyer or a white friend in the advertising business. I had been an editor of black publications so long, he contended, that I could no longer think as a white man. Perhaps he was right, I reflected, counting all the years that I had been editing black publications and wondering whether I had so absorbed black perceptions, speech, and culture that I had ceased to think and react as a white man, not only on racial basics but even in everyday matters. I recalled joshing from my white friends about my constant use of such jive terms as "chick" and "cat," how I would flare up angrily when I read a news story that contained some racial affront to a Negro. I acknowledged that I shared more interests with Negro friends than with white friends, found more to talk about with black friends, and was more free and easy in our conversation about race. Most readers of *Ebony* assumed I was black, and never was there the slightest doubt about the "racial line" of anything I wrote. Because I associated more with blacks than whites, I was being constantly taken for Negro and did not bother in most instances to refute such beliefs.

My personal racial status was as much a maze of inane contradictions as the American racial scene as a whole, where definitions of who is a Negro have varied widely from state to state in the South and where even federal census definitions have changed repeatedly. I could choose to pass for Negro, as some white musicians did, such as Mezz Mezzrow (who detailed his experiences in his entertaining autobiography, *Really the Blues*) and singer Johnny Otis, or as John Howard Griffin did, who told his story in a *Sepia* magazine series and then in a best selling book, *Black Like Me*. It was far easier for a white to pass for black than for a Negro to pass for white. All I had to do was to say publicly that I was a Negro. Most Americans, black or white, would agree that anyone zany enough to accept all the handicaps of being a Negro must certainly be one. But I resented the entire notion of passing; in a sense it was an admission of guilt, an acknowledgment of deficiency if not inferiority in the abandoned race. That was no less true for a Negro passing as white than for a white passing as Negro.

The racial truth in America is, as James Baldwin wrote, that "color is not a human or personal reality; it is a political reality." For me as a white editor of black media, that tenet had much meaning, when my publisher focused *Ebony* to white standards and then told me I was "not a real white man." What then truly was I? I found myself in a quandary when I sought to define my standing in an America that insisted on wrapping people in neat packages and putting a racial label on them.

My situation was as confusing as that of white-skinned but Negro NAACP secretary Walter White and his tanned but white wife, Poppy Cannon, who were once asked by journalists in Turkey whether it was true that they were an interracial couple. When they replied that indeed was the case, one reporter turned to the Negro leader and bluntly asked: "Mr. White, what caused you to marry a colored woman?" White explained that it was he and not his wife who was Negro and then tried to untangle the twists and turns of America's race problem that foreigners find so puzzling.

My own case made me wonder whether even Americans could comprehend the queer contradictions of my situation at *Ebony*, where my views were dismissed because I was "not a real white man," while the black publisher geared his editorial judgments to the norms of white advertisers.

The most unusual example of my being assumed to be Negro occurred at the most improbable of settings—a nudist camp. I had heard that an Indiana camp had several Negro members and had arranged with the nudist movement's Midwest leader, an elderly lawyer named Alois Knapp, to shoot a picture story on the blacks attending a weekend regional convention at Roselawn. After getting my credentials at the campground entrance, I was introduced to the world of nudism as I strolled through some woods and headed for the assembled delegates in the buff. Our host soon spotted me and my photographer, David Jackson, very obvious standouts since we were both fully clothed. In the midst of his discussion of membership regulations, he quickly departed from his subject and turned to the minority status of nudists.

"In our movement we well know what it is to be in the minority. We have been pushed around because of our beliefs and have had to fight the law as well as public opinion. Sometimes as a minority, we feel very much alone. But we are not the only minority in America. There are others, as I found out several weeks ago when I got an invitation to speak at a Negro church on the South Side. I was glad to go because I know the way the Negro minority in this country is treated. When I arrived the minister gave me a warm welcome and then introduced me to his congregation in a way which I thought was a real tribute. He told his people: 'I want you to meet Alois Knapp, who even if he has a white skin has a black heart.'

"In meeting these colored people, I got to appreciate more what it means to be a minority. And so I'm glad that we in the nudist movement don't practice racial discrimination in our ranks. We minorities have got to stick together. I am pleased that we have here today at Zoro Nature Park an important representative of *Ebony* magazine, which I understand is the biggest Negro publication in the world. It does my heart good to introduce Ben Burns to you. I want you to meet a man who may have a black skin but he surely has a white heart."

Flabbergasted as the nudists broke out into applause, I nodded in acknowledgment but refused to make any remarks after Knapp's expression of solidarity with Negroes (of whom I was not one) by nudists (of whom I was certainly not one). I pleaded that I was at the camp as a journalist to watch the proceedings, not as a speaker to address the group. Hurriedly Jackson and I searched for the promised black nudists, who turned out to be a couple of tots brought to the camp by white friends of the children's parents.

Each time I was mistaken for Negro became for me a thrill of personal fulfillment of a mission, an indication that I was being successfully melded into the black world. I never felt that I was a paragon of virtue or that I deserved any special recognition or plaudits for my assumed role. I found myself agreeing with New York mayor Fiorello LaGuardia, who once said, "I don't think a man should get a medal just because he recognizes the legal rights of another man. If I were to denounce segregation, it would be like saying, 'I don't beat my wife.'" Noted white South African author Breyten Breytenbach stated the point another way: "People expect if you are of white background and you're fairly intelligent—and became involved in the struggle of black people—you must be some kind of saint."

Having committed myself wholly to Negroes' attainment of fair and equal status, I measured my effectiveness in reaching for that end not only by the efforts I devoted to editing black publications but also by the extent of my integration into black life. I endeavored to become in every sense a "brother" by virtue of my oneness with Negroes in values and customs, interests and concerns, reactions and resolutions. Since my skin color did not qualify me for that role, I hoped that I could pass muster based on my racial orientation, my familiarity with the black heritage, my communion with racial aspirations, my unstinted sharing in the sadness as well as joys of everyday black life.

Yet I had to acknowledge the verity that I could never truly pass as black, that my objective was betrayed not only in my physical appearance but also in my personal lifestyle. Realistically, I recognized that my pose could be no more than a charade to fill the editorial role I had assumed by sheer coincidence at its inception, but which had magnified enormously. In truth, as a white editor of black magazines, my racial standing was much like West Indian author Caryl Phillips's description of his experiences living in white working-class London: feeling like "a transplanted tree that had failed to take root in foreign soil."

10

Staff Troubles and Anti-Semitism

*Just being a Negro doesn't qualify you to understand the race situation
any more than being sick makes you an expert on medicine.*
                                 Dick Gregory

In the first years after *Ebony* began, while I was still bubbling over
with idealism, still obsessed with the black "cause" and committed
to working with a crusader's zeal to make the magazine successful,
I tried in vain to inspire similar fervor in our mixed bag of writers and
subeditors. I sensed a baffling lack of genuine attachment or loyalty to
the magazine reflected in the apathy among many of our editorial crew.
Lacking personal devotion to the magazine either as a good job or as a
worthy institution, many settled for sophomoric writing and showed little
initiative in originating photo story ideas. While racial pride may have
been ingrained in their being, pride in *Ebony* as a racial organ was often not similarly reflected in their copy. I was stunned when one day a
particularly straightforward editor razzed me, "Burns, you know you've
spoiled Johnson. He expects everyone to throw themselves into their work
like you."

"Maybe you're right. But when I like to do something, I get excited about
it and can't help throwing myself into it," I admitted.

"But what's the point of getting all het up? This is only a job."

Still, I was "het up" in those early days of *Ebony*, and mine was more than
"only a job." I was determined to prove my editorial creativity as well as shape
a well-rounded, consequential publication. I had also taken up the challenge
of waging battle for the cause of racial equality, despite the limitations placed
on me by Johnson's "positive" approach. He readily concurred in my glum
assessment of the staff, but he had no solution other than to periodically fire
the worst.

At a loss to explain the problem, I turned to Marxist thinking, which still influenced me, and attributed *Ebony*'s staff flaws to inferior wage standards at their former jobs at Negro weeklies, which had given reporters little motivation to perform better.

I refused to harbor even the slightest thought of the stereotypical notion of "racial traits" to account for the editorial inertia, since I was well aware of the very high caliber of any number of black writers. And any doubts I might have had at that time about Negro journalists' ability based on my early days at the *Defender* and *Ebony* were in any case dispelled by the high quality of a later generation of black journalists, who penetrated the media and fully demonstrated the highest professional skills in every capacity from city desk reporters to national network anchors.

As at the *Chicago Defender*, I found myself at *Ebony* more racially knowledgeable than most of our staff. Both Johnson, an omnivorous reader, and I bemoaned to editors their poor reading habits and lack of intellectual curiosity. At one time he decided, as a quick fix for the staff's insular interests, to provide everyone with a copy of *Time* magazine each week. This, he hoped, would encourage them to read and also help them to learn about magazine writing style. Another time, he decided to offer cash prizes for the best story ideas each month. The staff immediately responded with a deluge of suggestions, some of them better than others. That scheme, however, soon fell victim to one of Johnson's periodic economy waves.

Payoffs to writers became his concern when he one day intercepted an irate letter from a nightclub owner to one of our editors complaining that a story about one of the club's entertainers had not appeared, although the editor had been paid a sizable sum of money. The editor, who had been with us for only some two months, was promptly fired. After this grievous instance of payoff, I alerted readers that never was "any type of gratuity for articles" accepted by *Ebony* or its editors and reported that a culpable writer had been dismissed for "violating that rule." My warning acknowledged the prevailing practice at Negro weeklies:

> Unfortunately the practice of paying for stories has not been unusual on some publications. But from the beginning, *Ebony*'s policy has been to refuse to accept any money for publishing articles and to make the same ironclad rule for its writers . . . Sometimes we do not and cannot know when someone representing *Ebony* solicits or accepts money for a promise to get a story in the magazine. We would appreciate information in this regard and will take appropriate steps to halt the practice.

However, the ever vigilant Johnson did not depend entirely on outside tips for ferreting out editorial payoffs. Almost every letter that came into our building was opened at the reception desk to thwart any employee with "sticky fingers," as Johnson put it.

My disheartening problem with some editors and photographers over second-rate work sometimes could take an ugly turn, if and when a frustrated staff member would grasp for the most convenient defense: accusing me of lack of racial understanding or even outright prejudice. Fortunately, only a few took advantage of this ploy. One was Milton Smith, when he turned in his first article. When I proceeded to criticize his piece and asked him to rewrite it, Milton shook his head, grimacing, and told me, "There's nothing wrong with this story. You just don't understand the fine points because you're white."

Though incensed by his remark, which I had heard before from other writers, I gave my standard reply: "Look, Milton, I've been a colored man for a long time, maybe not as long as you, but long enough to know the score. That line has been used on me before, and it won't work. Why don't you just rewrite the story the way I told you, and let's forget that you've got a little more tan than I have. Your tan doesn't make that much difference."

With a shrug, the chastened Milton returned to his typewriter and did as I asked. When his article appeared in *Ebony*, he came into my office with a gracious smile and commented, "You know, this makes a good story. Thanks for the swell job of editing that you did."

That was something new for me; rarely did anyone at *Ebony* ever thank me for rough handling of copy. I tried to reciprocate: "You wrote a good story, that's all."

"Thank you. We'll make a good team together."

And indeed we did, Milton becoming one of my closest friends on the staff although he was no doubt the most overtly anti-white Negro I had ever met. In his contacts with whites, he was invariably able to pressure even the most biased into defensive postures by the pugnacity of his verbal onslaughts. In time I came to admire and respect his sharp story sense and his remarkable perspicacity in gauging the intrinsic character of both whites and Negroes. Music helped strengthen our close friendship. I discovered that he also loved classical music, and together one summer evening we went to Ravinia to hear the Chicago Symphony Orchestra. On the way home with my car radio tuned to a station that was playing Brahms's *Double Concerto*, Milton joyously accompanied the music with vociferous "oom-pahs" and ardent gestures.

To the incorrigible Milton, every day was another battle in the race war, and he gloated in the many personal victories he won in this endless conflict. He relished calling the few whites who worked at *Ebony* "white niggers" and took delight in tormenting them with racial jibes. On his first visit to our apartment, when I served him a martini, he complained: "What, green olives? Don't you have any black olives for your colored guests?" At another social evening at our home, he spoke forthrightly about the bitterness some Negroes hold toward whites, while denying his own vindictiveness and insisting that to him race was a big joke and that was why he jested about it. As our assembled guests sat mesmerized, Milton went on, "You don't know what bitterness really is. Now take a friend of mine"—and he spoke the name of one of the most famous black writers in America—"he really hates white people, even though his wife is white. Once he told me that every time he had intercourse with his wife, he felt he was getting revenge on the white race for all the terrible things that have been done to Negroes. And funny thing, he says he is much better in bed because of his feeling."

Milton took particular glee in baiting *Ebony*'s "white man in the darkroom," as he was jokingly called, pinkish, blonde Bob Florian, whom we had hired from a part-time job at *Life* at about the time of race riots in suburban Cicero. Florian, who lived in Cicero, was quite naive about racial relations, and he took a merciless ribbing from Milton without wincing. Once he became the laughingstock of the office when he innocently asked Milton: "Say, is it true that Negroes have a push day on Thursday every week?"

"Why, where'd you hear that?" inquired Milton, ready to pounce on Florian.

"Well, a fellow out in Cicero told me that, when I said I worked at *Ebony*. He claims every Thursday Negroes go out of their way to push some white person, sort of a club where everyone takes a pledge as a kind of revenge for getting pushed around by white people all week." Actually the chimerical rumor about push clubs had originated during the war years at the same time as the bigot-inspired reports of Eleanor Clubs, which were supposed to be groups of militant black domestics who named themselves in honor of Mrs. Roosevelt because of her open sympathy for Negroes.

Bob's indiscreet query provided Milton with just the kind of opening he savored, and with a straight face, he said: "Sure, it's true. I belong to a push club." Thereupon he shoved Bob with his shoulder, and then repeated his action every Thursday until the tired joke had run its course and Bob had been enlightened by someone. I always suspected that Milton was behind another racial prank involving Florian, whose darkroom had become a retreat where photographers and editors hung out. Because Florian complained that constant staff visits cut into his print production, I laid down a rule against social visits to the darkroom. Up went a waggish communiqué on our bulletin board:

JOHNSONLAND, Ill. (Special)—Eviction of Negro photographers and editors from the darkroom of the Johnson Publishing Company late Thursday brought a strong protest from the local NAACP branch.

Photographers David Jackson and Isaac Sutton, following protests by Robert Florian, white darkroom supervisor, were summarily evicted following a brief meeting with Ben Burns, white executive editor. The men charged that Florian, a native of Cicero, Ill., has for a long time sought to make the darkroom lily-white. "We will take this case to the Supreme Court if necessary," said A. L. Foster, state NAACP head. "If Jackson had been evicted from a 'whiteroom' we would have no quarrel, but to evict him from a darkroom—this is carrying segregation too far.

Florian and Jackson had been continually involved in professional friction, and in a perverse sequel to the darkroom incident, when Florian was dismissed by Johnson on the same day as the Supreme Court ruling outlawing school segregation, Jackson was triumphant as he was able to take over the darkroom for himself. "It's a great day for the race," he gloated.

It was with Jackson that I had my most aggravating racial confrontation, over his insistent charge that I was prejudiced against blacks. In all my years of working at black publications, he was the only colleague who openly accused me of being anti-Negro (I knew others sometimes felt that way from their churlish demeanor and glowering stares, but they never spoke openly). Jackson obviously did not regard me highly from his starting day at *Ebony*. He had come to work as a beginner in magazine photography, although claiming previous experience in white studios. Placed on the payroll by Johnson at a low tryout salary to cover routine assignments, he proved incompetent and temperamental. I at first attempted to point out what I believed were the faults in his pictures, but my constructive criticism seemed futile. I knew he was doing his best, but that did not measure up to creative magazine-quality photography. Under the unceasing pressures of deadlines and short-staffed with untrained people, I had less and less time to give calm, considered advice to novice staffers, and I became more blunt in my reproofs to Jackson.

Taking umbrage at my continued chiding, Jackson limited his response for a time to scowls. When he went into the hospital for ulcer surgery, the standing joke in the office was that I had caused his ulcers. The climax of our wrangling involved his assignment to get photos of a West Side tailor who created smart uniforms for many big-name black bands. I had been led to believe that the tailor was Negro, but Jackson returned to report: "He's not colored. He's a kike."

I was certainly aware of the widespread anti-Jewish feeling in the Negro community, which Richard Wright had openly delineated in his *Black Boy*: "To hold an attitude of antagonism or distrust towards Jews was bred in us from childhood." Yet in my years of working with blacks, I had never confronted blatant anti-Semitism. Momentarily taken aback that right in my office I was hearing the standard expletive of anti-Jewish bigots, I recoiled defensively and caught my breath as I pondered just what to say. How could I respond calmly and not lose control?

I restrained my temper and asked Jackson, "What is a kike?"

"You know, a Jew."

"But what makes you think this fellow is a kike, as you call him?"

"Well, he's over there in Jewtown and he looks like a kike."

"Jewtown? What's that?"

"Over there, around Maxwell Street."

"And how does this kike look?"

"You know, long nose and he talks with his hands all the time like the Jews."

"Long nose? Well, I've got a long nose. Do I look like a kike?"

"I don't know."

"Well, I am a kike. But you know there are lots of people with long noses that aren't Jews. Lots of them are colored too."

"Maybe that's so."

"You know, it's a mistake to think you can tell what people are by their features. And it's just as wrong to call someone a kike as it is to use the word *nigger*. You think you can tell what someone is by looking at him but you're wrong. Now take my wife. You've met her. What do you think she is?"

"I don't know."

"Well, she has a short, wide nose like a lot of Negroes. A lot of people think she's colored, but she's Jewish. Do you think she looks it?"

"No, I'd never take her for Jewish."

"Well, she is. The point I'm trying to make is to show you how wrong you are in judging people by their looks and then putting an insulting label on them. I take it you don't like Jews."

"Not much."

"Maybe you've had some bad experiences with Jews. But don't make the same mistake that white people make in judging Negroes. They see one Negro who is lazy, eats watermelon, and smells bad, and right away they say that all Negroes are the same. Do you get what I mean?"

"Yeah, I guess you're right."

But I knew that Jackson was far from convinced by my polemic. Now in addition to disliking me for my criticism of his photos, he had a new reason to resent me: I was Jewish. For months our touch-and-go relations simmered until our bickering finally boiled over when Jackson blurted out what he had wanted to say for a long time: I was prejudiced against all Negro photographers.

His denunciation of me occurred during a chance meeting with editor Ed Clayton in Johnson's office. For a moment there was complete silence, as all of us paused breathlessly to recover from his remark, tossed out like an explosive grenade. Such an accusation at a Negro magazine amounted to a betrayal of all the principles for which the magazine stood. Incredulous, livid with anger, I was momentarily speechless. Finally, Johnson spoke up: "That's a very serious charge you're making, Jackson. You know Burns has been with us longer than anyone on the staff. No one has ever accused him of prejudice in all those years. You're the first one."

"But it's true. I swear it," Jackson insisted. "He never gives an assignment to a Negro photographer when he can get a white photographer. And he always says their work is better. He doesn't even like Gordon Parks and his stuff is in *Life* now."

Clayton quickly came to my defense: "That's not true, Jack. I've heard him praise Gordon's stuff, and whenever you do good work, he doesn't hesitate to say so."

"Let's talk about you, Jack," Johnson interceded. "That's what this is all about. That's how this started. We got together to find out why we're not getting better pictures from you. Burns isn't the only one who says your pictures are sometimes bad. Clayton and I have told you that many times. Are you going to say that we're anti-Negro, too?"

"I don't say all my pictures are good," Jackson defended himself. "But they're not all bad the way you'd think to listen to Burns."

Unable to contain my exasperation any longer, I jumped into the fray: "Let's forget about pictures for a minute. There's something more important involved here. For the first time in all the years I've worked with and for Negroes, I've been accused of being anti-Negro, and I deeply resent what Jackson says. I feel extremely hurt, since I don't think anything worse could be said about me. I've known the way Jackson has felt for a long time, but this is the first time he's had the guts to come out in the open and say it. I'm glad he said it because I want to get straight with him. He claims I don't like him and his pictures because he's Negro. Nothing could be further from the truth. His color has absolutely nothing to do with my opinion of him or his pictures. I've cussed out many other photographers for turning in lousy pictures, and most of them are white. If his claim that I'm prejudiced against blacks is true, then I've no business working here and ought to be fired now. If it's not true, then Jackson ought to straighten out his thinking."

Johnson turned to Jackson and told him, "I think you owe Burns an apology. In fact, I insist on it. I've been very lenient with you in the past and given you all kinds of breaks, but this is one time I'm going to be stubborn. Either you apologize or else you can resign." In the end Jackson capitulated and offered me an apology. I was not mollified and remained disturbed by the quarrel, which had left me despondent and doubting myself. Was there a scintilla of truth in Jackson's self-serving contention? It was an exacting test I faced over and over in my years of editing black publications. In Jackson's case I found myself innocent, recognizing that blacks as well as whites can be tempted to seek a racial scapegoat for their woes. If Jackson after our confrontation found me not disposed to esteem him, no doubt he was also more inclined than ever to loathe me as a "kike." Between the two of us had developed the worst sort of racial barrier, an almost impenetrable gulf. Ruminating over our unfortunate confrontation, I found myself regretting that what had begun as a mundane difference over an everyday work problem had devolved into a commonplace racial scrap. The after-effects persisted for days and weeks, as I tiptoed gently in my critiques of staff, while wondering whether there would ever come a time when Jackson and I could agree that our mutual dislike had nothing to do with race. As tennis star Arthur Ashe put it many years later: "I'm looking forward to the day when a white man can look across the room at a black man and say, without guilt, 'I don't like him'—without it having to do with race. And a black man should be able to do the same thing. Then we'll have real equality."

Swept away by the spirit of interracialism during my tenure at *Ebony*, I believed that in the 1950s significant progress had been achieved in alerting and sensitizing much of white America to its grievous racial problems. Accordingly, I visualized the potential for *Ebony* to extend its readership outside strictly Negro confines. After writing so many effusive pieces about the growth of interracial tolerance and integration, based on that illusory premise I counseled Johnson that the moment was ripe to court newly aware whites to subscribe to *Ebony*. He agreed to attempt a subscription sales campaign directed at whites through a series of expensive advertisements in major metropolitan newspapers as well as several magazines, plus a solicitation mailed to select lists of white liberals. But hopes that subscription checks would swamp us proved deceptive. My assumptions proved erroneous, and clearly I had badly miscalculated the possible interest of white readers in a black magazine; the response to our ads was disheartening, not even covering advertising costs. Our *Saturday Review of Literature* advertisements, hoping to capitalize on the praise for *Ebony* from columnist Bennett Cerf, elicited no more response than did our advertising in the tabloid *New York News*. Compliments could not be converted into white readers.

Our failure to attract white readers for *Ebony* was confirmation of everyday discussions of race relations in *Ebony*'s lunchroom, where skeptical staff members reflected the larger black community in scoffing about endemic white attitudes and white liberals' newly avowed concern for Negroes. Almost every day someone would relate another witless comment by some white liberal, who would unconsciously betray his or her prejudices by a chance remark or action. With my interracial principles, it was always startling for me to hear of these incidents reflecting how ignorant most whites still were concerning black people's beliefs and emotions. Even to well-meaning, open-minded liberals at that time, race relations was a relatively new discovery, and their awkwardness in racial matters was immediately evident to aware blacks, with the result that both races were uncomfortable.

In the often grotesque pattern of U.S. race relations, well-intentioned whites were sometimes pressured by rigid racial rules to abide by and even enforce segregation. One such instance in the deep South involved an ostensibly unbiased white New York publicist and the first appearance of a black singer at a big hotel in Miami Beach, Florida. Up to the debut of Joyce Bryant at the Aladdin Room at the Beach's newest hotel, the glitzy Algiers, no black entertainer had ever performed at a Miami Beach hotel. Miami Beach had a rigid curfew on black menials, who were forced to return to the black neighborhood of Miami before dark.

The hotel's press agent was an attractive white New York woman who had sought several years previously to write fashion stories for *Ebony*, and she welcomed me warmly for the dazzling Joyce Bryant opening, offering to cooperate fully in setting up any photos I wished. She even put a white bellboy at our disposal to carry the equipment of our Negro photographer, Bertrand Miles, a strange sight indeed for Miami Beach.

"Things have changed here," she assured me as Miles and I began shooting photos of Joyce Bryant in a bathing suit at the Algiers swimming pool. Friendly hotel guests watched and joined in welcoming the stunning performer, whose jet-black skin was set off dramatically by her silver hair.

All went well until the owners of the Algiers, three white male New Yorkers, arrived and sullenly hauled their press agent off into the hotel lobby. When she walked out to the pool again, she informed me with sudden coldness of a change of affairs: "I'm afraid we can't allow any pictures of Joyce anywhere except in the nightclub."

"What seems to be the problem?" I asked, even though sensing what the objections would be.

"Well, the hotel owners feel that since Joyce only sings in the nightclub, that's where the pictures ought to be." Obviously a black singer "socializing" with the hotel's white guests around the swimming pool was too radical a change for the New York owners to risk in Miami Beach.

"But no one seems to object. Certainly none of the guests said anything," I protested.

One of the florid-faced owners who had been listening on the sidelines could contain himself no longer and burst in: "There won't be any more pictures except in the nightclub. This is Florida, not New York. You don't do things down here that way."

"How about pictures of Miss Bryant in the dining room and lobby?" I spoke up.

"Absolutely not. Nothing in the hotel except in the nightclub."

Into the club we went for our photos, and I told the publicity manager, "I knew it was too good to be true."

"Don't get the wrong impression," she responded. "We're absolutely un-prejudiced, but you know we have to live down here."

We finished our work and returned to the Lord Calvert, the all-black Miami hotel where we, as well as Joyce Bryant, were staying because of the ban on Negro guests at Beach hotels. There I received a telephone call from the worried Algiers publicist: "Say, I'd like to make a request I hope you won't think unreasonable. I was talking to the hotel owners and they're worried about the pictures you took around the swimming pool before they got there. I'm going to ask you to kill all the pictures that show Joyce at the pool with the hotel in the background." Despite her avowed commitment to racial equality, her job compelled her to comply with the most repugnant Jim Crow restrictions as interpreted by bigoted New Yorkers. She would do nothing to upset the social segregation of Negroes as dictated by Dixie standards, even while professing her strong belief in racial equality. Too many white Americans also fell into that trap of talking integration but blindly following old-line Jim Crow ways.

11

Racism on the High Seas and in Europe

The more uncivilized a white man, the more he fears and hates all people who differ with him.
André Gide

In my youthful wanderings, impelled by insecurity and disillusionment, I sought ceaselessly for some anchor that would help me make sense out of a senseless world and also offer a way to earn my living in a challenging, intellectual pursuit. After some eight years of working as an editor for publisher John Johnson—the longest I had ever stayed put on a single job—I found myself in a challenging career and yet at a dead end. I had wearied of my endless, futile confrontations with Johnson over *Ebony*'s policies. I recognized, too, that I seemed to lack direction and aspirations for tomorrow and wondered whether I was suffering from burnout. I also doubted my editorial leadership, exasperated by my failure to mold a concerned, creative staff. I disliked being a boss, which too often forced me to be impatient and grumpy with apathetic writers. Under the pressure of deadlines, I was less and less tolerant of turgid copy, of the petulance of writers. No longer could I follow the expedient of the early days of *Ebony* and simply take copy away from an editor and write an article or caption myself; there was too much work to do.

I also had to bear in mind constantly my vulnerability as a white supervising black writers; anyone could accuse me of racial prejudice, always a convenient weapon for an incompetent employee to use in response to my criticism. Although I resisted the temptation to softpedal my comments for fear of being charged with racial bias—was not that feeling in itself a passive kind of discrimination, I wondered—I inevitably became overly prudent in my relationships with staff members. I knew that I was commonly the object of staff resentment as being too carping and caustic with writers and editors, exacting in my editorial goals, viewed as a workaholic who was unreasonably hard on staff in hectoring them to keep pace with my interracial commitment, and overly ambitious in my role as a white "outsider."

My blighted hopes, increasing frustration, and pent-up anger after eight years working for Johnson's publications added up to a fresh wanderlust. Now that I had a comforting cushion of savings, I was once again inclined to think about travel. "Travellers, like poets, are mostly an angry race," wrote African explorer Richard Burton, and so it was with me. Paris beckoned as offering a spell of relief from work and also fulfillment of my pledge to Esther of a trip to Europe. I rationalized that *Ebony* was now well established and steadily growing in circulation, so that with enough planning I could make good on my pledge.

As a first step I applied for a passport. Its issuance was a matter for concern since many fringe leftists were being denied passports on political grounds in the late 1940s. Not until many years later, under the Freedom of Information Act, did I learn what a stir my application had made at the State Department and FBI.

If I had put my leftist political past out of mind after *Ebony* became accepted as an establishment organ, the overzealous FBI and other government agencies had not. In the 1940s clandestine surveillance was maintained on my developing career in Negro journalism, as can be seen in the detailed report I was able to obtain: twelve single-spaced pages in which the FBI summed up my editorial activity from my initial reportorial job at the *Daily Worker* up to 1950. I became FBI File No. 100–3690-55 in its Washington bureau and 100–2817 in the Special Agents file in Chicago. However, much of what the FBI—as well as the CIA, State Department, and army intelligence— purported to uncover about me during the early war years remains classified as "confidential" despite my efforts to pry loose other pages of records under the Freedom of Information Act.

What triggered the recapitulation of my past was issuance of a passport to me on March 31, 1950. It set off a series of frantic messages between the State Department and FBI, as if I were about to depart on a secret spy mission to Europe. When I was able to penetrate the FBI's curtain of stealth and obtain piecemeal copies of its documents, I ascertained that a diligent covert watch had been focused on me as a former Communist who had infiltrated the Negro press. Ashley J. Nicholas of the Passport Division of the State Department first alerted the FBI to my passport on April 11, 1950, apparently setting off the renewed watch on me. When the Chicago FBI office was informed that I had applied for a passport, agents asked permission from Washington to interview me personally "in view of the subject's termination of his activities with the Communist Party." The memo of August 15, 1950, continued:

It is believed that by interviewing this individual information may be obtained concerning activities and members of XXX [deleted] Communist Party who have been known to associate with the subject in the past. In addition the interview is also expected to establish conclusively if Burns has severed all contact and connections with the Communist Party and consideration will be given to the possibility that Burns may offer to place himself in a position which would afford him an opportunity to furnish information of value.

Under J. Edgar Hoover's name, the FBI on September 28, 1950, dispatched by special messenger to the State Department and to Colonel Robert A. Schom of the CIA a memorandum on my political trespasses. The cover letter concluded, "These data are being furnished to you for your confidential information and should not be disseminated outside your Department." Oddly, by the time of Hoover's memo I had already sailed for Europe in early May and returned in June—not on any surreptitious business but as just another tourist. Incredibly, nothing in FBI files recorded my 1950 passport (No. 231402) issued by Ruth B. Shipley, passport division chief.

Not until two months after the Chicago bureau's request to interview me did a response come from Hoover's office: "The Bureau does not believe it advisable to interview this subject at this time particularly in view of his position as Executive Editor of *Ebony* magazine. Authority is not granted for this interview." Possibly the growing eminence of *Ebony* and my status as its editor dictated caution. Six months after the FBI alert to the CIA on my plans for a trip to Europe, another memo in response was sent by the CIA's assistant director (whose name was deleted from the records furnished to me) on April 9, 1951, to Hoover and the secretary of state. This memo reported, "No record has been found of Bernstein's [the name on my passport] passage. Should any information on him come to our attention in the future the bureau will be advised." This was almost a full year after I had sailed to Europe and come home!

The cloak lifted on my extensive 1950 file when I finally was able to obtain partial records from the Justice Department, which spelled out how busy the FBI had been in tracking me down for a decade: in 1947 and 1949, inspection of the records at Hill's Reports, Inc., a credit agency, to confirm my home address, employment, and marital status; in August 1949, a "pretext" phone call, as the FBI termed it, to a neighbor at our

Jackson Boulevard apartment building to make inquiries about me; in 1950, a check of our mailbox when we moved to Lakeside Place; another "pretext" phone call to *Ebony* on August 19, 1949, to learn of my status there; in 1949, a review of my student records at Northwestern University. Nothing startling was turned up anywhere in those inquiries, but much detail about my past radical connections was credited to so-called informants of "known reliability" whose names were blacked out in the now "unclassified" dossier.

My departure from the Communist Party was mentioned in 1950, but the account of my trial and expulsion was expunged in some three blacked-out pages except for the mention of *Daily Worker* articles reporting my ouster for "white chauvinism and for aiding the enemy" and the follow-up censure of several party members for "fraternizing" with me. A puzzling element was the identity of the informant in late 1951 whose wild imagination conjured up and credited me with preposterous plotting. Out of the office of L. B. Nichols of the FBI, on December 20, 1951, a bulletin was dispatched to key operatives and the Chicago bureau. It credited a New York City source "contemplating doing business" with *Ebony* as the origin of the fanciful "information":

> XXX [deleted] stated that in connection with their inquiries they had been advised by XXX [deleted] of Chicago that this publishing company is actually backed by an individual by the name of Benjamin Burns who is in actuality its true owner and that Johnson is merely a figurehead. XXX [deleted] stated that Benjamin Burns had made two or three trips to Moscow. Burns is white. After his trips to Moscow, he seems to have come into a large sum of money without explanation which he utilized in financing these publications. XXX [deleted] thought this was a peculiar situation and thought we might desire to have this data for appropriate attention. XXX [deleted] pointed out that XXX [deleted] the information furnished by him did not appear to be prejudiced because of any competition but was reliable information. XXX [deleted] also advised that XXX [deleted] indicated that some Congressional Committee planned to investigate the Johnson Publishing Company and *Ebony*.

The FBI message concluded, "It is recommended that this memorandum be referred to the Domestic Intelligence Division to determine what our files contain regarding the above and to take what action that appears appropriate in connection therewith." There was also a "request that the passport records of the Department of State be examined to corroborate or disprove the allegation that Burns had made trips to Russia." (Only some thirty years later did I first travel to Russia—and unfortunately I came back without any "Moscow gold.")

The only follow-up to those sweeping charges from the mysterious tipster that I can find in the FBI records is an acknowledgment from the Chicago office of its receipt and the message to J. Edgar Hoover that its request "for authority to interview the subject" more than a year earlier had been denied. "In view of the above it is believed no further investigation of the subject is warranted at this time and no further action will be taken," read the Chicago bureau reply. But the ham-fisted FBI tail on me was by no means at an end.

When I asked John Johnson for two months off for an extended vacation in Europe, I fully expected that my audacious request would be turned down. But surprisingly he not only acquiesced but also shocked me by suggesting that he and his wife Eunice go along with Esther and me on the projected trip. I could sense that he, too, was worn out from our five years of concentrated labor in bringing *Ebony* to full fruition and was also ready for a long holiday. I initially hesitated over his proposal to accompany us, but my second thoughts not only weighed how impolitic it would be to reject my boss and his wife as tour companions but also calculated that I would have less guilt about leaving *Ebony* for so long if Johnson went along to Europe with us. Esther, who had become friends with Eunice Johnson on a visit to Haiti, welcomed the idea of touring Europe together, and we carefully began our travel planning.

For Johnson, who relished the comforts of home and strongly resisted any departure from his resplendent Michigan Avenue office complex, his astonishing decision to "tag along" on the trip to the Continent was motivated by more than just the idea of a vacation; he was going to Europe to learn for himself whether it was true that racism was not pervasive there as in the United States—as indeed I, too, wished to discover. Traveling with the Johnsons we had no choice but to change our plans to go "on the cheap," since that was not their style. Right from the start we encountered "the race problem" when we discussed what accommodations to book on the *S.S. Caronia*; I was inclined to travel second class not only to save money but also to evade wearing a formal dinner jacket. But Johnson would not think of second class. "Look, all my life I've been living second class," he pointed out. "Any time I get a chance to do anything first class, well, that's it." There was no reply I could possibly make, even though I would have to pay the first-class fare as well as first-class hotel rates.

Our travel agent booked first-class outside doubles for us on the *Caronia* to Cherbourg and on the *Île de France* returning from Southampton, as well as working out a first-class itinerary at Europe's finest hotels: the George V in Paris, the Negresco in Nice, the Danielli in Venice, the Bauer au Lac in Zurich, and Claridge's in London. Sailing day early in May 1950 was the usual mad routine, with Johnson scurrying about Manhattan to buy a last-minute supply of easily laundered nylon shirts, which had become the postwar mark of the American tourist in Europe. Esther's family turned out in force on shipboard for a farewell gathering until finally the ship's lines were cast off. Down the bay we joined the Johnsons at the starboard railing to gaze at the Statue of Liberty, and I sensed ironical symbolism in Johnson's remark as we viewed the statue and departed America: "You know, this is the first time I've seen it."

To Esther, after we had stretched out on deck chairs, he said with an inscrutable smile, "You know, I was glad to meet your family. Funny thing—I was always suspicious of you, but I guess I was wrong. Now that I've seen your family, I believe that you're white after all." All four of us burst out laughing. The Johnsons had known us for almost a decade and always suspected that somewhere there was a "black skeleton" in our family closet, that something was "just not right" with a white man working for black publications. Coming to New York Johnson finally got a good look into the "closet" and assured himself that Esther's snub nose, broad face, and full lips were not Negroid but perhaps Mongolian, the result of some ancient invasion of Russia where her parents originated.

The *Caronia* voyage proved rather disappointing. The formalism of the "stiff upper lip" set in first class was exasperating, and wearing a new conservative blue suit rather than a tuxedo reinforced my "out of place" feeling. If we thought we had left "the race problem" behind when we sailed out of New York Bay on the *Caronia*, we learned differently at our first shipboard dinner. Headed for our assigned dining room table, we found ourselves the focus of frigid stares from other passengers, not knowing whether they were directed at Johnson's brown skin, represented the standard frosty demeanor of the British upper class, or perhaps were just part of the first-day formalities of sizing up one's fellow passengers. As we approached our table, we turned to each other in astonishment. Sitting there was "the problem"—in the shape of a young Negro woman and child! All of us immediately had the same thought: Jim Crow. Clearly, we had been seated together as the only Negroes on board, the maître d' assuming Esther and I were colored since we were with the Johnsons.

There was no retreating, no making a scene in front of the sedate dining room audience. Determined to be on our best behavior, we took our seats, nodded to our assigned table companions, and introduced ourselves. Our table mate identified herself as Barbara Depasse from New York, traveling to Paris with her three-year-old daughter Suzanne (who grew up to become a Hollywood television and movie producer) to meet her father there. We then settled into small talk about mutual friends in Harlem. Nothing was mentioned about "the problem" that was haunting the table. Finally, before we reached dessert, our new friend broke the ice and openly addressed the subject that was on everybody's mind.

"I hope you don't mind, and I want you to know how much I enjoy your company, but it's pretty obvious that we have all been put at the same table because we're colored, and I won't take it," she said angrily. "I'm afraid I've been brought up never to accept discrimination, and I won't stand for it here anymore than any other place. I specifically asked the steward for a separate table for two because I know a child disturbs other people. I see there are plenty of vacant tables for two, but he put me at this table with you. While I certainly appreciate meeting you and would like to stay here, I'm going to stand up for my principles. I hope you won't mind if I insist on getting another table with my daughter."

"Oh, but we agree with you completely," Johnson told her. "We can see you on ship everywhere else. You go right ahead and make all the noise you can. We'll support you."

"Good! I'm going to talk to the steward right away. Why don't you come to my cabin later and I can tell you what happened."

When Barbara had left the table, Johnson chuckled, "This is going to be good." Our dessert was dispatched quickly as we hurried to finish dinner and get to Barbara's cabin for a full postprandial report. There she was sitting triumphantly, all smiles. "Well, I did it! The steward just fell over apologizing. I told him that I didn't stand for that kind of thing in New York and I wouldn't take it on a ship that is supposed to follow European customs. He admitted he had placed us all together because he thought we'd like it since we are all Negroes. And I said that we called that Jim Crow in America, and it is Jim Crow here, too. I really got hot and threatened to go to the captain. But he was nice and apologized. He claimed he usually seated people of the same nationality together because they liked it that way."

"I've heard that one before," chimed in Johnson.

"Anyway, he said you folks asked for seats together. I explained that you were friends and had come on ship together. Anyway, it's all settled now. Suzanne and I have a table of our own and she won't bother anyone."

"Well, I'm sorry you won't be sitting with us. We enjoyed your company, and Suzanne is certainly no trouble at all," I told Barbara. "But I guess you've got to stick to principles. Maybe the steward will learn from this not to try it again."

Then Johnson spoke up, "Funny thing about all this, though. I hate to disappoint you, but you know the Burnses are not Negro. They're white."

Barbara's eyes opened wide, and she clapped her hand to her mouth, appalled. "Oh, I'm so sorry. How could I make that mistake? I want to apologize if I caused you any embarrassment."

Johnson burst out laughing until tears came to his eyes. Barbara joined in the animated conversation that followed, but somehow I could not help feeling that deep down she believed she had somehow demeaned us by mistaking us for Negro.

Other than Barbara, we made no friends on the voyage. Other passengers, like her, also took for granted that our association and travel with Negroes indicated that we, too, were Negro. When we danced in the ballroom one evening, I with Eunice and Johnson with Esther, that sight confirmed their suspicions, judging from the hostile stares directed at us. On the high seas in mid-Atlantic, we learned that we were still not far from home and conventional racist thinking.

The upper-crust frigidity during our shipboard crossing diminished somewhat at the top-bracket hostelries on the Continent, but nevertheless, as on the *Caronia*, I felt like an interloper, ill at ease in confronting the pompous decorum at swank hotels, with their uniformed doormen, fishy-eyed desk clerks, and obsequious flunkies always dogging one's every step. I never learned to take for granted their fawning greetings and always felt like a trespasser walking into staid lobbies with other guests staring frostily at the four of us.

On our arrival in Paris and the George V Hotel, we commenced a routine in checking in at the front desk, which continued at every hotel we stopped at. Even though we had confirmed reservations, all of us well knew that was not the final entrée to a hotel room for Negroes. Black GIs may have been a familiar sight in Europe during the war, but in exclusive hotels in the postwar years blacks were infrequent guests. Too many accounts from Negro travelers related how upon their arrival in a hotel lobby, their written reservations turned out to be "a clerk's error," the actual mistake being that the would-be guest's color could not be determined from a wired request for space. Consequently, at the George V, which was a favorite American tourist hostelry, and at all hotels after that, we agreed that I should always enter alone, while our taxi or car was still at the curb being unloaded, and confirm our reservations at the front desk. Once I had signed in, the managers could not very well change their mind when they saw Johnson and his wife walk in. We were never rebuffed anywhere using that strategic maneuver, but we did learn that racism was very much alive in Paris.

The French do not discriminate, we had been told by francophiles, but discovered otherwise on our return visit to the George V after touring France, Spain, Italy, and Switzerland. When we first arrived in Paris, our genial hosts on several occasions had been Nicole and Eddie Barclay, wartime friends of *Ebony* staff member Allan Morrison who were then getting started in the record business. Some weeks later after we had left on tour, Nicole telephoned the George V to learn if we had returned to Paris. When she asked for John Johnson, she was told he was not registered. "But I am sure he is there," Nicole told the registration clerk. "He is a Negro. Perhaps that will help you find him."

"But we do not accept Negroes at this hotel, Madame."

"What did you say?" asked the unbelieving Nicole.

"We do not have any Negro guests here."

"Who am I talking to? What is your name?" Nicole asked warily. Abruptly the phone was hung up.

Assertive and obstinate as she could be effervescent, Nicole immediately telephoned back and asked for the manager. He proved evasive on the question of acceptance of Negro guests. Infuriated, Nicole decided to follow up by summoning her brother-in-law, who was a high police official in Paris. She and the prefect of police in uniform together descended on the George V to confront the manager. Cornered, the manager quaked at her declaration that she would take him to court, while the gendarme at her elbow added the threat to slap a padlock on the George V if any further discrimination against Negroes was reported there. When we finally arrived back in Paris and returned to the George V without incident, Johnson queried the manager about the incident. But he denied Nicole's story. "That cannot be," he asserted. "We take everybody here, even though some Americans may object. We take anybody who can pay their bill."

This was an entirely different Paris from the still spiritually shattered city I had first seen just months after VE Day. The world's most beautiful city was beginning to regain its prewar sparkle. My first trip there had been a work assignment with limited time to play tourist, but with the Johnsons we did not pass up anything in the *Guide Michelin*, from Sacré Coeur to Versailles. At

Bricktop's, the Pigalle club operated by the much publicized Negro celebrity hostess, Johnson was buttonholed by Art Buchwald, then a columnist for the *Paris Herald-Tribune*. Buchwald never made use of the interview, however, since the ever cautious Johnson was reluctant to utter anything controversial that would make headlines back home.

In our European grand tour, Esther and I were consistently surmised to be colored by most whites as well as Negroes whom we met, and we played our assumed roles to the hilt. If we were invariably misidentified, Johnson was even more so. In the lobby of the George V, we were approached by a husky, bespectacled man, whom I recognized as the American author, Paul Gallico, remembering him from his years as sports editor of the *New York News*. Extending his hand to Johnson in a friendly shake, Gallico struck up a conversation and then said: "Aren't you Canada Lee?" Johnson and I could not suppress a laugh. Johnson looked nothing like the former boxer turned actor, and he quickly set Gallico straight. But before he could explain who he really was, Gallico talked on: "You know, Lee once boxed for me in the Golden Gloves when I was sports editor of the *News*. I was sure you looked like him. By the way my name is Gallico, Paul Gallico." I smiled at the recurring demonstration of the old chestnut that to whites all Negroes look alike

We discovered the truth of that cliché as we traveled through France and Italy. Wherever we went in the countryside as well as in cities, the immaculate Johnson seemingly was viewed as an oddity by Europeans, who stared at him as if they had never seen American Negroes before, at least well-groomed, obviously wealthy Negroes. Every so often Johnson would be stopped and asked if he were Joe Louis or Duke Ellington or Louis Armstrong—black names familiar to Europeans. It quickly became apparent that to many Europeans, as to many Americans, a wealthy black must be a celebrity.

The same concerns about Negroes that worried white Americans also plagued some racist-minded Europeans, as we gathered upon our arrival in Spain. Deciding upon a side trip to Barcelona, we left our baggage in the picturesque medieval town of Carcassonne at the Hôtel de la Cité and crossed the border uneasily under the hostile eyes of Spanish soldiers with submachine guns on their backs, a disquieting holdover from the Spanish civil war. When we checked into the most elegant hotel in Barcelona, the Ritz, the scowling hotel clerk insisted we surrender our passports to be turned over to police, a request that disconcerted Johnson.

Throughout our travels he had seemed to treasure his passport as a precious guarantee of his return to America, handling it guardedly as if it were a ticket to paradise. To give it up was traumatic for him, even though he was assured by the clerk that "it's just routine." But it was not "routine," as we soon learned. We had been in our rooms only a short time when the phone rang and Johnson was informed that a journalist was in the lobby who wished to interview him. How had a reporter discovered Johnson's presence so soon after our arrival? Was he really a journalist, or was he a plainclothes detective? All of us scented trouble in the making. In nervous anticipation we all headed for the lobby to confront the "reporter," who immediately identified Johnson as publisher of *Ebony*, "the world's largest Negro magazine." After some perfunctory queries, he began asking ill-boding questions such as "What do you think of Paul Robeson?" and "Are most Negroes Communists in the United States?" Did the fascist immigration officials, scouting for Communists, believe we were on some kind of spy mission? The interrogation disturbed Johnson so that he cut short our planned stay in Spain. The moment he was able to get his hands on his passport once again, he was ready to head back to the French border.

If Europe was a racial Zion, obviously we had strayed out of its celestial precincts. In French restaurants there were embarrassingly named desserts like "La Négresse," which turned out to be vanilla ice cream with chocolate syrup. Nowhere in America had I ever seen as many Mammy-type advertising posters as I did in a week's tour of the French countryside. Every fifty kilometers, or so it seemed, a pop-eyed, Jolson-mouthed, jet-black face would peer from a roadside sign for a restaurant or *buvette*. Supersensitive as I had become in my color-consciousness to derogatory racial images and slights, I was disturbed along with the Johnsons by the frequency of the caricatures, which were already virtually taboo back home.

In London Esther went shopping with Eunice for a brown cashmere sweater at an exclusive shop and was told by a salesgirl, "Sorry, but we're out of stock right now. Must you have nigger brown?"

What was criticized and condemned as racist in the United States was viewed as quaint by tourists in Europe, we discovered to our dismay. At one of the most popular Paris nightclubs, the Rose Rouge, we watched nearly nude Africans painted in blinding tribal colors performing bump-and-grind "voodoo dances" and marveled that what was described as stereotyped "shake dancing" in America was considered "folklore" in Europe.

In Switzerland we were confronted with the most overt instance of racism during our journey. Coming down to breakfast at the elegant Bauer au Lac, the only empty table had not been cleaned, and we sat down waiting for our orders to be taken. After some fifteen minutes a surly waiter arrived but made no move to replace the coffee-stained tablecloth or even brush the crumbs off the cluttered table. Returning with our food, he placed our orders on the dirty table. Esther could not restrain herself and burst out, "Don't you clean tables around here?"

The waiter responded, "Not for breakfast."

"But all the other tables are clean," insisted Esther.

The waiter remained silent, finished serving the food, and then turned away, mumbling something of which we caught only one word, "Schwarz." Rushing to the front desk, Esther told the concierge what had happened. Again, she received silence and a shrug of the shoulder.

In our first-class cabins aboard the *Île de France* headed back home, once again we were assumed by other passengers to be "colored" by token of our being with the Johnsons. Even the few other Negroes on board accepted us as such. One woman, the daughter of prominent black architect Paul Williams of Los Angeles, befriended Esther and constantly referred in conversation with her to "our people."

Having been initiated and accustomed to being so often mistaken for black at home in Chicago, Esther and I were mainly amused in our European experience of "passing." But we could recognize that Africans and Arabs as well as Asians living in Europe faced almost the same color line in housing, employment, and day-to-day living that prevailed in the United States. What we and the Johnsons were able to confirm unmistakably was that racism in Europe varied from America mostly in less outright and more subtle discrimination.

12

The Richard Wright Squabble

What black men do to other black men is no better than what white
men do, and no better because it is done by blacks.
Eddy L. Harris

You know, these white men are no smarter than we are," John Johnson announced to me with an exultant grin. "They've got the same headaches we have, and they don't know what to do about them any more than we do."

Sitting in our New York offices some months after our return from Europe, Johnson was summing up his visit with the circulation manager of the financially shaky, pocket-sized magazine *Quick*. Now extremely confident of his acumen as a magazine publisher, Johnson toyed with a truly audacious idea: to become the first black to publish a white magazine. *Quick* was widely reported to be about to go out of business despite a weekly circulation of more than 1 million, and Johnson eyed those readers covetously. Using as a pretext the possible purchase of *Quick*'s magazine racks, Johnson had arranged to meet its circulation manager to sound him out on why *Quick* was in trouble so as to determine how he might add the sinking publication to his growing chain of magazine properties.

Both Johnson and I had come back from Europe supercharged with vitality and had immediately plunged into an ambitious expansion program, launching two new publications in quick succession: *Jet*, a pocket-sized weekly with capsule coverage of Negro news, and a romance monthly titled *Tan Confessions*. Like *Ebony* and *Negro Digest*, both had been openly styled after white publications—*Quick* and *True Confessions*, respectively—and both were immediately successful. Now fancying himself in the big leagues of publishing, the insatiable Johnson boldly weighed the acquisition of *Quick* as his breakthrough entry into the white magazine field. In the early 1950s that idea was grandiose indeed; rare was a black who had gained entry into the highest reaches of the white business world. At that time black business executives were always relegated to black products and black customers in such fields as hair and skin care, insurance and banks, newspapers and funerals.

The field for Negro magazines seemed saturated. *Ebony* topped picture publications; its main competitor, *Our World*, went out of business a few years later, in the mid-1950s. *Tan Confessions*, started in November 1950, soon had a circulation of more than 300,000, fulfilling the potential indicated by our reader surveys, which had shown that "confessions" were the biggest selling white magazines in black communities. The minuscule weekly *Jet*, in which I unabashedly cannibalized *Quick*'s format, displaced *Negro Digest* in our magazine list in November 1951, after the *Digest* ceased publication. Soon *Jet* also netted more than 300,000 sales every week, far exceeding the highest circulation of any of the Negro weeklies, which were increasingly becoming more like community and neighborhood newspapers with less coverage of national black news. (At one time we contemplated publication of a black version of *Time* magazine, but we dropped the idea when *Michigan Chronicle* publisher Louis Martin tried it and failed.)

The demise of *Quick* seemed a propitious moment for an attempt to crack the white magazine market, and despite my fatiguing work load, I encouraged Johnson's dream of regenerating *Quick*. An impromptu session with *Quick*'s circulation chief gave Johnson some promise of a possible turnaround in its bottom line through his typical expedient: keeping overhead to a minimum and using a bare-bones, low-paid editorial crew. To Johnson, *Quick* appeared to be overstaffed by Cowles Publishing, the parent company of both *Quick* and *Look* (which also folded in following years). But what finally caused Johnson to decide against pursuing his scenario was dread that advertisers in *Ebony*, perhaps 95 percent of whom were white, would think that he was becoming "uppity" and stepping out of his "place" in invading the white magazine field, and that they might in consequence pull their advertising from *Ebony*. As with many of his major decisions, this one was purely instinctive, the gut feeling of a Jim Crow–inured southern black who had learned early in childhood how to judge whites by visceral reactions and behavior in race relations. That early education of blacks was aptly summed up by Beryl Markham: "What a child does not know and does not want to know of race and color and class, he learns soon enough as he grows to see each man flipped inexorably into some predestined groove like a penny in a banker's rack." It was something Johnson sensed deep down, and I had to agree that his fears of white resentment were probably well founded.

Once Johnson was quoted by the *Los Angeles Sentinel* as saying, "The only way to succeed is to learn the rules and to try as nearly as possible to play by those rules. I learned the rules of the game. It wasn't easy but I learned them." In deciding against the notion of publishing a white magazine, he was following the white "rules" as he had learned them. The project was dropped, but out of playing with the idea, Johnson did confirm his considered reflection that "white men are no smarter than we are" when he discovered that the basic problems of *Quick* and *Look* were essentially the same as those of *Ebony*. He resigned himself to his limited role as a black executive in the publishing business.

Ebony thrived in its beginning years by publishing what others would not, what both white publications and Negro newspapers either shunned or neglected. As the magazine prospered, however, a more influential concern for Johnson was "what gets or loses advertising." Always for him there was the specter of advertising agency objections to some outspoken or offbeat feature in our pages, and consistently his editorial judgments were predicated upon what white advertisers would think.

After our return from Europe I had settled into passive resignation and obedience to this fact of editorial life at *Ebony*. Yet although I sought to temporize our policy differences, on occasion I disagreed vehemently with his prohibitions. One of our most jarring policy confrontations shook our day-to-day publisher-editor relationship despite all our congenial experiences traveling together on the Continent. The contretemps revolved around an article I had assigned to Richard Wright during a visit to Chicago from his postwar home in Paris.

Wright was a longtime friend whom I had always liked for his jovial conviviality and keen sense of humor, which contrasted so vividly with the fury and vehemence in his novels. He and I had had no contact since our days together on the *Daily Worker* some thirteen years previously. He turned up at *Ebony*'s offices in the fall of 1950, arriving from the Palmer House during his stay in the city to shoot some background scenes for a movie version of his *Native Son*. Out of Johnson's hearing, like a couple of refugees who had found a new sanctuary, we joshed in our private reunion about old times at the *Daily Worker*. I broached the idea of his writing a piece for *Ebony* on his observations and reactions in returning to the city where his literary career had begun. Wright agreed to the munificent $500 fee I offered him and assented to an announcement in *Ebony* that he would be our Paris correspondent.

If I believed I had scored a coup in lining up the celebrated author as an *Ebony* contributor, my elation was soon tempered when in due course his manuscript, "The Shame of Chicago," arrived from his Paris refuge. It was a tart, devastating portrait of the plight of the black ghetto, which Johnson rejected. He immediately vetoed my scheduling of the article, concerned over how advertisers would react to Wright's scathing condemnation of the racism that plagued Chicago. For several years *Ebony* had been boasting about the new prosperity of black Americans, and here was Wright contradicting everything the magazine claimed—in effect, erasing at one stroke the glowing image that Johnson had sought to project.

For months Johnson and I wrangled over my insistence that Wright's article be published. I had, after all, solicited his views, and I believed strongly in full freedom of expression for writers, even if in opposition to *Ebony*'s editorial policies. I was embarrassed to have persuaded Wright to contribute his world-recognized writing talents to *Ebony*, only to have to inform him that the publication I edited was too conservative to tolerate his militant racial views. Although I disagreed with parts of Wright's one-sided tirade on his return to Chicago, I believed that his article deserved an audience. But Johnson remained intractable in refusing to publish Wright's piece, until finally, more than a year after its submission, he agreed to a compromise in the face of my incessant nagging: the angry fusillade against Chicago racism could be published only if I agreed to write an editorial rebuttal to it based on Johnson's own racially moderate views.

I found the editorial extremely difficult and painful to formulate, veering between candid confession and Chamber of Commerce flackery in describing black life in Chicago:

> Essentially Wright has done a brilliant job in spotlighting the sins committed against the Negroes of Chicago's invisible city—the colored dwellers hemmed into the South Side slums by unseen, unwritten restrictive codes enforced by terror and violence of white bigots. Returning to the city after twelve years, Wright found the same slums he left. He found the same abominable racial discrimination, the same helplessness and hopelessness that results from slum living. There is no question that these exist in abundance in Chicago.

To induce Johnson to agree to this statement was a major triumph for me, but then I had to pay the price by ripping relentlessly into Wright's portrait of Chicago racism to reflect Johnson's views:

> When it came to the better side of Negro life in Chicago, Wright was wearing blinders. Like so many Negroes, distressed and distraught by the bitter pill of racial bias, Wright has become so schooled in striking out in blind fury at the slum way of life that he has failed to perceive the remarkable advances

made by Negroes in Chicago since the depression days. The facts of Negro life in Chicago tell a story not unlike that of any big city anywhere in the world. We have our slums, to be sure. But we also have blocks and blocks of fine Negro apartments and homes, which are newer, more roomy and more modern than 90 per cent of the flats in Paris, of which Wright is such an avid admirer . . . Go down the line of what most people in the world consider the measure of better living—food, clothing, shelter, job security—and the Chicago Negro is better off than most Frenchmen. Too often some of our race leaders have sacrificed truth on the altar of militancy. The Negro in America has enough legitimate grievances, enough righteous causes for indignation without distorting truth. Let us occasionally mix pride and self-esteem with discontent and belligerence.

The scurrilous editorial was one that I wrote with a sickening sense of dejection. Once again I agonized over my untenable position as editor of a magazine whose racial policies I so often differed with. As always, I considered the alternatives and could find no comfort in the prospects of what I would confront if I exited *Ebony*. The never-ending fear of probable exposure of my Communist past always had to be taken into account. Word had drifted back to me from a public relations contact that a *Time* correspondent, Ruth Mehrtens, in compiling an article on the newest addition to Johnson's publications, *Tan Confessions*, had inadvertently stumbled over reports that I had formerly worked for Communist dailies. The worried days until her story ran—happily without any mention of me—were an importunate reminder of my vulnerability in a political climate that was on the threshold of the McCarthy era.

When I informed Wright that his "Shame of Chicago" was finally, reluctantly published by Johnson after a year on my desk, I also ventured to ask him for another article for *Ebony*. Believing that his recognized byline had much reader appeal and wanting to remain on good terms with him, I suggested that as a follow-up he write about his life in Paris, a subject that I believed could not possibly be as controversial as the Chicago piece and would not arouse the ire of advertisers—and Johnson. Obviously in need of money, Wright immediately cabled that his article was on the way to our office. It arrived with a long explanatory letter, most of it asking for more money. As yet he had not seen his Chicago article in *Ebony*, he wrote me, but he had heard from close friends "that Johnson had to write an editorial explaining and disagreeing with what I said." Then he cautiously explained his newest commentary: "I thought and thought and came to the conclusion that if I simply wrote about Paris itself it would be what everybody says. So I tried in the opening pages to give a two-page quick background, then went into the

closing events of my life in New York which made me decide to leave, then I
tried to give a general idea of what life in Paris is like. The style is more or
less like that I used in the Chicago piece."

Reading that preface, I immediately scouted trouble with Johnson. When
I routinely sent the manuscript to him for his perusal, comments, and
approval—sometimes I felt his masthead listing should have been "publisher
and censor"—I had deep doubts that the article could pass. It contained
sentences such as, "I tell you frankly that there is more freedom in one
square block of Paris than there is in the entire United States of America!"
As was his consistent practice, Johnson first postponed a decision, sending
me a curt memo: "I will let you know in a few days on this."

It was not days but weeks later that he informed me he had decided
irrevocably against publishing Wright's article. "In the other article, he
was just attacking Chicago," Johnson maintained. "Now he's going after all
America. We can't print that."

Once again I espoused an author's right to be heard, but perhaps my
arguments for Wright's essay this time were not as strenuous; for one thing
I felt Wright's thesis overall was less trenchant than in his first article,
even if more provocative. Yet as before I felt he deserved an audience and
believed his commentary would help gain circulation, if only because of the
unquestionable sales value of his byline. But Johnson claimed that some
of his statements bordered on the "subversive," citing such bold, sweeping
passages as: "America's barbaric treatment of the Negro is not one-half so
bad or inhuman as the destructive war which she wages against the concept
of a free person, against the Rights of Man, and against herself!"

For months the article remained on my desk while I hoped that perhaps,
as in the first instance, I would catch Johnson in a milder mood and persuade
him to agree to its publication. But that moment never came. As executive
editor, I recognized that it was my disagreeable chore in the end to inform
Wright as gently as possible that *Ebony* would not publish his controversial
views. But I balked for once at "covering up" for Johnson and suggested that
he himself write the rejection letter. Between the two of us nothing was done.
Wright finally impatiently cabled a demand that we either print his article or
relinquish our rights to it. He followed that up by a letter in which he gingerly
conceded: "Frankly I have come to feel, because of your silence and the non-
publication of the article, that the sentiments I expressed in that article were
a little too strong for your magazine. I don't quarrel with you about this; you
are on the home scene and you know better than I do what kind of impression
you want *Ebony* to make." He suggested that perhaps he could persuade a

white magazine, such as *Atlantic Monthly*, to publish the article, since there it would "do the most good" and "carry the moral burden of printing articles that might harm Negro publications in the eyes of the Government." But the *Atlantic* turned him down, too.

Little more than a year later, *Ebony*'s rejection of "I Chose Exile" was one of the first items of conversation when I had a reunion in Paris with Wright. Before my arrival I had written him, "Perhaps I can explain the facts of American magazine life to you a little better when I see you." In his welcome to me Wright proved his usual genial, gregarious self, greeting me warmly as a long-time friend and making no allusion to our conflict. He invited Esther and me to lunch at his spacious Left Bank apartment at 14 rue Monsieur Le Prince. Talking freely at our initial meeting about Johnson and *Ebony*'s refusal to publish his article, he said with a knowing smile, "Frankly, I didn't expect him to use it." We met socially with Wright and his family several times during that visit; our children played together and enjoyed a marionette show in Luxembourg Gardens near his apartment. Never in our conversations did Wright attribute to me personally the blame for *Ebony*'s refusal to publish his Paris article; he clearly recognized that it was Johnson who had killed it. Even though the rejection had left Wright with a bitter aftertaste—and he was anything but the forgiving type—he nevertheless remained cordial during our stay and gave us valuable advice on how Americans could fare best while living in Paris.

I was stunned and aggrieved after our warm fellowship in Paris to find myself bearing the brunt of later recriminations in biographies of Wright written after his death in 1960 by Michel Fabre and Addison Gayle (the latter mistakenly lumping me with Johnson as *Ebony*'s "publishers.") In his book Fabre, professor of Afro-American studies at the Sorbonne, provocatively stated that Wright was engaged in a "continuing feud with Ben Burns, his 'white friend' from *Ebony*." His statement was based on an article I had written for *Reporter* magazine in 1956. Much of its contents reflected my conversations with Wright on the day-to-day discrimination I had observed against African Negroes and Arabs in Paris, who like American blacks were relegated by the French, I wrote, to the dirtiest and most servile jobs, while half the "colonials" were unable to find any work at all. To me the visible predicament of France's darker minorities differed only in numbers from that of blacks back home. Wright readily conceded as much to me but warned: "You can say or write anything you want over here, but don't get started on France's colonies. Whoop, the police will be on your neck and out you go in forty-eight hours. There's no explanation—just out you go!" I quoted this comment of his in my *Reporter* article.

No doubt Wright was rankled by my quotation in the *Reporter* of his honest appraisal of the French version of racism and my notation that he "wrote not a word" about his dilemma. Probably he feared that I had placed him in jeopardy and that he might be expelled from his French refuge; the McCarthy era was then reaching its zenith, and he was terrified at the prospect of being forced to return to America. Certainly I did not wish to endanger his status in Paris, but I did not fully comprehend how relentlessly the French government could crack down on foreign critics of their colonial problems at home.

For authors Fabre and Gayle, I rather than Johnson became the villain, Fabre charging that my *Reporter* article "was justifying American racism" and Gayle describing the *Reporter* as "a cold-war journal" and claiming my article expressed "similar sentiments . . . found in the remarks of informers."

Fabre posed prosecutorial questions about me, hinting at the worst: "Could he have been acting on behalf of certain reactionary forces that wanted to discredit Wright? Was he jealous that Wright was safe in exile? Or was he deliberately trying to provoke an incident?" This was outright speculation and fantasy.

When these statements came to my attention, some years after the book's publication, I exchanged correspondence with Fabre to refute his distorted accusations, particularly his inference that I was somehow part of anti-Wright plotting. Fabre in his reply claimed that it was Wright, not he, who believed I was involved in some kind of reactionary conspiracy and attributed the confusion over attribution to the translation of his book from French: "Maybe it was clear in French and the fact that the same tenses would be used in English for near fact and supposition made it less clear." But I reread his text and replied to his letter, "I cannot but conclude once again that as written these assumptions were projected as yours, not Wright's." Seeking to establish my true feelings in the dénouement of the controversy about Wright and his work, I wrote Fabre:

> Suffice to conclude by saying once again that while I differed with Dick on some of his extreme viewpoints, we were on the same side politically far more than opposites. I always had the greatest respect and admiration for him as an outstanding writer . . . and I still do despite what one would assume from reading both Gayle's and your observations about our relationship. Regrettably too often people on the same side politically have a tendency to fall out and quibble with great emotion over strategies to attain a better world rather than concentrate on battling the real enemy. Certainly

I cannot but regret that I have been cast in the role of being anti-Wright because we differed somewhat on our approach to fighting racism wherever it appeared, the U.S. or France.

In yet another book on Wright, *Daemonic Genius*, published in 1988, Margaret Walker came closest to the truth about how "I Chose Exile" was rejected by Johnson despite my objections. She intimated that my 1948 ouster from the Communist Party exposing my "radical connection" plus "the hysteria of the moment" with a renewed government crusade against Communism "may have been factors in the rejection" by Johnson. However, Johnson's knowledge of my Communist past was nothing new, dating back to the first days we worked together for Alderman Earl Dickerson and my editing of *Negro Digest* and *Ebony*. But no doubt the renewed anti-Communist "witch hunt" of the early 1950s figured in Johnson's jitters, as Walker suggested. She described my role at *Ebony:* "It was impossible to tell from his swarthy appearance whether Burns was white or black. Johnson had no reason to suspect his political affiliations. He was simply a very competent and capable journalist, a white liberal, and almost indispensable to this new but thriving black business venture."

To my mind Johnson's projected breakout from his segregated role as exclusively a "Negro publisher" through acquisition of a white magazine like *Quick* was well grounded, based on my belief that the goal of racial integration was crucial for black Americans in their herculean striving to redress old wrongs and improve their status. In my early years at *Ebony* I had consistently sought to stress that objective of integration in picture stories ranging from the first black students at white southern colleges to the ultimate integration, interracial marriage. But I eventually learned how mistaken I was in judging black aspirations based on my own belief in racial mixing as basic to the elimination of inequity in American life.

After *Ebony*'s introductory years, I found myself repeatedly rebuffed and opposed, both by Johnson and by my sub-editors, in assigning and scheduling anything but the most acceptable of integration articles. In time I discovered that more than the negative reaction of white advertisers was involved; to a substantial percentage of *Ebony* readers, and some of our editors, integration amounted to what they dubbed "amalgamation." To them, amalgamation meant the dilution of black identity, traditions, and pride, the abandonment of black exaltation and nationalism. Many race-proud blacks viewed integration as a delusive "bill of goods" sold by white liberals to unsuspecting blacks and, like writer Gloria Naylor, were opposed to what she derided as an "amalgamous America." To James Meredith, the first black student at the University of Mississippi, integration was "the biggest con job ever pulled on anybody."

Particularly the target of scathing resentment by stand-pat champions of black culture and character was any sanction of intermarriage. For a black man to take a white wife was considered by race-conscious blacks a cardinal offense, akin to "turning his back on our people." Especially angered by intermarriage articles were black women, who saw themselves as rejected and humiliated when black men took white wives. Yet invariably these features in *Ebony* spurred newsstand sales. Since as *Ebony*'s editor I was held responsible for declines or gains in our circulation, I was initially apt to favor publication of such interracial articles. But as *Ebony*'s advertising revenue increased, there came to be a tacit injunction on anything but the most ordinary of integration stories. I was hesitant to contest Johnson's proscription too strenuously lest my loyalty to the black cause be doubted.

In my personal views, my eagerness in espousing the principles of racial integration was slowly doused as I observed the contagion and fanaticism of black nationalism spreading and infecting even some of my fellow editors. Back in the 1920s the showy fanfare of the Marcus Garvey movement had enlisted many thousands behind the concept of black power, and I could sense those same goals again emerging even before the Black Muslims and their leaders—Elijah Muhammad, Malcolm X, and later Louis Farrakhan— resurrected the Garvey spirit and enlisted new zealots to their extremist cause.

Ebony's editors rarely expressed open support for the nationalist movement, but likewise they rarely voiced any opposition to it. The prevailing view among most, whenever expressed candidly, was that although they did not support black extremists like the Muslims, they could not oppose them as long as the white world was upset by them. In that racial milieu, the principle of integration was bound to become a casualty.

Although I could appreciate the need to stress black pride to counter so many negatives in black life, I also was disturbed to sense racial thought moving inexorably toward black extremism. To me "nationalism" had always connoted concepts such as jingoism, fanaticism, and xenophobia. Tagging "black" onto "nationalism" unsettled me, as I found black megalomania fully as noxious as theories of white supremacy. I vacillated as I pondered whether interracialism and integration really lead to and result in assimilation, amalgamation, and the loss of racial identity. If racial pride could engender "black is beautiful" sloganeering, would it not also breed egregious black nationalism and its converse of white superiority theories?

Renowned civil rights thinker Dr. Kenneth Clark refuted this separatist trend in a *New Yorker* interview published on August 23, 1982: "As for the supposed justification for black separatism in any form, I do not believe that genuine pride in oneself can be based on anything as external as color. I do not accept the pride argument from 'Black Power' people any more than I do from white supremacists. In both cases, it's racism."

Recognizing that when racial awareness explodes into exaggerated group loyalties, it can also, tragically, translate quickly into racist counter-movements and self-segregated extremist groups, I found my outlook for the future becoming more and more pessimistic. I could see that integration would be overwhelmed by black nationalism, as manifested in the 1990s in the Nation of Islam's official organ, *Final Call*: "We believe that the offer of integration is hypocritical and . . . is intended to prevent Black people from realizing that the time in history has arrived for the separation from the whites of this nation."

Still troubling to me was my continued personal failure to penetrate into black social circles. I had to acknowledge that for all my noble intentions, my personal endeavors to "integrate" even with fellow editors had somehow become largely futile, with few exceptions. Much as I sought to mix with staff members when away from the office, I was not succeeding too well in these efforts. My social friendships were still predominantly with whites. The blunt reality was that I had little in common with most of the other editors except the black cause and our work.

On our return from Europe I found myself also drifting away from social contacts with Johnson, despite our one-time congenial friendship. In our early days Johnson and I would occasionally visit each other's homes for dinner. Such dinner occasions became rare after our European trip. More and more he now played the role of boss, as financial success elevated him to higher status and adoption of a more autocratic management posture.

When *Fortune* magazine in later years selected Johnson as one of the "Toughest Bosses in America," it cited his "standout callousness" and quoted an *Ebony* employee as saying that "just like in a plantation, he is lord and master." *Fortune* described him as a "brutally hostile" boss who exploded in "wild temper tantrums" and "firing threats." For his part Johnson conceded, "I'm tough. I make no apologies." He then went on to talk of "the days of Alexander the Great and Napoleon . . . I'm trying to be that kind of leader . . . I'm considered a legend in my time."

In truth, ours had never been a normal warm friendship. Never did I get to know Johnson intimately, to speak to him of personal problems; inevitably, in our rare social meetings our conversation was always professional talk. Some years later, when I read Johnson quoted in *Reader's Digest* as saying, "A man ought to have the right to live with his own people," I felt that his remark echoed the kind of segregationist sentiment many a white Dixiecrat might express. It gave me a better understanding of possible reasons for our failure to develop a closer relationship.

If I had believed and hoped that our close contacts in Europe would close the ever widening breach in our editorial thinking and smooth over my exasperation with day-to-day work pressures, I was disheartened to find on our return that our rapport was no better and my work pressures were just as severe. If anything our discord widened and my work burden was increased by the addition of two new magazines to edit. I had determined during our travels to bend more on our return and reconcile myself to the problems I had confronted upon our departure, but I found that the more successful *Ebony* became, the more distant Johnson became, the more completely he dominated the direction and choice of *Ebony*'s contents, and the more he constrained my editorial options.

As the *New York Times* later accurately reported, "Johnson . . . makes all the major decisions for the company, including selection of the cover and inside articles for *Ebony*." An article that appeared in the United Airlines magazine typified Johnson's domineering editorial regimen: "I believe my success is a miracle. I issue edicts and statements and policy as though it were the final word and I'd gotten it from on high."

My outlook for the future looked more and more bleak as Johnson seemed to revel in his power and I became more and more his echo. My thoughts turned again to retreat and flight, to travel and escape.

My many months of contention with Johnson over Richard Wright's articles were but one phase of a succession of basic differences with him over his obsessive concern for "what advertisers would think." (In the *Black Journalism Review*, he later justified this concern by saying, "I knew I could not be talking about things that people I was appealing to would not support and expect them to support me.") Though I had thought myself resigned to his conformist stance, somehow my previous forbearance was now lacking.

As always in the past when faced with job problems and stress, I felt a strong urge to get away. Although it was little more than a year since I had broken away to Europe, I was ready for another trip. Again I was lured by Paris. I also had thoughts of writing a book on my experiences working for

Negro publications, something I had long considered but always shrugged off because of lack of time and energy.

In making travel plans I had to consider a new component: might I be able to renew my passport in view of the growing anti-Communist hysteria in the government? Senator Joseph McCarthy had been loosed on the national scene, and his Red-baiting demagogy continued to haunt America from 1950 until he was finally brought to heel by a Senate vote of censure in 1954. Anyone with the slightest suspected tinge of Red was being denied the right to travel outside the country by the State Department's refusal to issue him or her a passport. I suspected that despite my open rupture of all ties to the Communist Party, I still could not pass a check of my past by the FBI and State Department.

Yet impulsively I broached my travel ideas to Johnson, asking for a two months' leave for the summer of 1952, pleading that I needed a break from my heavy work load and wanted to take my family on a trip to Europe. Surprisingly, he once again acquiesced. Immediately I reserved space on the *Île de France* for the whole family for a sailing on May 16, 1952, and proceeded to fill out applications for our passport renewals, determined to test my status with the State Department and FBI. A month later my fears were confirmed when a letter from Ruth B. Shipley, chief of the passport division, informed us that our passports might not be renewed because "it has been decided that your proposed travel would be contrary to the best interests of the United States." The letter was the first confirmation in writing from a federal agency that I was under watch by Washington as a Communist, even though I had long feared and suspected such scrutiny.

But if I was subject to surveillance by federal agents, why had they not read the *Daily Worker* and seen the virulent denunciation of Ben Burns as an "enemy" of the party back in 1949? If the FBI was so careless, then why should I not call its attention to its shoddy spying efforts? I was apprehensive that such a step might lead to an FBI request that I become an informer to prove that I was indeed anti-Communist. Nonetheless, I was resolved to clear my name.

In a letter to Ruth Shipley, I requested a meeting with her to appeal the rejection. It was undoubtedly the most difficult letter I have ever written in my life, as I tried to refute the charge that my projected travel to Europe was "contrary to the best interests of the United States." I knew that the standard quid pro quo for FBI clearance of my name was confession and contrition, which I was willing, though not eager, to undergo in order to be able to travel freely with a renewed passport. But I was unswerving in my steadfast resolution never to take the next step for FBI blessing: turning informer.

How could I phrase a letter to the State Department that would receive a sympathetic ear? I well knew what the State Department and FBI had in mind and addressed my letter to that imputation, avoiding any mention of informing. After much pained reflection, I assured Shipley in my letter: "I know that I can prove to your complete satisfaction that neither I nor my proposed trip overseas would be contrary to the best interests of the U.S., as your letter states. I feel that the State Department's letter to my wife and myself is a reflection upon our loyalty to this country."

Certainly I could honestly and unreservedly make that testament, even though I remained critical of much that I found disturbing in America, such as race relations. My brand of "loyalty" was well described by Mark Twain: "My kind of loyalty was loyalty to one's country, not its institutions or officeholders." I would have liked to have quoted to the State Department the eloquent words of abolitionist William Lloyd Garrison: "My country is the world; my countrymen are mankind."

Agreement to listen to my appeal came from Shipley a week after my letter was mailed, and on May 5 Esther and I went to Washington for the first time, nervous about what we would confront when we walked into the State Department offices. We met with Ashley J. Nicholas, assistant chief in the passport division. He described our meeting in a memorandum, released to me years later under the Freedom of Information Act:

> I told Mr. Burns that he had been refused a passport under the policy of the department to follow the spirit of the McCarran law in denying passport facilities to persons we had reason to believe are Communists. Mr. and Mrs. Burns stated that they had been members of the Communist Party for a number of years, having joined during the depression but that they had withdrawn from it after the end of World War II when they became convinced that the Soviet Union was following a policy of aggression.
>
> I asked Mr. Burns whether he had ever talked to the FBI regarding his experience while a member of the Communist Party. He stated that he had not. I stated that the best way in which Mr. Burns could convince the government that he is no longer a Communist would be for him to go to the FBI and answer fully all questions which they might desire to ask him concerning the Communist Party. While Mr. Burns did not specifically say he would do this I get the impression that he would.
>
> He is anxious to avoid all publicity and stated that for that reason he did not wish to appear at any public hearings, such as before the Committee

on Un-American Activities. I told Mr. Burns that if he went to the FBI
office in Chicago and cooperated with that agency he should so advise the
department and return the passport renewal fee which had been refunded.

What Nicholas did not record was our consternation when we walked out of
his office, now irrevocably confronting the question I had long feared would
face me: would I talk to the FBI and become an informer in exchange for
issuance of my passport? I had no doubt about my response when I left
Washington, despondent and convinced that any future European trip was
off. I was inconsolable and told Esther I did not ever want to return to the
capital—and indeed I did not for more than a score of years.

Back home in Chicago I decided to go through the motions of what I was
convinced would be a vain gesture and mailed our passport renewal fees to
the State Department. I expected any day to receive a telephone call from the
FBI asking me to appear at its office and believed my refusal would spell the
end of our overseas travels. But the telephone call never came, even though
two teletype FBI messages marked "urgent" (both copies obtained later under
the Freedom of Information Act) were dispatched to the Chicago FBI office
detailing my past and describing my interview with the State Department, and
advising Chicago FBI agents:

> Subject stated he is departing for Chicago this evening and will contact
> FBI office in Chicago and will talk to FBI freely re his activities . . .
> Passport division requests bureau advise it re cooperativeness of subject
> and stated passport renewal depends on subject's willingness to cooperate
> with government.

Under J. Edgar Hoover's name in June was dispatched a later message to
the Chicago FBI impatiently asking whether I had shown up at that office:

> You are instructed to advise the Bureau by return mail whether or not the
> subject has appeared at your office to relate his Communist activities and
> affiliations as he indicated that he would do to Department of State on
> May 5, 1952. In the event the subject has appeared at your office, you
> should advise the Bureau concerning the details of the interview.

The response from the Chicago bureau was:

> There is no information available to indicate that subject has appeared in
> this office or has attempted to contact the office regarding his Communist
> activities and affiliations, as he indicated he would do to the Department
> of State on May 5, 1952. No further action is being contemplated by this
> office in this matter.

My failure to appear at the Chicago FBI office was then reported orally to Ashley Nicholas at the State Department by an FBI agent who sent a message to J. Edgar Hoover that Nicholas "understood the situation" and would "advise the Washington Field Office in the event of any further contact with the Passport Division by the subject in the future." But the FBI waited in vain for "the subject" to show up. Why the FBI did not dispatch an agent to face me at my home, to confront me and pressure me to talk about my Communist years, I cannot fathom. Why FBI agents did not follow up my visit to the State Department remains puzzling to me to this day. Did my status as editor of the foremost Negro publication cause the FBI to hesitate for fear of unfavorable publicity? Whatever the reasoning of the FBI and State Department, I was thankful not to have the FBI come knocking at my door or calling at my office. I put Europe out of mind.

This created another predicament: how could I explain to Johnson why I was suddenly canceling our European trip? To level with him about our passport troubles with the State Department and FBI was out of the question, since I did not want to bring the matter to his attention. Since Johnson had already consented to my extended leave, I decided not to cancel my travel and informed him we had changed our plans. Instead, Esther and I chose a destination that would not require a passport. One June morning we piled into our Buick with our brood and headed for California, visiting national parks along the way.

To my astonishment, more than a year after our passport denial I opened my mailbox one morning and found our passports with renewal stamps on them. We felt like freed prisoners, passports in hand once again. What had prompted the State Department to renew our passports despite my unwillingness to turn FBI informer, I could not even guess. Certainly, the anti-Communist hysteria had not abated, and the Red-hunting Senator McCarthy was still riding high. Whatever the reasons for the decision, I was intent only on using our passports as soon as possible. But could I persuade Johnson once again to allow me a long leave of absence?

The germ of a solution came one evening at a dinner party with Roi Ottley during a discussion of my long projected book about my experiences at *Ebony*. He offered to contact his literary agent, Gertrude Algase, and recommend the proposal to her. While on a trip to New York on *Ebony* business, I arranged a meeting with Algase, and on Ottley's recommendation she gave me the go-ahead on the project based on an outline I would submit. In little more than a month she had lined up a contract and a $750 advance from the publishing firm of G. P. Putnam & Sons.

Despite my passport renewal and a book contract, I still had a formidable hurdle to cross: agreement from Johnson for a six months' leave, which I believed would suffice to write the planned book. In my proposal to him I emphasized that a book on my experiences at *Ebony* would be a detailed account of the magazine's success that not only could be used in sales promotion but also would become a part of the history of Negro journalism. As usual he took several days to respond. When he finally did agree, it was with the proviso that I work on as many advance issues of *Ebony* as possible before departing for Paris. Thereupon, I began to push hard to assemble as much as possible of the contents for three or four future issues of *Ebony*.

Many years later I learned that the FBI was still watching me as I left the country. In my FBI dossier is a message from the Chicago office on July 31, 1953, two weeks after we sailed for Europe, advising J. Edgar Hoover that I still had not appeared at its offices for an interview and continuing:

> XXX [deleted] advised that Ben Burns, Executive Editor, *Ebony* Magazine, had sailed for Europe on about July 15, 1953; XXX [deleted] that Burns left Chicago accompanied with his wife and his two young daughters. The Washington Field Office is requested to ascertain from Mr. Ashley J. Nicholas, Assistant Chief, Passport Division, Department of State, if the subject was issued a passport, and if so, to report all pertinent data relative to his travel to the Chicago Office.

Once again the FBI agents had erred, this time reporting me with "two daughters" instead of two sons and a daughter.

Not until October did the State Department send a response to the Chicago FBI agency, informing it that our passports had been renewed in March "under the personal authority of Mrs. Ruth Shipley, Director of the Passport Office." In a registered letter to Hoover, the Chicago office then seemed to be washing its hands of the case of Ben Burns, since I had severed my Communist ties, been issued a passport, and allowed to travel to Europe:

> Since the subject's expulsion from the Communist Party, the Chicago Office has not received any information reflecting that the subject has been active in behalf of the Communist Party, therefore it is felt that continued investigation in this case is unnecessary and therefore it is being placed in a closed status.

But the Chicago office was wrong; J. Edgar Hoover was not yet ready to close the book on Ben Burns, as my voluminous FBI file later showed.

13

Paris and Parting

There is no way now in the last decade of the century to convey—
convincingly—the stupidity, the idiocy of the average white person's
idea about the blacks.

Doris Lessing

As much as Paris has been glorified in song and story, for me no description could fully capture its magic. On my third visit in the summer of 1953, for the first time I was in Paris not as a working journalist or gawking tourist but as a temporary resident, arriving with my family for a six-month stay. Thanks to the advice of our friend Nicole Barclay, we had packed light, yet our baggage still seemed overwhelming when viewed in customs. Nicole had located a furnished apartment for us in the shadow of the Eiffel Tower at the reasonable rental of $400 a month, and she also met us at the train station to welcome us to Paris and help ease our way through customs. We settled into our apartment at 65 avenue de Suffren, a fourth-floor, two-bedroom flat in a turn-of-the century building with a bird-cage elevator that could hold three people at most.

Our busy day-to-day routine in Paris revolved around the school schedules of our children and my morning writing hours, as well as the classes that Esther attended at the Alliance Française and the famed Cordon Bleu cooking school. Whatever free moments we found were devoted to absorbing all that Paris had to offer.

Paris provided not French lessons for our family but also lessons in "jive talk." One afternoon while we were sightseeing I recognized bebop musician Babs Gonzalez with his Scandinavian woman friend. We talked, and Babs began relating how much "bread" he was making in European "gigs." I had to interpret when my son Rich whispered to me, "Is he a baker?" There followed an outpouring of "jive" expressions from Babs when he visited our apartment, and our children were fascinated with this new language. They began to use terms like "nitty gritty" long before most whites had ever heard the expression. ("Nitty gritty" already was common "jive" vocabulary in 1953, although *Webster's Ninth Collegiate Dictionary* dates its origin in 1963.)

Another visitor to our flat was Mezz Mezzrow, who had passed as Negro in the jazz world and whose book *Really the Blues* caught the flavor and flair of black music better than any other writing up to then. Mezzrow looked more like a conservative businessman than the pot-smoking wild musician he describes in his book.

My immersion in the Negro world, which encompassed reverence for black music and musicians, beckoned me to Parisian nightspots where such luminaries as Sidney Bechet and Bricktop had become popular postwar fixtures. It was in one evening of casual club crawling that we encountered jazz pianist Lil Armstrong for the first time. We quickly became close friends with the ex-wife of the great Satchmo, and she became an occasional visitor to our apartment for lunch or dinner. Frequently we would join her for an evening on the town.

Meanwhile, at my typewriter I faced the problem of how best to recount in a book the *Ebony* success story and its evolution to its predominant role in the world of black media. If I thought I had escaped my disaffection at the magazine by my retreat to Paris, I quickly learned how mistaken I was. No sooner did I begin recycling the past in my daily disciplined routine—writing for four hours each morning—than I began to experience all over again the emotional trauma of my constant strife with Johnson over *Ebony*'s policies. I had to decide just how revealing and detailed my account could be, how critical and candid I could be without endangering my return to the Johnson staff.

As I wrote I could feel Johnson standing over my shoulder as always, monitoring my every sentence, shaking his head and remonstrating at my slightest criticism of his policies. In contrast to all my previous writing, invariably hurried as we raced against deadlines, I now worked at an agonizingly slow pace, painfully recalling the past in words that became more labored with every new page of manuscript. My writing was dominated by feelings of frustration and resentment, even anger, directed not only at Johnson but also at myself. While my editorial role in the creation of *Ebony* as the most successful publication in Negro history was the most significant accomplishment of my journalistic career, I now had to face up to the uncomfortable truth that it was in some respects also among my most disappointing memories.

I realized that I would have to settle for a shallow anecdotal account of my tenure as a white editor of a black publication. My writing became easier after I accepted that limitation, even though I was saddled yet again with reflecting

Johnson's positive approach, much as I differed with it—and him. I omitted my own somber assessment of the plight of most black Americans and also my unhappiness over my difficult relationship with Johnson. What I set forth on page after page was not what I believed or how I truly viewed my *Ebony* years, but in the end a flawed work best not published at all. Nonetheless, I had committed myself to turning out a book, and so I plodded on.

During my months in Paris, I would periodically break into my daily writing quota to send off letters to Johnson detailing some of our more offbeat doings in trying to become Parisians and relating our frequent contacts with American blacks living or visiting in Paris. I received no response until I informed him of our planned return to Chicago at the end of December via the West Indies on the French ship *S.S. Antilles*. To my surprise a cable was delivered to our apartment one morning reading:

> As you well know, I am a great procrastinator when it comes to writing letters. I have been planning to write you for weeks and somehow just haven't gotten around to it. Knowing I have waited so long that even airmail may not reach you before you board ship for home, I am sending this cable to say that all of us have missed you very much and we are all looking forward to your return to Johnson Publishing with much anticipation and pleasure. The staff is much increased and I think we can promise you that the pace will be slow and easy enough for you to really think and function as an executive editor should. Give my best regards to Esther and the children. Hope you will be in Chicago in time for the Christmas party on December 24th. Johnny

The cordial, conciliatory tone of the cable was a surprise not only for Johnson's belated acknowledgment of the heavy burdens piled upon me as editor in past years and his promise of relief, but even more so for his first open confession of his habitual tardiness and his grudging recognition of what my leadership role should be as executive editor. I was skeptical of his professed change of heart as well as of his promises, but after months without a paycheck, I had no choice but to find some comfort in his words and to attempt once again to find some common ground in our tumultuous relationship.

Our homeward journey of more than two leisurely weeks at sea followed a roundabout route from Le Havre, island hopping from Martinique through the Caribbean, with stops in Venezuela and Colombia. It gave me the chance to see a part of the black world unfamiliar to me.

Back at my Chicago desk I soon learned that nothing had changed in my situation, for all Johnson's promises. While I was away, Johnson had clamped even tighter editorial control on his magazines. He had the printers deliver a set of galleys and then page proofs to his office, and he checked every article and caption, every photo and title, often revising or cutting entirely anything he did not approve of. Much as I fretted over the situation, I soon yielded once again to his control of *Ebony*'s editorial policy and resumed my prodigious work load.

In my absence two new monthlies had been initiated—*Copper Romances*, a spinoff of *Tan Confessions*, and *Hue*, a pocket-sized feature magazine similar in format to *Jet*. Neither was in any way imaginative in concept or contents, and they were not faring too well in sales. I was immediately enlisted by Johnson to infuse them with life, to save them from their impending demise with the tried-and-true formula of sensationalism and sex. I did not have much stomach for the shabby role and routinely suggested standard circulation gimmickry, but for nought. Both eventually joined the list of Johnson magazines that did not survive.

During our Paris stay I had maintained an uneasy watch in the *Herald-Tribune* on distressing events in Washington, where Senator McCarthy was making front-page headlines with his wild accusations of Communist taint against so many in public life. The broad sweep of his "Red scare" tactics was a reminder of my own vulnerability to possible informers as well as of what I assumed the FBI already had in its records concerning my Communist past. Even though I was now back in my editorial sanctum and receiving a steady paycheck again, I still was alarmed by every new sensational headline about McCarthy's ranting on supposed Communist Party influence in the army. The tawdry drama was played out daily on television. If McCarthy could seek out some of the lesser lights he was now pursuing, why not me as well?

In this worried state, I had another serious cause for anxiety: a clash with Johnson over my book manuscript. I had completed the book shortly after our return from Europe and foolishly had allowed Johnson to read it, thinking that perhaps he would have some constructive suggestions for revisions. Much as I had tempered my description of my *Ebony* years in keeping with his racially positive thinking, he was shocked by my account. Claiming that I had indiscreetly divulged confidences about the inner operations of his magazines and had revealed many undisclosed aspects of black life, he insisted that I shelve the book. "It's just as though you told every personal family secret about your own private life," he fumed. "You've given away everything Negroes have been keeping to themselves for years, every secret way they've learned to live with white folks and get along. There's not a single thing in it that's not true, but you just can't publish a book like that!"

"You mean even though it's true?"

"Sure, it may be true, but I'll call it all a big lie if it's published. White people—and Negroes, too—are just not ready for the truth. You've taken everything you've learned about Negroes and spilled it all to white folks. And they're not ready yet!"

In defense of my writing, I argued that I had omitted much of what I had heard and seen during my *Ebony* period that could be controversial and embarrassing and had soft-pedaled other parts. I could not be totally honest and inform him that in addition I had deleted all discussion of my deeply felt differences with his editorial policies. My argument was in vain. He would not agree to my suggestion that I work on revising the manuscript, insisting that my half-year of labor be junked. So intent was he on halting the book's possible publication that he offered to reimburse me for the advance I had received from the publisher if I would agree to shelve the manuscript. Implicit was the threat of my dismissal if I did not agree to his terms. My choice was self-evident: with no quick prospects of another job, I caved in to his demand.

Although nothing changed on our return from Europe in my fitful relationship with Johnson, what did change was my family's housing, and that in turn shackled me more than ever to my job at *Ebony*. After an upsetting contact with one of our son Rich's inferior teachers before our departure for Europe, I was determined to better the schools our children attended. We began our hunt for a house in the North Shore suburbs with their better schools, and the search quickly became a loathsome reminder of the ingrained bigotry at home in America. Chaperoned by a podgy, smooth-talking real estate agent, Esther and I checked out some dozen or so elegant residences in the North Shore suburban bastion of Chicago wealth. Even though these were in our projected price range, we were so hesitant to make a commitment that the agent pressured Esther, "I guess I've shown you just about everything we have on our list right now. Surely you must have seen one home that pleased you."

"Yes, there were several we liked very much," Esther conceded. "But there's one thing that bothers us. It's not about the houses but rather about the neighborhood. You see, for one thing we're Jewish, and while I know there are a lot of Jewish families living on the North Shore, we're cautious and worried since several we know have had problems."

"Why, we have no prejudices of any kind up here."

"Well, I hoped not. You see, my husband works for Negro magazines and we have many Negro friends. We were wondering what would be the reaction of neighbors when they see us entertaining our Negro friends."

The real estate agent grimaced. Then she warned us openly, "I guess you'd better not look for a home up this way." At the time her pronouncement, reflecting the prevailing racial climate, was enough to halt our house hunting.

But shortly afterward a phone call from another suburban agent we had contacted informed us of a promising possibility for us in our price range in Wilmette: an old Victorian house, "a handyman's special," as these venerable but neglected houses were sometimes termed. Agreeing to look once again in the north suburbs despite our initial setback, we were fascinated by the design and craftsmanship of the vast three-story, dozen-room house just a block from Lake Michigan. While recognizing that we would no doubt be exposed to anti-Semitism and racist hostility to Negro visitors, we weighed those negatives against the positive potentials of 519 Forest Avenue and resolved to bid for the rambling Victorian.

The asking price of $31,000 seemed astronomical to me—and other doubts also perturbed me. Were we anchoring ourselves to a locale where we would risk endless problems with neighbors? Was I turning my back on my professed racial principles in considering a move to a community where Negroes were unwelcome? Were better schools for our children worth the rupture from our past lifestyle? Weighing all these doubts, we finally agreed that for all our uncertainty, we should buy the house. I was able to cushion our monetary commitment by persuading Johnson to make us a $4,000 loan to cover some of our balance after arranging a mortgage. In April 1954 we moved into our new home and, with the original blueprints in hand, set about remaking what was once a sumptuous house, built for a wealthy Colonel Frank Knox in 1899.

On a gray Monday afternoon in late September, nine months after our return from Europe, I was sitting at a desk at the W. F. Hall Printing Company reading page proofs of *Jet* magazine, as was my routine on the day the weekly magazine closed, when messenger Robert Winkfield arrived and handed me an envelope from Johnson. I opened it casually, thinking it was some last-minute correction he wished to make in a story. I was shocked to find that the letter, strangely addressed to "Dear Burns" instead of his usual "Dear Ben," was notice of my dismissal as executive editor. The letter was a staggering surprise, especially delivered in the unlikely setting of the Hall printing plant. Confirming my instinctive fears about the years-long tensions between us, the letter read:

> It is always difficult to end any association which has lasted for twelve years and so you understand my reluctance in writing this letter asking for your resignation as executive editor of Johnson Publishing Company. I don't

mind telling you that it has been on my mind for quite a long time and is being done now only because I feel that it is the best thing for the magazines. In talking with you, I've gotten the feeling that you are not personally aware of changes in thoughts and attitudes which have been going on in the Negro community and in the country as a whole. The overemphasis on sex, mixed marriage and other similar stories, which characterized and sparked our early growth and that of other publications, are no longer popular. You may recall that I announced at a general editorial meeting several months ago that these types of stories were to be banned from all our publications. You, of course, openly disagreed with me at that time and I didn't object to your opinion because I felt it was your privilege to do so. However, instead of falling in line with the new policy and doing what you could to make it work, I have had the feeling that you have actually worked against it and have hoped that it would not work out. You have embarrassed me with articles that you knew I did not want published, you have left out material which I have specifically requested be published, you have insisted on running questionable photographs which you knew might get us in trouble with the post office. The general effect of all this has been that I no longer have confidence in you and I no longer have faith in your loyalty to the company. And frankly, I am beginning to have too many questions about your editorial judgement on stories that will sell. All in all, I feel I have no choice except to ask that your services as executive editor be discontinued, effective immediately.

The letter included two weeks' severance pay and stated that the loan of $4,000 made to me for my house would be considered canceled as termination compensation. The letter concluded: "I shall, of course, be happy to write letters of recommendation if you want me to."

For moments after reading the letter I sat in dazed silence, until I was able to relate the news to *Jet* managing editor Ed Clayton, who had accompanied me that day. The letter's impact was so shattering that I bolted out of the plant, tears filling my eyes. When I arrived home, I could not restrain convulsive sobs as I broke the news to Esther. Then came moments of bitter rancor combined with self-reproach as I sought to pinpoint what had actually provoked my sudden dismissal. Seemingly, Johnson was reluctant to confront me personally and had waited for an occasion when I was out of the office to dispatch a special messenger to hand me my dismissal.

To this day I do not know precisely what triggered Johnson to fire me, in spite of the claims made in his letter. No unusual quarrel over a mixed marriage or sex story, and nothing else particularly combative, except for our ruckus over my abandoned book, had occurred in the preceding weeks.

Contrary to his charges that I had inserted articles he did not want and omitted those he did want, in actuality Johnson and I had been at peace for months. Submitting to his close perusal of every word and photo, every caption and title in *Ebony*, I had sought to follow his bidding like a loyal foot soldier. Much as I was upset by his rigid curb on what little discretion I had previously had, I was not inclined—especially after becoming financially burdened with our Wilmette house—to insert any editorial feature in our pages that I knew he would frown upon.

In just nine months Johnson had switched from an enthusiastic welcome for my return from Paris to condemnation and rejection of my editorial role. What had changed in the interim? Certainly my editorial abilities had not, but the political climate of the country surely had. Had the Red scare and McCarthyism finally caught up with me? Doubtless the FBI was fully capable of the worst of "dirty tricks." Could Hoover's agents have shown Johnson my Communist record to pressure him to get rid of me? (In his impressive book, *Parting the Waters*, summing up the civil rights movement, author Taylor Branch claims that "the FBI did not lack friendly contacts in the upper echelons of the Negro press" and specifically cites *Ebony* and *Jet* among examples of FBI "contacts.")

If not FBI intrigue, what was the actual cause for making me jobless at a time when I was deep in debt, reduced to a zero bank balance after our European expedition and the purchase of our Wilmette house—possibly the worst time to lose a job in all the years I worked for Johnson? Had the well-circulated open criticism of *Ebony* for having a white editor finally been too much for Johnson to resist?

Any of these could have been the true reason for Johnson's firing me. The least likely seemed to me the reason given by Johnson in his letter, and the most plausible was the threat of McCarthyism, though this was not something Johnson could very well openly admit, given the revulsion felt by much of the black community for the Red scare. What disturbed me most was Johnson's fallacious pretext for my dismissal—his contention that I was responsible for his own editorial policies in exploiting sensationalism and sex for circulation gains. When Johnson some years later in a *Fortune* magazine article sought to blame me for the sex and sensationalism in *Ebony*, I responded in a letter to the editor:

> The facts are that Mr. Johnson, and no one else, as any of his employes over
> the years will testify, always set and retained close to his vest the editorial
> policies of the magazine. It was his appetite for quick circulation gains
> that brought about the policy of sensationalism—and it was my assignment

as editor to find yet another sex, mixed marriage, passing or scandal story that fitted the formula he set. Due credit for the sex and sensationalism belongs solely to Mr. Johnson, who was its author. Certainly I had no motive whatsoever to champion sex in the magazine since the dollar benefits went to him rather than myself. I do resent being made the "white scapegoat" in this matter and want to set the record straight once and for all.

My own cause had been in another area entirely from sex articles: I well remembered the days when we had argued hotly over my attempts to put more militancy rather than froth into *Ebony*. I could honestly look back over almost a decade of *Ebony*'s existence and trace step by step how my efforts to engage the magazine in the battle for racial equality had been continually subverted by Johnson in his desire for more advertising. I could recall his veto time and again of articles like Richard Wright's and others that might offend conservative advertisers and his demand that *Ebony* have "hot" titles to increase newsstand sales. Repeatedly I had backed down after all my protests, had given Johnson what he wanted, and had at his behest toned down anything with a scintilla of racial militancy.

The weeks after my departure from *Ebony* were agonizing and confusing, not only because of our financial straits, but even more so when the emotional hangover began to have its debilitating effects. For the first time in more than fifteen years I was without a job. For days I remained overwhelmed by what at the time seemed one of the most disastrous moments in my life. This was actually the first time I had been fired from a job, and I felt a sense of shame and humiliation. I was even beset with doubts about my editorial abilities. A brief moment of solace came in a letter from the most senior of *Ebony* editors, Allan Morrison, who wrote me:

> I was shocked by the news of your removal as edit chief of JPC. As usual, I received the news late and secondhand. I am frankly puzzled by it all. But the longer I live, the more I seem to brace myself for the unexpected. One day I expect a rational explanation of why you were released, but so far I have not heard one. I want to say at this juncture that the years spent under your direction were on the whole deeply meaningful to me. I think I learned a great deal and improved on my still woefully inadequate craftsmanship. I hope your family is in good shape and that you are suffering no serious psychological ill effects from the break with Johnny. I am sure he would be the first to credit you with a major share in the upbuilding of the magazine.

Looking back at that traumatic moment in my life, in retrospect my departure from *Ebony* a decade before the black revolution of the 1960s was a precursor of what undoubtedly would have been my fate eventually. My position as *Ebony*'s top editor would have been untenable in the face of the black militancy of the 1960s, which rejected integration and the proffered hand of any white. Despite my early exit before those momentous years, I could still find in my initial dozen years in the Negro press much gratification in whatever small way I was able to participate as an editor in promoting the cause of racial equality, and I hoped for "more to come," to use the traditional editorial phrase.

IV

1955–1977

14

My Second-Best Career

Publishers are all cohorts of the devil, there must be a special hell for them somewhere.

Goethe

Job hunting for the first time since the Depression years was strange and humiliating after my dozen years of steady, secure employment, first at the *Chicago Defender* and then at John Johnson's magazines. I had forgotten what an ordeal it could be to repeatedly submit resumes, especially when I had to cover up for the glaring gap of my eight years after college graduation working first as a house painter and then on Communist newspapers before finding a career in the Negro press. Always on my mind was the lingering realization that extremist renegades remain forever suspect and not exactly welcome in their new métier despite their avowed change of heart. In the first gloomy weeks of my job search in the limited consumer magazine field in Chicago, I quickly became discouraged, irritable, and then morose when informed time and again that I was "overqualified" and "oversalaried," mostly because of my $25,000 annual salary at *Ebony*.

After three months of unemployment compensation and fruitless job interviews, totally discouraged at my bleak prospects, I finally decided in desperation to accept a $15,000-a-year job in a magazine factory with the nondescript name of Publishers Development Corporation.

There I found myself in time editing no fewer than five monthlies simultaneously—two "girlie" magazines, *Modern Man* and *Cabaret*, another "flesh" periodical titled *Art Photography*, and then *Guns* magazine and a trade publication, *Guns Merchandiser*. I edited the latter two of these magazines, despite my lifelong aversion to guns and the fact that I had never fired a pistol or rifle.

A year later in April 1956 I received a propitious telephone call from George Levitan, the Texas publisher of the black monthly, *Sepia*, and soon

after I was making my reentry into black journalism. I had long observed
Levitan's amateurish publishing efforts in Fort Worth and had little regard for
Sepia, a pathetic attempt at a black picture magazine, and even less for his
string of shoddy confession-type monthlies with names like *Bronze Thrills* and
Jive and later tawdry additions titled *Soul Confessions, Soul Teen,* and *Hep.*
Sepia had occasionally come across my desk at *Ebony*, and I had flinched at
its crudeness, both in editorial content and printing quality.

I had heard secondhand accounts of the eccentric white millionaire who
published *Sepia*, and when he phoned to meet me at Chicago's Hilton Hotel, I
informed him that I already had a full-time job and would not be available for
additional work. A compelling salesman, he insisted he just wanted to discuss
the black magazine field with me, flattering me, "I know you're the best man in
the business." Wouldn't I at least have dinner with him? I finally succumbed
to his doggedness and thereby began a long off-and-on association with the
unlikeliest publisher in the history of Negro journalism.

My initial encounter with Levitan was almost enough to send me scurrying
out of his executive suite where he rattled about alone in three huge rooms.
He was togged out in the same garish Texas uniform he had worn at our initial
encounter when I was at *Ebony*: a prodigious ten-gallon hat, black string
tie, and a pair of $15,000 cowboy boots studded with diamonds set in the
Statue of Liberty's torch embossed in the rich brown leather. Levitan, always
wearing his extra-dark sunglasses, invariably had a smile and a warm strong
handshake for everyone he met. Although he spoke with but a slight trace of a
southern accent, his "y'all" mien and thinking were all Texas. I was amazed to
hear this anomalous white publisher of black magazines speak of his editorial
people as "hands," as if they picked cotton on his plantation.

We talked shop for a while, he intently probing to find out more about *Ebony*
and Johnson, and I seeking to learn more about his operations in Fort Worth.
How *Sepia* continued to stay in business was beyond my comprehension—
until I learned of Levitan's skinflint payroll for his skeleton staff. In our
discussion he was effusive in his flattery, seeing in me, as the founding editor
of *Ebony*, an opportunity to upgrade *Sepia* to *Ebony*'s standards. It was Ben
Burns who had "made *Ebony*," he repeated again and again, and why could I
not do the same for *Sepia*? He insisted that I move to Texas and take over his
editorial department, offering to give me complete latitude in editing *Sepia*.
Not easily discouraged despite my disinclination to switch jobs or to become
a Texan, Levitan in his droning voice continued his sales pitch, painting a
rhapsodic picture of life in Texas. Working for him, I could attain a new forum
in Negro journalism and compete with *Ebony*, he pointed out, seeking to

seduce me with the hint that editing *Sepia* could be my chance to strike back at Johnson for abruptly dismissing me.

Resolutely, I resisted his pleading and projected perquisites. I would not consider a move to Texas for my family. We now had too much of a stake in Chicago's North Shore to leave. Yet I was drawn in spite of myself by the lure of a possible return to black journalism. All my years of experience with black newspapers and magazines bade me grab Levitan's tantalizing offer and once again put to use the special knowledge I had acquired in my years in the Negro press. But in the end pragmatism won out, especially when Levitan's pinchpenny salary offer was projected against our family's needs. I informed him that I could not take the job for his salary offer, but suggested an alternative: I might consider editing *Sepia* on my own time at my desk at home as a part-time adjunct to my normal working hours in Chicago. He speedily accepted my proposition, which encompassed lining up all articles and photos for *Sepia* each month, assembling and editing copy, laying out pages, writing captions and headlines, proofreading galleys, and pasting up the final dummies—all for $200 weekly to the best of my recollection. I rejoiced to be reentering black journalism, even if in a limited fashion.

Flying down to Fort Worth to become acquainted with his business routines, I met the sparse staff he employed and was jolted by their limited editorial know-how and the jammed sweatshop conditions in their restricted office space. If Johnson was a tyrannical "tough boss," Levitan equaled him with his gruff, iron-fisted commands and southern paternalism, exemplified by his insistence that everyone punch a timeclock (he had little tolerance for tardiness). I learned more of Levitan's background: he had arrived in Fort Worth from his native Michigan at the age of twenty-one after working at a variety of jobs, starting as a lumberjack at the age of fifteen. In Fort Worth he hired a horse and wagon to collect manure and gravel. He became a junkman during the Depression years, picking up used plumbing fixtures and selling them to poor families at a high profit. During the war years his long-warehoused stash of plumbing supplies proved a bonanza, since nothing new was being manufactured. Levitan graduated from junkman to "salvage business" status, reaping a small fortune selling used fixtures. He then expanded into any fading business he could "salvage," if he could buy it at a bargain price; his purchases included a couple of floundering Negro magazines that caught his fancy as a challenge to his business acumen.

In taking over the black periodicals, he sought to temper his typically condescending southern ways in his relations with his "hands," but his views and manners were by then too ingrained to change for all his sweet talk and token kindnesses. When I first met him, he sought to exude sympathy for blacks and their aspirations, but he could not shake off his musty notions of black lassitude and incompetence and his deep-rooted convictions about white superiority.

My trip to Fort Worth was a revelation in southern race relations from the moment I arrived at Love Field in Dallas, where Levitan picked me up in his big coffee-colored Cadillac (one of six autos he owned, including a white Rolls Royce). On the twenty-five-mile ride to Fort Worth, over and over he sought to impress me with his munificence to his employees, even while demeaning their abilities and boasting of his astute business sense. Located in an ordinary factory-like structure adjacent to a federal low-income housing project, his vast personal office at 1220 Harding Street near downtown Fort Worth was as flamboyant as his car with its twelve-foot-long desk set against a background of wall-to-wall drapes with a bucking-horse motif. Before lunch in the grungy company cafeteria where all employees ate without charge (a sign read "Return No Food," and no one did), Levitan pointed out the large organ in his office and then summoned an employee, Ulysses Rivers, a stout, quiet-spoken, seemingly timid fellow in his thirties. Like some old-time plantation owner showing off the talents of one of his fieldhands, Levitan sat Rivers down at the organ and boasted: "Rivers has a good voice and sings in his church choir. Rivers, sing Ol' Man River for Mr. Burns." I was abashed and held my tongue, while Levitan explained that Rivers's normal job was typesetting on the IBM setup that produced all his magazines.

In contrast to Levitan's gargantuan office, the least important office space was the small editorial room, where a constantly changing mix of part-time, pick-up writers and editors were crowded together, desk to grubby desk cluttered with stacks of papers and magazines. My main contacts in the plant, as it was appropriately called, were two hard-working, dedicated women who seemed completely out of character in editing the raunchy confession articles with screaming lurid titles they spliced together each month. The predominant was Edna Turner, the sometimes crotchety but well-intentioned editorial doyenne who now and then stood up to the brusque, hot-tempered Levitan and some of his daft fatuities and dealt with the vagrant flotsam of freelancers who furnished most of the randy contents of the Good Publishing Company pulps. The ablest of the duo was Eunice Wilson, reticent but efficient watchdog over everything that went into the company's magazines. She seemed most out of place in examining the bawdy romance-type picture material or editing the sexual sagas that were the basic grist of the Good magazine chain.

While Levitan constantly decried the ineptitude of his meager staff, what was extraordinary to me was their ability to produce as much as they did, given their lack of editorial skills. Levitan maintained a tight rein, allowing little opportunity for editorial imagination or initiative. Author John Howard Griffin, who wrote his best selling *Black like Me* for a *Sepia* series in 1960, worked for Levitan's periodicals on a part-time schedule and once apologetically described Levitan's modus operandi in a letter he sent to me from his home lest his complaints about "the boss" be intercepted. "Everything that comes in and everything that goes out (except for some of my letters to you) is read, so we have no choice but to write exactly what we are told. I'll ask you to make no mention of this, since your letters are read before they reach me." He sought to explain some of the "strange missives" I was sent by him and others in the office: "The occasional ill-tempered and childish letter you receive from the office is always *dictated* and does not reflect any of our feelings of high esteem and admiration for you."

Levitan was a most genial host while I stayed at his fashionable ranch home in an exclusive residential section of Fort Worth. Treating me to a whopping T-bone steak dinner in the old-time Cowtown section, Levitan recounted the extraordinary saga of how *Sepia* began, his version supplemented by information gleaned from staff members over the years. Its genesis, a publication conceived in 1944, a year before *Ebony*'s start, was a monthly compilation of true stories written in black street language, with no corrections or copy reading allowed. The magazine concept for the *World's Messenger* in the original projection of its founder, Horace J. Blackwell, was to publish the stories in what later came to be called black English, which supposedly would give blacks "a form of expression where at least they can say what they feel," as one of his early editors, Adelle Jackson, recalled (she was quoted in a dissertation by Janace Ponder at North Texas State University). "If the story was in third grade language, that's what Blackwell wanted. Some of the writers had never been to school and stories showed it. But no matter how crude, they stayed," Jackson recounted.

Born out of wedlock in Kansas to a white father and black mother, Blackwell, even though very light-skinned, disclaimed his white ancestry and became a champion of black racial awareness at the used-clothing store he operated on East Tenth Street in Fort Worth, where he sold Negro publications. He prospered enough to decide to become a publisher himself to "deliver a message to the world" (hence the name *World's Messenger*). Full of racy stories, the monthly sold well enough to encourage Blackwell to initiate another venture in mid-1946, this one a pulp tabloid, *Negro Achievements*, that was the forerunner of *Sepia*. Conceived as a news magazine emphasizing what its title said, the monthly soon veered off into religion and sex and its logo added a descriptive underline: "Featuring All True Stories, Consisting of Negro Accomplishments, Love, Romance." Such titles as "God Spoke to Me and God Leads Me Now" and "What Will I Be Doing When Jesus Comes?" were featured along with sordid sex narratives like "How I Went Astray" and "Cheap Love Can Cost a High Price," written mostly in the ungrammatical black English that Blackwell believed reflected "true Negro life." Contributors were advised in blunt words of the kind used in the stories: "Your picture must accompany the story, and don't send us any little bit of old faded pictures."

Constantly in debt, Blackwell related in his November 1949 issue under the title, "Yes, I Am Going to Die," that he had cancer and was struggling to prevent white printers from taking over his magazines because of his unpaid bills. In bitter words, he told of his fear of white ownership after his death and concluded: "There is not a white man in the United States who can publish a Negro magazine." But a month later he was dead, and in eighteen months a white man, George Levitan, was publishing Blackwell's magazines.

Faced with losing her job because of the threat of foreclosure after Blackwell's death, editor Adelle Jackson looked for a financial angel, black or white, to rescue her from being "tossed out into the street," as she related later. Hearing of a local businessman who had a reputation for salvaging failing firms "just to get a piece of the action," she contacted Levitan for an investment in Blackwell's debt-ridden magazines. He turned her down, saying he knew nothing of publishing: "I just wouldn't put any money into something unless I could own and run it." Tempted by his words, immediately she agreed that indeed he should "own and run it" with complete control. To her it was the only way to save her job, as little as she was paid. Levitan then with dramatic flourish assumed the publisher's role and with an accountant's touch actually turned a profit of $500 his first month at his new desk. In a supposedly beneficent gesture he raised Jackson's salary from thirty to thirty-five dollars a week.

In a couple of years Levitan changed *World's Messenger* to *Bronze Thrills*, continuing to appeal to barely literate readers with grubby romantic tales—though no longer written in ungrammatical black English—that made *True Confessions* seem like fine literature. *Bronze Thrills* was a highly profitable "salvage" operation, and its success was enough to spark his ambition to create a publishing empire. He installed a large rotary offset press to print all his magazines in a new building addition after changing the title of *Negro*

Achievements to *Sepia*. Not only did he add other pulp titles in the confession field in which he had no competitors—he himself came up with names like *Jive* and *Hep*—but also he was confident he could begin to compete with the most successful black magazine ever, *Ebony*. But for all his audacious ambitions, his staff was not up to the challenge; *Sepia* bore no more resemblance to *Ebony* than *Playboy* did to the *New Yorker*. On one occasion he sought to compete with *Ebony* by buying out another black picture magazine, *Our World*, when it became defunct. But at the auction sale of its assets including its title, John Johnson outbid Levitan, paying $14,000 to kill *Our World* forever. Then when Levitan heard that I had been fired from *Ebony*, he believed that installing me as *Sepia*'s editor would fulfill his fantasy of competing successfully with *Ebony*.

Despite the Texas-style warmth of my reception, what I observed at Levitan's "plantation" and all my instincts impelled me to reject the proffered *Sepia* editorship and instead take the next plane back home to Chicago. But my eagerness to get back into the black media, the most gratifying editorial work I ever had done, overwhelmed my better judgment. *Sepia* could be my last chance ever to edit a black magazine, I feared; the opportunity was too enticing to forego, no matter what difficulties I would face in lack of competent staff support, typographical mechanics, and printing quality, plus the certainty of complications in coping with Levitan's hidebound prejudices and inane caprices. Despite my fears, it was a gamble I could not resist. I returned home to Wilmette anxious to begin my new journalistic adventure.

Given only a couple of weeks to close copy until the initial deadline, I went to work on my first issue of *Sepia* imbued with revived energy. As in the early days of *Negro Digest*, I employed a variety of pseudonyms to give the impression of a substantial staff rather than a one-person editorial operation. Never did I exceed $2,500 in editorial costs for the contents of any single issue, including all the photos (color transparencies for the cover and eight pages of color on inside pages) and six or seven articles. The total budget per issue was an amount less than some magazines paid for a single article.

As I had feared, I soon ran into impediments with Levitan. My attempts to tone down the overt sensationalism that was his simplistic notion of a way to increase readership swiftly proved in vain. Yet though deferential to his periodic intrusion into my editorial direction, I still was able to bring about drastic improvement in *Sepia*'s contents and appearance by radically overhauling the magazine's contents with racially aware pieces that Johnson never would have agreed to publish in *Ebony*. But Levitan was unhappy that there was no quick consequent dramatic increase in circulation as he

had hoped. His shortsighted idea of magazine sales was limited to placing
Sepia on newsstands in the expectation that circulation would automatically
increase. When I sought to persuade him to budget a minimal amount for sales
promotion, he balked, and he even refused to begin accepting subscriptions,
claiming it was too complicated to set up a mailing department. I became
resigned to *Sepia's* restricted readership, never exceeding 100,000. Then
I bowed out altogether when Levitan complained that I was spending too
much for editorial material. "I realize that you have been handicapped due
to budget," he wrote in one of his rare letters. After two years as *Sepia's* chief
editor, I was informed that his Fort Worth staff would resume assembling all
the magazine to save on expenses. However, my initial stint with *Sepia* proved
to be the prelude to a long, seven-year tenure as editor some dozen years later.

On my other job at the Publishers Development magazine shop, out of
character and alien as I was to the gun crowd, I still managed as editor
to capture their distinct parlance and zeal when I began shaping the pages
of *Guns* magazine. But even in this role I could not escape the stealthy FBI
stamp on my past. One feature I started at *Guns* was "My Favorite Gun," a
short piece by celebrities on their personal choice of sports weapons—the
type of editorial big-name gimmick I had employed in my years at *Negro
Digest*. The first of these were written by movie stars, such as John Wayne
and Clark Gable. I sent one of my requests for a "My Favorite Gun" piece to
FBI chief J. Edgar Hoover. There was no answer from him for some weeks,
but finally a reply came from his secretary noting that he was out of town and
adding, "I know that Mr. Hoover will appreciate the interest which prompted
you to write." But then followed in weeks a curt rejection of my request,
claiming lack of time. Years later I learned the actual reason when I read my
FBI dossier. My letter had set the FBI wheels to turning, and the Chicago
bureau was informed by Washington:

> On the basis of this letter alone, no data in Bufiles could be identified with
> Burns or his magazine. You should therefore check your files to determine
> the background, character and reputation of Burns and his publication,
> including your recommendation as to whether the desired statement should
> be furnished. Bufiles reflect numerous references to the name Ben Burns.
> 100–369055 reflects Communist connections on the part of one Benjamin
> Bernstein, whose aliases include Ben Burns, white Executive Editor of
> *Ebony* Magazine and also connected with *Tan Confessions*, but this incoming
> does not contain sufficient information to identify the correspondent with
> any of the references.

The Chicago FBI office then put its agents to work and set the Washington FBI office straight; I was indeed the same Ben Burns in its records as a former Communist Party member. I soon received a letter from J. Edgar Hoover: "I regret that exceedingly heavy pressure of official business makes it impossible for me to assist you." It was not to be the last time I heard from him.

During most of the Depression years of the 1930s when I first became a Communist, rarely did feelings of dread about police harassment or even possible imprisonment enter my mind; such dangers were commonly accepted as part of the expected "dues" paid for party membership. But never was I actually involved in any grave tangles with the law. My passport problems in 1952 were in essence only a minor legal blip. J. Edgar Hoover and his agents may have been persistent in tracking me in page after page of FBI reports, but never was I charged with violation of any law. It was only when I unwarily assumed a humdrum, humbling job as editor of a "girlie" magazine that I blundered into legal troubles. When I agreed to become *Modern Man*'s editor, I was not aware that the periodical, as well as *Cabaret*, was being scrutinized by puritanical watchdogs offended by the magazine's airbrushed nudes. Soon I was unwittingly thrust into a legalistic quagmire that brought me into court to face criminal charges for the first time.

Just a few months after Hoover had rejected my invitation to write for *Guns*, I heard indirectly from him through a federal indictment of its associated magazines, *Modern Man* and *Cabaret*, for violating obscenity laws. Obviously, the FBI had been scouting for some time to find some evidence to prosecute George Von Rosen, the publisher of those magazines, and his ranking personnel, including me. Adduced by the FBI as a particularly heinous "criminal offense" was the January 1956 issue of *Modern Man*, in which I had used a stock picture from the Graphic House agency as part of a photo package on an artists' ball in Paris. A former *Ebony* writer, expatriate black novelist William Gardner Smith, who now worked for Agence France-Presse in Paris, had provided the text for a spread titled "The Unmasked Ball of Paris" about the annual Nuit de Montparnasse, held to choose the best artist's model. Among the photographs was one of a topless French model who in her pro-American fervor had devised a U.S. flag motif in her bikini-style costume. Printing that shot proved a ruinous decision.

The FBI threw the book at us through the U.S. attorney's office, charging that both *Modern Man* and *Cabaret* were "obscene, lewd, lascivious and filthy matter of indecent character." "Desecration of the flag" was what the Cook County state's attorney's office termed it, and it threw in the obscenity charge to boot.

In the days when I was a vulnerable Communist, I might have accepted my
arrest and perhaps even prided myself on being in jail, viewing imprisonment
as a mark of martyrdom to the cause. Now, however, I worried what our children
would think and say about their father's indictment. How would I tell them
what obscenity meant? What would their schoolmates say to them? Beset
by anxiety, I wondered what wildly distorted headlines could be fashioned
by newspapers if my one-time Communist ties were disclosed: "Red Plot to
Spread Obscenity," "Red Convicted in Porno Trial," "Expose Red Scheme to
Peddle Smut." Caught in the unfolding legal drama, I resolved that tangling
with the law was not for me and that I must leave Publisher's Development,
even though leaving meant once again facing whatever limited choices I could
make in mid-career. The county case was heard first, and in judicial chambers
it was agreed that we would be cleared of obscenity charges but penalized with
an insignificant fine for desecration of the flag, with an understanding that an
appeal would be filed with the state supreme court—a plea-bargaining, face-
saving arrangement for both sides. The desecration verdict was overturned
by the higher court on appeal.

The federal case, on the other hand, dragged on for months during which
Hoover's office hounded the Chicago FBI office and the U.S. attorney's
office with more than a dozen teletypes demanding swifter, more vigorous
prosecution to obtain maximum punishment. Finally Hoover was advised by
his Chicago office that Assistant U.S. Attorney Frank McGarr (later to become
a federal judge) had decided that "some copies of the magazines included in
indictment were not in his opinion obscene." An understanding was reached
between the lawyers to dismiss all personal counts.

Why Hoover and the Justice Department had chosen to single out *Cabaret*
and *Modern Man* for their morality crusade even though other periodicals
published similar topless photos I could only guess. When I later reviewed in
my FBI dossier the long succession of interbureau teletypes from Hoover to
Chicago, I began to conjecture whether my imprudence in asking Hoover to
write on "My Favorite Gun" for *Guns* magazine had reminded the government
of my Communist background and alerted it to my connection to *Cabaret* and
Modern Man. I now had to begin prospecting for job opportunities under a
dual handicap: my former Communist ties and an obscenity indictment.

Recognition that I was going to have to begin my working life anew when not
yet forty-five years old was extremely painful, especially when I faced my
sobering belief that in the field of journalism the traditional direction for "has
beens" was public relations. Dejected as I was at this career crossroads, I was

not yet mentally ready to follow many ex-journalists who had chosen public relations. Admittedly, it brought financial rewards, but it also meant having to accept the toadying to clients and the writing and peddling of mundane press releases to editors that is the essence of the publicity trade. But for me at that moment public relations, which I considered journalism's perdition, represented a refuge from my complex legal ordeal. I was now forced, in the words of George Bernard Shaw, "to do what we can in this world, instead of what we would like to do."

Soon I found myself working with the small but quite aggressive public relations agency of Max Cooper & Associates. With no more than a handful of accounts—a sporting goods store, a television sports show, and a jazz nightclub, among others—Cooper was still struggling to make ends meet with his bare-bones payroll of a couple of secretaries and some freelance help from moonlighting newspaper people. A born gambler, he was willing to chance that together we would succeed by pooling efforts with a third partner, former MGM flack Al Golin, in the reshaped firm of Cooper, Burns & Golin. His idea also was possibly to turn my past association with Negro publications into a vehicle to line up new accounts based upon my supposed "expertise" and contacts in black media.

I sought to discourage Cooper's casting of me as a "racial expert"; I had long been disenchanted by too many of that "hustler" breed while I was editor of *Ebony* and the *Defender*. But he insisted that my resume would be an excellent entrée for the agency in presentations to businesses seeking to win black patronage with the new awareness of the growing black consumer market. My own strong belief was that most businesses soliciting the black market would do better retaining a black consultant. When little encouragement and no new clients were forthcoming, in the interim I went to work on some of Cooper's ongoing accounts, assigned to do publicity on a television bowling show. In my few years with the agency, however, our client roster climbed to more than twenty accounts, running the gamut from airport motels to the national McDonald's fast food chain at the time of its infancy, and we became an assured business success.

My career in public relations began with yet another editorial endeavor: another black magazine to edit. If in becoming a public relations agent I thought I had bade farewell to print journalism, I soon found that the high-flying Cooper had other plans for me. He had a brainstorm of plunging into the magazine business to capitalize on my long editorial experience with Negro publications: why not create a black version of *Playboy*, but more restrained and less raunchy, a black men's magazine that would appeal to younger men. Cooper proposed to attempt this gamble on a limited budget, one of numerous side ventures in which he engaged during the years I was with his agency.

I was not enthusiastic about his idea to publish a tame black version of *Playboy*, based on my editorial background with both black and "girlie" publications. To me, prospects for a black version of *Playboy* seemed to be less than promising. My negative judgment was founded on my observation while at *Ebony* and *Jet* of a rather straitlaced attitude toward nudity even among urban, middle-class Negroes who would have to constitute most of the potential readership. Many *Ebony* and *Jet* readers had protested when revealing photos or offbeat sexual stories had appeared in those magazines. Even though romance-type publications, such as *Tan Confessions* and *Bronze Thrills*, had found an audience among less educated blacks, I could not be convinced that an upgraded sex-oriented magazine was likely to be successful. I told Cooper plainly what I thought, though without rejecting his proposition, because I was enticed by the thought of returning to the Negro magazine field. After I agreed to draw up a prospectus, Cooper surprised me by turning up ten financial angels to invest $3,000 each into the new publication. Although short of the initial $50,000 goal, this was enough to signal "go" for *Duke*, the name chosen for the new magazine for its connotation of courtliness and suavity, as personified by Duke Ellington.

In gathering the contents for the initial issue, with a target issue date of June 1957, I was again alone in soliciting and piecing together manuscripts, pictures, and artwork, just as I had been in the first months of *Negro Digest* and *Ebony*. Once again I had to persuade writers to work for virtually nothing on the pledge of higher payments "if and when," a pledge many had heard previously in the early days of *Negro Digest* and *Ebony*. In the final weeks as *Duke* was shaping up, I realized that I was back where I had started some fifteen years ago: a one-man editorial staff.

Closer to our kickoff issue I enlisted the part-time help of a quondam colleague at *Ebony*, Dan Burley, again in one of his regular sieges of unemployment. He helped solve the dilemma of how to present *Duke* to the public editorially. Although most of the contents were of black authorship, the ownership and editorial staff were white. I informed Cooper that we had somehow to project a black image editorially, even if a false one, as in the case of the first issues of *Negro Digest*, when John Johnson rather than myself was listed as editor. Feeling that we had to have a known black writer as ostensible editorial chief, I asked Burley if he would agree to be listed as editor of *Duke*. He readily assented, but as I expected he wanted some compensation to front as *Duke*'s editor. We agreed on a paltry forty dollars a week, for which he turned up at our office twice a week to write assorted feature pieces.

Editorially, *Duke* had shaped up as a polished, well-rounded professional product in which I could take personal pride even though my name did not appear in the magazine. With outstanding graphics, both in art and photography, we also had a top-ranking line-up of writers. The first issue included sensual, racially aware fiction (mostly book excerpts) by the likes of James Baldwin, Langston Hughes, Chester Himes, Ray Bradbury, Erskine Caldwell, and Robert Lowry. Jazz articles were contributed by name musicians such as Duke Ellington, who selected his all-time dream band for *Duke*; Billy Taylor, who wrote a provocative piece, "Negroes Don't Know Anything about Jazz," describing black musicians' lack of knowledge of the historical background of the music they played; and Gene Krupa, who sat down in our office with Burley to dictate his article contending that "what white musicians have been doing for almost a half century is to beg, borrow and steal the racial asset of jazz from Negroes."

Even when the first 50,000 copies of *Duke* went on sale, my outlook for its future still remained very pessimistic, based on problems such as arranging speedy and widespread distribution through retail outlets to assure recouping printing and paper costs. Even though we began publication with scant resources, *Duke* was kept alive for six months, even if often only barely, with average monthly sales in excess of 30,000, considered promising for a new publication. Tardy payments by distributors helped to speed our demise. *Duke*, as a soft-pedaled black version of *Playboy*, professed grandiloquently that it would "cater to the sophisticated, urbane tastes of Ivy-minded males. We see its market as a select group of quite worldly gentlemen and some of their lady friends." In due time we confirmed that *Duke*'s market was indeed select—far too select to pay printing bills.

By the time of our November 1957 issue, so little remained of the initial $30,000 investment that even the irrepressible Cooper expressed doubts about being able to continue publishing *Duke*. Ironically, the final issue of *Duke* with Duke Ellington on our cover proved the best selling of all our issues, moving upward to the 75 percent sales mark, a quite respectable figure for newsstand-only distribution. Then *Duke* was dead, another name among the more than one hundred Negro magazines interred during the past hundred and fifty years.

For me it was time to return full time to public relations, and I recalled the words of Proust, who noted that so often we end up doing the thing at which we are "second best."

For all my distaste for public relations, I turned out to be a competent practitioner of the craft, which in my mind was much like Shakespeare's description in *King Lear* of "that glib and oily art to speak and purpose not." But I soon came to despise the public relations business, rankled by every aspect of it but most of all by the demeaning "salesmanship" needed to sell a story. The more contact I had with journalists, the lower my opinion of the breed—particularly the newsroom freeloaders who would always be prospecting for some under-the-table handout, such as free carpet cleaning from a client in exchange for a column item. In one instance, a Pulitzer Prize–winning reporter offered to "take care" of our motel client if our agency would arrange for the motel to use the exterminator service the reporter operated in his spare time. Client contact was another sore point, but eventually I learned to tolerate even the most loathsome of business executives who paid our agency to see their names in print regularly.

Shortly after I joined the agency, we marked our most significant client breakthrough, which helped build the agency into one of the most successful in the nation (in its present-day incarnation). I was leafing through a neighborhood newspaper one day in 1957 when I noticed an ad for the opening of new drive-in chain restaurant and suggested that these new franchise-type restaurants might be a potential client prospect. We phoned to try and make a date to see the firm's top executive at his office. Surprisingly, even though he was informed that we were selling publicity services, he gave us an appointment for the next day. I was never much of a salesman, but in my public relations career I knew I had to swallow my distaste for selling. Part of my assignment as an agency executive was to be a "pitchman," and I accompanied partner Al Golin to make our standard spiel to the McDonald's chief, who turned out to be a genial former salesman of malted milk machines, named Ray Kroc.

It is said that the easiest prospect to sell is a salesman, and this proved to be true in Kroc's case. He was the best salesman I ever encountered, in a lifetime of exposure to sales pitches. We had come to sell the dynamic Kroc, but instead he sold us on the virtues of the McDonald's fast food idea as we sought to convince him of what publicity could do for McDonald's. In our wildest dreams we could not possibly have imagined that in a couple of decades McDonald's would become the world's biggest restaurant business and "Big Mac" would be part of the American language. In less than a half-hour with Kroc, we made him as much of a believer in publicity as we became believers in McDonald's, and we walked out of his office with his commitment to retain our agency at an initial fee of $500 a month.

Kroc, who several years previously had assumed the franchising rights to the assembly-line system of serving hamburgers started by the McDonald's brothers in San Bernardino, California, was an ideal client, giving us virtually free rein in what we wrote about his commonplace hamburger business. Some of our inventive yarns ventured into the realm of fantasy in our efforts to achieve maximum exposure in every possible news medium for McDonald's and for Kroc personally. McDonald's became a national and then a world institution, gaining its universal recognition in part by the early deluge of news clips generated by our agency. Cooper, Burns & Golin gained recognition too, eventually becoming one of the nation's leading public relations firms as Golin-Harris Communications.

15

Back at the *Defender* and Off to Africa

For me, the black contains the silhouette, the essence of the universe. . . .
Black encompasses all colors.

Louise Nevelson

A welcome happenstance in 1962 provided me with an opportunity to return to the black press and make an exit from public relations. "How would you like to take over as editor-in-chief of the *Daily Defender*?" was the challenge thrust at me by my former sponsor, "Doc" Lochard, exactly twenty years after he had first hired me in 1942. Lochard's surprising bid to me was not a query so much as a statement of certainty that I could have the top editor's post for the asking, based on his discussions with publisher John Sengstacke. Here was fresh air to revive my spirits, an opportunity to return to the field of black journalism, which had been my first love.

Lochard and I had been in contact off and on during my *Ebony* years and after, maintaining cordial relations even though I was initially embittered after he dismissed me in 1946 from the staff of the *Defender*. Lochard himself had later been let go by the *Defender*, and he had taken a stab at starting his own weekly, the *Chicago World*. Its quick demise was a hard blow to him personally, but soon he was back in the good graces of the *Defender*'s publisher, this time as chief editorial writer rather than editor-in-chief, ghosting Sengstacke's speeches, and steering the newspaper's course. The *Defender* by then had become one of only two black dailies in the country, even though it was sloppily edited, inferior to both the black and the white press in news coverage and in typographic style. I was confident I could perform some journalistic magic and turn the *Defender* around, even though this would be my initial experience in editing a daily newspaper. The *Defender* salary offer was less than I was earning in public relations, but I happily quit the Cooper agency nonetheless.

My return to the *Defender* was spotlighted by a two-column announcement on the front page that detailed my impressive twenty-year record in black journalism. The downtown dailies took some slight editorial note of the black daily's unprecedented step in naming a white editor; columnist Tony Weitzel of the *Chicago Daily News* wrote that "with the appointment of Ben Burns as editor-in-chief, the paper is practicing what it preaches—integration!"

As the first white editor of a black daily newspaper, I knew I faced a multitude of racial problems. From the first, Sengstacke was wary about negative reaction in the black community, and to temper the expected objections to designation of a white editor, he appointed a black editor to an important post, too. My photograph was run adjacent to that of black editor Lloyd General, who had been named editor of the weekly *Defender*. On my arrival at the *Defender*, I was assigned to a large private office at the back of the open newsroom, so as not to be too visible to the visiting public.

In the heat of August I plunged into my challenging new job. I was delighted to return to the clickety-clack of the Linotype and the smell of printer's ink in the composing room, and I was filled with optimism despite my apprehensions about the reportorial staff, whom I immediately assessed as underpaid and undermotivated. Never had I labored as doggedly as I did at the *Defender* in the following months, once again deeply committed to a cause and determined never to have to return to a public relations job. Knowing it was inevitable that I would confront staff resentment, I was overly cautious in tackling the many flaws of the *Defender*. Yet the sparks flew even with my most prudent attempts at correcting its lax inaccuracies, tatty make-up, and incomplete, lackluster news coverage. Just as I had been in my earlier stint with the *Defender* and later with *Ebony*, I was still a white interloper. At the staff Christmas party with Dick Gregory as the invited entertainer, I became the butt of his jest when the militant-minded comedian pointed at me and jibed, "What you doing here—trying to pass for colored?"

While I well understood the staff resentment of a white boss at a black newspaper, I sought to shrug off and ignore as much as possible the open hostility, sticking firmly to the principle that my color was irrelevant in my attempt to better the *Defender*. I sought to win the respect if not the liking of the staff, most of whom were polite if not friendly. But several continued to exhibit open antagonism. The gifted staff editorial cartoonist, Chester Commodore, was the most forthright in his resistance to my every suggestion. In a matter of weeks he walked out, and I had to search for another artist for editorial-page cartoons. In striving to attract and train new editorial talent and to remake the *Defender*, my most grievous handicap was Sengstacke's reluctance to pay any but the lowest salaries. The total editorial staff budget was a meager $110,000 yearly for some fifteen editors and reporters. I soon learned, when I sought to expand the editorial department slightly, that Sengstacke would not budge on financial matters.

I still irrepressibly scouted for black writing talent, but I found it almost impossible to persuade established writers to accept editorial work at the *Defender*. I had to recognize that the paper's reputation as an employer was so overwhelmingly negative that only the least qualified writers would agree to do editorial work there. I realized I would have to make do with the insufficient staff talent I had, striving to be a teacher as well as an editor, much the same role I had assumed in *Ebony*'s early days. The *Defender* under my editorship was no doubt improving somewhat after my initial months of arduous labors, but I began to wonder how long I could maintain the killing pace I had set for myself.

I was nearing a closing deadline down in the composing room late one afternoon when the office receptionist phoned me there to say there was a man named Meredith in the front lobby, insisting on seeing me personally about a "hot story."

"Did he say what it's about?" I asked, wary of the continual influx of people to the *Defender* with supposed "hot stories."

"He says he's going to be the first Negro student at the University of Mississippi," I was told.

"Sounds like some kind of nut," was my response, since I well knew that at that time a black student at the University of Mississippi, for decades the prime bastion of American apartheid, was as improbable as a black in the Oval Office. "Why don't you switch the call to the city desk and let him talk to a reporter."

Later I walked through the city room and observed a clean-cut youth quietly talking to a staff member, who then related to me that this fellow named Meredith had indeed enrolled at the University of Mississippi and expected to start classes there, even if he was killed. Knowing the Jim Crow policies of Mississippi, I did not take seriously the written interview with its high-flown claims and made the mistake of burying it in the back pages of the *Defender*. How wrong I was! Before long Meredith was on the front page of just about every daily newspaper in America, when 3,000 federal troops were called out by President John F. Kennedy to put down rioting and allow Meredith to enroll.

If judgmental errors, like my failure to take Meredith seriously, are part of every newspaper editor's apprehensions in weighing news value, to me another hazard as *Defender* editor was my responsibility for any indiscretion on its news pages. As in my years at *Ebony*, when there was a grievance concerning news coverage, I served as the white scapegoat and bore the brunt of complaints. A typical instance was a news account in the *Defender* of a speech by Olympic hero Jesse Owens in which he espoused his usual gradualist tenets on race relations. A couple of days after our story was published, with a provocative headline not flattering to Owens, I was surprised when he barged into the composing room one evening to confront me with clipping in hand, shouting, "Ben, what are you trying to do to me?"

I tried to explain that our story was based on a United Press account. I sought to cover up by blaming an overly militant copy reader for the sensational accusatory headline written without my approval—a devious ploy I had learned at *Ebony* from John Johnson, who sometimes went so far as to claim that the offending writer had been fired. Owens charitably accepted my excuse, and we remained friends.

Inevitably, I became involved in South Side politics, since one of the high points for the *Defender*'s bottom line occurred during political campaigns, when both parties felt obligated to court the black vote. Substantial dollars were budgeted by candidates, both white and black, for advertising in black newspapers. For white candidates, courting the black press was vital, since this attention would supposedly demonstrate their recognition and regard for the black community they usually ignored between elections. With the advertising space designated for the *Defender* usually came the obligatory press releases labeled "Must" with a big rubber stamp by the advertising department. Though I detested the practice, I had no choice but to abide by the custom. There was always a groveling parade of minor-league candidates and their hangers-on to solicit *Defender* endorsement, and I was often the target of their solicitations, even though political policy and deals were determined "upstairs," in the publisher's office.

By the time I became editor-in-chief, the one-time scam of marching into the city editor's office and depositing cash in his desk drawer had become too flagrant to maintain. Instead, the politicos and their managers were all smiles and promises in wooing the *Defender* for support. But after a legislative election one manager of a victorious candidate came into my office to offer his thanks and a fifty-dollar bill for our support. "I'm sorry I can't take this," I told him. "I've never taken any money for a story for my support and I won't start now." Crestfallen, he shook his head in disbelief and left. But he did send me a bottle of Scotch, which I reluctantly took home but later on second thought regretted accepting.

As in most offices the *Defender* had its share of staff politics, and I could not avoid being entangled in the cliques and their intrigues, much of it along racial lines. As the boss I had a coterie of followers who kowtowed to me. I flattered myself into believing they were showing respect for my know-how rather than making up to the boss. Then there were a few holdouts who never forgave me my whiteness. Another anti-Burns group believed I was too critical and too demanding in my attempts to bring about change at the *Defender*.

With all these thorny problems, I loved what I was doing every day: the excitement and drama of piecing together a daily newspaper, the challenge every day to shape a fresh, informative, entertaining product unlike anything else in America. (The only other black daily, the *Atlanta World*, was a pallid paste-up of wire service copy and publicity handouts, with little national coverage of the racial scene, though it had strong coverage of local politics and events.) The *Defender* had enormous potential in impact, significance, and prestige, but I wondered whether I could ever realize its possibilities. Did I have the stamina, both physical and mental, to overcome its limitations, given the *Defender*'s inadequate staff, tight finances, and shortsighted management? After all my years working for the black press, I finally had to acknowledge realistically that a white editor could not assume leadership of a black institution without inevitable resentment, misunderstanding, and eventually open opposition. The daily grueling pace I had set for myself, as well as the emotional toll of simmering racial acrimony, in the end proved too much for me, and I decided to resign after less than a year as the *Defender*'s editor.

While a score of years had passed since I first faced contemptuous cold stares when I went to work for the *Defender* in 1942, relations between black and white Americans still frequently remained fossilized by bitterness and hatred. Yet things became even worse when "Black Power" emerged as the prime theme of the black revolution. The chasm between the races became almost unbridgeable, even while the nation was supposedly desegregating. The bulk of white Americans gave only lip service to the nation's laws prohibiting racial discrimination, and for their part vast numbers of incensed blacks rejected proffers of friendship from white liberals. Many blacks continued rightly to maintain that whites could never put themselves in the mind of a black person.

After my long experience in black journalism, I have to agree that white Americans can never really know or understand what it is like to be black. And conversely, just as Holocaust victims could not fully communicate the total reality of their experience, so too blacks cannot ever convey a full sense of what it is like to be black. Essayist Pico Iyer has contended in *Time* magazine that "in suggesting that a white cannot put himself in the shoes or soul of a half-white, or a black, they would impose on us the most stifling form of apartheid, condemning us all to a hopeless rift of mutual incomprehension." Iyer has fallen into the traditional trap of blaming the messenger for the somber message. It is not so much whites' inability to know and feel the black experience that is to blame for continuing American racism as the continued failure to react to racism with much more than tokenism.

Despite the enormous advances made by African Americans during and since my years in black journalism, the country by and large still holds fast to prevalent socioeconomic color lines of many years' standing. A vast percentage of blacks remain plagued by poverty and ghettoized in segregated inner city "reserves." Although the law proclaims racial equality, the United States has a long road to travel to anything like color parity in fact. Perhaps South African novelist Mark Mathabane has most realistically projected the future for African Americans: "Given the pervasiveness of intolerance and prejudice in this country, I cannot believe there will ever be a clear path for minority children to follow, free of obstacles and racism."

In the inflamed racial climate of the 1960s, for a white to edit a black newspaper had become obviously impossible. I decide to leave the *Defender*, my decision a recognition that I was no superhero able to transform its editorial maladies, staff attitudes, and the ingrained shortsightedness of its top management. By then I had also come to recognize realistically that trapped in the innate contradictions between commercial success and racial militancy, black journalism had faced a perpetual dilemma from its founding in 1827. During all the intervening decades, the accepted thinking of black publishers was that the very racial belligerency that garnered readers for them inevitably lost advertising revenue, while diminishing militancy in their pages lost reader support and loyalty even as it increased advertising. African American newspapers chose to favor militancy over advertising. With *Ebony* magazine John H. Johnson challenged that conventional approach; he rejected racial militancy to win millions of dollars in advertising. Yet although he upset the general precept of the black press, he nevertheless was able to win a vast readership, unprincipled as his journalistic path might have seemed in some eyes.

The major role I played in *Ebony*'s early success could have been a source of much pride for me, but I never quite adjusted to *Ebony*'s deliberate disregard for the ongoing plight of so much of black America. I resigned myself to accepting the principles of black capitalism and the limitations they inevitably placed on *Ebony*, but I never became fully reconciled to its editorial policies. Eventually I came to understand that black journalism—whether the *Defender* and *Ebony* under black ownership or *Sepia* under white control—was as fully dedicated to profits as any other business venture.

Disenchantment and a degree of financial security, plus my weariness with everyday office tensions at the *Chicago Defender*, dictated my final exit from black journalism. As I had done in the past, I plotted my escape by requesting a leave of absence and booked a trip to Europe with my family on the *S.S. France* in June 1963. There would be no editor's post for me on my return, I knew. With my few years of public relations experience, I was confident that I would be able to find employment in this expanding field.

When I walked out of the *Defender* for the last time, the historic civil rights movement was in its birth pangs, and black ghettoes were beginning to explode in violence. In the following years my only role was to watch from the sidelines. When I returned from Europe in the fall, the *Defender* editor's chair was occupied by Chuck Stone, a highly talented, provocative black writer whose forte was upsetting black institutions and customs as much as white ones in hard-hitting prose he flaunted in a front-page column. Knowing the publisher's sensitivity to controversy, I presumed that he was bound to tangle with Sengstacke and that his days were numbered, and so it was. He and a succession of editors since then lasted not much longer than I had.

For me the magnetic pull of journalism had begun in high school and then, combined with my leftist political leanings, became the vehicle for expression and protest. It also provided an escape from my ghetto origins and then the first illusion of some small power to influence the world, to have some trivial voice in attempting to shape the future.

At Negro publications that illusion became almost a reality, as the politicians in Washington who wrote the laws actually paid some attention to what we wrote in black newspapers and sometimes even responded in terms of legislation—or else were worried enough by our writing to post an FBI watch on us. During and after World War II the *Defender* and the black press generally even merited White House attention, so effective was our outcry against blatant discrimination in the armed services as well as on the home front. We were cause journalism at its finest; we were read, we got attention, and we even achieved some results.

If at *Ebony* magazine that outcry was muted, my tenure at the magazine did perhaps leave some small mark in the inspiration and motivation it may have provided for many of the youthful African Americans who followed its upbeat "first-only-biggest" features. As John Johnson has stated, "The magazines will live forever because they are a record that cannot be erased. They're in the libraries of the world." To have played even a minor role in a significant chapter of black journalism at the *Chicago Defender* and *Ebony* is a memory I cherish.

After my departure from the *Defender* and a summer's stay in Europe, returning to Chicago I went back to what I considered the purgatory of journalism, public relations—this time as a salaried employee rather than partner at Cooper & Golin. Several years later I was able to establish my own public relations firm. I could not resist moonlighting once more at home when in 1970 publisher George Levitan again summoned me to edit *Sepia*. I assembled monthly issues of *Sepia* at home until 1977, while still running my downtown public relations business. I resigned from *Sepia* and shut my public relations office in 1977 to fulfill a long-time ambition to drive across the Sahara desert and into black Africa in a Volkswagen camper. Levitan died in 1976, and the demise of *Sepia* followed two years later. Leaving black journalism and the public relations field meant the end of working for a living and the commencement of the period the Spanish appropriately describe as *jubilado*, a time to relish, enjoy, savor, luxuriate in my remaining years of life with travel about the world and, in the words of Samuel Johnson, "instead of thinking how things may be, to see them as they are."

Index